W9-CRL-751

MICHAEL MARSHALL

The Gospel Connection

Foreword by
Presiding Bishop Edmond Browning

MOREHOUSE PUBLISHING
Harrisburg, PA • Wilton, CT

© 1990 by Michael Marshall

Morehouse Publishing
Editorial Office:
78 Danbury Road
Wilton, CT 06897

Corporate Office:
P.O. Box 1321
Harrisburg, PA 17105

All rights reserved. No part of this book may be reproduced or transmitted in any form or by any means, electronic or mechanical, including photocopying, recording, or by any information storage and retreival system, without permission in writing from the publisher.

Library of Congress Cataloging-in-Publication Data

Marshall, Michael, 1936–
  The gospel connection: a study in evangelism for the 90s/Michael Marshall.
  p. cm.
  Includes bibliographical references.
  ISBN 0-8192-1535-X
  1. Evangelistic work—Philosophy.   2. Episcopal Church—Membership.
3. Episcopal Church—Doctrines.   4. Parish missions—Anglican Communion.
5. Anglican Communion—Membership.   6. Anglican Communion—Doctrines.   I. Title.
BX5969.M37   1990   90-37965
269'.2—dc20   CIP

Printed in the United States of America
by
BSC Litho
Harrisburg, Pa 17105

To Canon Byran Green, who has faithfully
handed on the rich, Anglican heritage of
evangelism in a lifetime of
inspired and eloquent witness.

Contents

v

Foreword

General Convention in Detroit in 1988 called all Episcopalians to a Decade of Evangelism. My prayer is that we will use this decade to so deepen our commitment to be evangelists, sharers of the good news of Jesus Christ, that every decade will be a decade of evangelism.

Our tasks as the Church are to serve all God's people in the name of Christ, and to bring people to Christ. These tasks are inseparably linked and our work on one strengthens our commitment to the other.

In this setting, I welcome Bishop Michael Marshall's book on evangelism. We can be grateful to him for raising some of the central issues for serious evangelization, as well as for his practical suggestions, including ideas for preaching missions and for nurturing new converts in the Christian way.

I hope that this book will be for many the beginning of a new understanding of God's call to be evangelists, as well as a guide along the way.

Edmond L. Browning
Presiding Bishop

Acknowledgments

I am most grateful to Presiding Bishop Edmond Browing for accepting the invitation to write the foreword of this book and so to commend it to the Church. It does not, of course, mean that he agrees with all that is written in these pages. Rather, it is yet another example of his support and encouragement for the ministry of the Anglican Institute since its early days.

Without the intensely industrious and professional support of Georgia Streett, this book would never have been completed. In this, as in so many ways, she is a partner with me in the work of the ministry of the Anglican Institute.

The Reverend William Christian also gave considerable time to read the manuscript in its early stages and made many helpful suggestions that have been subsequently incorporated into the final work.

My thanks are also due to Allen Kelley for his patient and helpful support throughout the preparation of this book.

INTRODUCTION

"This will be a time for you to bear testimony," says Jesus in the midst of his apocalyptic prophecy in St. Luke's Gospel (Luke 21:13). The God of the end of all things sees the end of all things as a time and as an opportunity to witness to the reality of those things that have no end. For the times and the seasons of break*down* (when not "one stone is left upon another") are precisely the times and the seasons of break*through*. As we come to the close of the second millennium, many believe that these days constitute such a time and such a season: For although the gospel is good news for all seasons, yet it is especially good news at those very times and seasons when a convergence of circumstances suggests either individually (or as nations or even as civilizations) that we should stop and think it all out again.

For we live at a time when the false gods of our day are being discredited: the false gods of materialism, communism, and rationalism—to name but a few. On November 4, 1989, "the walls came tumbling down" as the Berlin Wall collapsed. On December 1 of the same year, Mikhail Gorbachev met with the Pope, and in the stunning photograph on the front of the *New York Times* the following

morning, history was both made and recorded for all to
see. There were the two leaders of two worlds keenly talking in the presence of Christ—majestically conspicuous in
an icon overlooking this shattering event. "Thou has con-
quered, thou Galilean" could well have subtitled that
photograph.

Yet, even as thousands of east Europeans broke through
the shattered Berlin Wall, the real significance of those
events still calls out for assessment and discernment, for
there will be no good news if those brave pilgrims only
exchange the sour wine of the communism of the East for
the bitter wine of the materialism of the West. To change
the metaphor: "A plague on both your houses!" There are
signs that the aggressive and acquisitive materialism of
the West is already also failing to produce the goods it
promised to its distracted worshipers. Drugs, violence,
AIDS, alcoholism are but a few of the obvious symptoms
that the gods of affluence and materialism have failed
miserably to bring happiness, wholeness, and that inner
contentment without which creative work and gracious
civilizations are not possible. And all this while the results
of greed and the abuse of the earth bring evident signs
every day in the skies, in the oceans, and in our climate
that the environment has been irreversibly raped to the
point where there will be serious, if not devasting, results
for our children's generation. For, "the fight for our planet,
physical and spiritual, a fight of cosmic proportions, is not
a vague matter of the future; it has already started," wrote
Aleksandr Solzhenitsyn. "The forces of evil have begun
their decisive offensive. You can feel their presence, yet
your screens and publications are full of prescribed smiles
and raised glasses. What is the joy about?"[1]

In a sense, the Christian perspective insists on speaking
by contradiction of joyful good news even at such times as
this: For when the credit of hedonism is low, that is the
time to order the real champagne of the gospel. For "when

these things begin to take place," insists Jesus in his contradictory counsel, "raise your heads and look up." Yes, such a time and such a season are indeed "opportunities to bear witness." It is precisely when the false gods are discredited that it is high time (God's time) to lift up the one true and living God: that "name that is above every name" and that refuses to go away from the pages of our history books. He is risen, and he is alive, and there he is on the front page of the *New York Times!* He refuses to go away after two thousand years of rejection, suppression, scorn, and indifference.

"The best metaphor for our world today," wrote Carlo Corretto, "is astronauts speeding through the cosmos, with their life-supporting capsule pierced by a meteorite fragment. But the Church resembles Mary and Joseph traveling from Egypt to Nazareth on a donkey, holding in their arms the weakness and the poverty of the child Jesus; God incarnate."[2] Throughout history, the churches (all of them) have been tempted and have frequently succumbed to the temptation to beat the world at its own game. In place of the worldliness of the world, we have so often only offered the worldliness of the Church: seeking to give to people what they think they want, rather than what God alone knows they surely need. A fully "gospelled" Church must be faithful in bearing only Jesus in its arms—God incarnate—and in holding him up to the world as the Truth, the Life, and the only Way out of the bondage, sin, shame, and sadness of Egypt, home to the heart of God where we all truly belong (that other Nazareth). For we were made by God and for God and, as St. Augustine discovered (at a similar moment in history when the world was crashing about his ears), "our hearts are restless until they rest in God" and God alone.

This indeed, then, is a "time to bear testimony" as the millennium hysteria mounts in a strange, mixed cacophony of confidence and loss of nerve; of idealism and morbid realism; of superficial happiness and a profound alienation and despair. "This will be a time to bear testimony," and that is precisely the task, the responsibility, and the privilege to which a Decade of Evangelization (heralded by all the mainstream churches) is calling us.

Yet it must be admitted that neither the Church of England nor the Episcopal Church in America has been particularly conspicuous in evangelistic zeal in recent history. "We have sub-contracted the work of evangelism to the Baptists, to the Pentecostals," the Reverend Tom Barnett claimed recently at a diocesan convention in St. Louis. "We have said," he maintained, "let them make new Christians and when they graduate, we will take them." There is enough uncomfortable truth in that assessment to give us cause to reflect with penitence as we begin the Decade of Evangelization. It does not always have to be thus and certainly not in a church that has known more sturdy and heroic chapters in its evangelistic history.

The principal purpose in writing this book is an attempt (albeit inadequate) to reclaim *evangelism* as a gospel word and as a joyful responsibility for the mainstream churches in general and for the Episcopal Church in particular. *Evangelism* is an entirely appropriate word in the vocabulary of catholicism. It also has its proper place in the language of tradition, reason, and Christian experience through the ages. It is a catholic, reformed, and reasonable exercise in the whole Church and more than that; for without it in *this* generation, there will be only a fragile and impoverished Church, if any Church at all, in the *next* generation. Let no one be duped: evangelism is not the exclusive property of the mass evangelists. It is ours, and it is high time we reclaimed it, cherished it, and began to exercise it conspicuously and conscientiously.

The Anglican Institute, of which I am privileged to be

the founding Episcopal director, has given me both the opportunity and the responsibility in the six years since it was founded, to concentrate on the ministry of evangelism—that is to say, on a ministry of the Word: the printed Word, the preached Word, and the Word through the media of video- and audio-tape ministries. That mandate and the means to exercise that mandate have been given to set me free as a bishop in the Church of God, to test again the deep waters of this ministry. The Episcopal Church, furthermore, has generously extended to me, through the House of Bishops as a collegiate member, hospitality and a ready welcome to enter almost every diocese of the Episcopal Church to practice that ministry among my fellow clergy and ministers of the gospel.

That ministry has been richly blessed. I have learned much and unlearned much at the same time. The following pages reflect some of what I have learned in thirty years of ordained ministry, fifteen years as a bishop (ten in a diocese), and just over five years as the Episcopal director of the Anglican Institute.

The central thesis of these pages stems from a deep conviction that the revitalization of our parishes is the key to the Decade of Evangelization. When a church, congregation, or parish is revitalized and renewed to what I have chosen to call *apostolic point*, it will inevitably become evangelistic and effective in evangelization. In many ways, this is a very low-key book, seeking to examine those basic ingredients in the life of the local community of faith that can raise up a congregation to be truly apostolic and therefore evangelistic. It takes for granted many of the insights of the renewal movement and in a real way is a sequel to a book I wrote in 1986, *The Gospel Conspiracy in the Episcopal Church*. This book was written out of the experience of the renewal movement in the Episcopal Church and has been widely used throughout America and Canada in study groups in parishes.

Chapter 8 rather painstakingly sets out, almost step by step, what an Anglican parish might do in order to prepare for a parish mission or evangelistic event. It subsequently outlines in some detail one kind of evangelistic event and mission service the author has found particularly effective and fruitful. It reflects in some detail the kind of requirements requested from any parish that looks to the Institute for a teaching mission or an evangelistic crusade in its parish or in a group of parishes.

Yet everything depends on the faithful and expectant response, especially by seminarians at one end and bishops at the other (and everyone between) if the Decade of Evangelism is to fulfill God's purposes and promises in our day.

For this is an urgent and timely call to our church to recover our evangelistic nerve and our passion for the gospel. This book offers but one brief and modest resource for parish clergy and congregations that wish to put all they are and have on the line of the ultimate concern and mandate of the Church, so tersely and yet eloquently expressed in the title of the Manila Manifesto (1989): "Calling the whole Church to take the whole gospel to the whole world."

Michael Marshall
The Anglican Institute
St. Louis, MO
January 6, 1990
Feast of the Epiphany

Notes

1. Cited in Charles Colson, *Against the Night: Living in the New Dark Ages* (Ann Arbor, MI: Vine Books, Servant Publications, 1989), 55.
2. Carlo Carretto, *The God Who Comes* (London: Darton, Longman and Todd, 1974), 83.

ONE

What Is the Mandate for Evangelism Now?

THE LARGER PICTURE

"It is highly likely that the modern world will witness a very significant outburst of evangelism as it heads towards a new century. The mood has changed drastically in the last decade. Most modern churches acknowledge that the Western world needs to be evangelized afresh."[1]

Presumably something of a similar insight had prompted recent resolutions at Christian gatherings calling for the 1990s to be a Decade of Evangelism. In some ways, the call for a Decade of Evangelism represented, when it came, a remarkable convergence of convictions. For example, the General Convention of the Episcopal Church in July 1988 called for a Decade of Evangelism in these stirring words when it resolved,

> that the 69th General Convention designate the decade of the 1990's a Decade of Evangelism during which we will reclaim and affirm our baptismal call to evangelism and endeavor, with other Christian denominations to reach every unchurched person in the nine Provinces of the Episcopal Church with the Gospel of Jesus Christ. . . .

The meeting of SOMA (Sharing of Ministries Abroad)

before the Lambeth Conference of 1988 spoke with white-hot passion of the burgeoning of evangelism in Africa, Asia, and in South America and called with a similar resolution for a Decade of Evangelism. It was not surprising, therefore, that the bishops of Lambeth, meeting subsequently at the Lambeth Conference of 1988, passed two significant resolutions:

> This Conference, recognizing that evangelism is the primary task given to the Church, asks each Province and diocese of the Anglican Communion, in cooperation with other Christians, to make the closing years of this millennium a "Decade of Evangelism"with a renewed and united emphasis on making Christ known to the people of His world.

A further resolution at the same Conference recommended "that Provinces and dioceses encourage, train, equip and send out lay people for evangelism and ministry."[2]

Now, it must be freely admitted that such aspirations can degenerate into little more than rhetoric and that high-sounding calls for a Decade of Evangelism might eventually add up to little more than a paper exercise and a decade of discussion about the possibility of evangelism! The cynic is naturally tempted to say that *evangelism* is now the "in" word and the new idolatry: it was *ecumenism* in the 1970s, *renewal* in the 1980s, and now it's *evangelism* in the 1990s! So what? What next? Furthermore, if the statistics for the declines in church membership, especially in the Episcopal Church of America and the Church of England, were to be projected for the next thirty years, it might seem that they would both be out of business by the beginning of the twenty-first century. Something has to happen for those two churches sooner or later within the larger Anglican Communion, which is in a much healthier state overall and continues to grow in converts daily. The picture, of course, is very different in other parts of the Anglican Communion where church growth has been clearly in evidence for many years. Worldwide statistics for Anglicans show no less than twelve hundred new Anglicans in the world every day, largely in the developing countries of the Third World. For, significantly, in those countries where Christianity is a minority religion, churches are growing (often dramatically) in numbers and at a pace. In such countries, the Christian communities have always seen themselves as being in a missionary situation, as a conspicuous minority that would not survive unless they went out of their way to make converts, to convince and convert those who have not yet heard of Jesus Christ or who were even positively hostile to the gospel.

So we need from the outset to get our heads up to see the larger picture and nothing less than a global vision as the context for the Decade of Evangelism in particular and worldwide evangelization in general.

"Philosophers," wrote Karl Marx, " have only *interpreted* the world differently; the point is, however, to *change* it." Surely the vision of Christians cannot be less than the vision of Marxists, for we also, as Christ's people, are in the business of changing the world and not merely of interpreting it. Interpretation is the work of philosophers, yet Christians are intended to be much more than philosophers or ideologists. For the mandate of Christ in his great commission still stands: "Go therefore and make disciples of all nations, baptizing them in the name of the Father and of the Son and of the Holy Spirit, teaching them to observe all that I have commanded you; and lo, I am with you always, to the close of the age" (Matt. 28:19).

Of course, some New Testament scholars apparently have reason to doubt the authenticity of these words ascribed to Jesus. However, there can surely be no doubt on reading the New Testament as a whole that the words of the Great Commission in St. Matthew's Gospel represent the declared intention of Jesus in his general charge

to the apostles and to his Church, namely, that the
Christian faith should be preached to the four corners of
the earth. "You shall receive power," says Jesus in the
opening chapter of the Book of Acts, "when the Holy
Spirit has come upon you; and you shall be my witnesses
in Jerusalem and in all Judea and in Samaria and to the
end of the earth" (Acts 1:8). So we need to set the situation
as it is today, not in the context of church growth (or
decline), past achievements, or future projections, decades
of evangelism or of decadence: "It is not for you to know
times and seasons" (vs. 7) cautioned Jesus before he gave
his promise of power. "But rather, what you *do* need to
know is that you are, indeed, my witnesses and that all the
necessary strength and power will be given to you to be
worldwide witnesses." So we need rather to settle for
nothing less than "the world for Christ."Yet,

> those who evaluate the progress of church growth tell
> us that there are 400 million more people in the world
> now without the Word of life than there were thirty
> years ago. This is the case despite the increased number
> of people professing to follow the Saviour. In fact, if the
> present trend of church growth continues, considering
> the projected increase in population, there will be more
> unevangelized people by the end of this century than
> there are persons living on earth today.[3]

In fact, the full picture is both more encouraging and
more discouraging at the same time. The twentieth century has witnessed nothing less than a phenomenal expansion of Christianity and for this we should give thanks to
God. "In this century this category of Christian believers
[i.e., the committed] has grown from about 40 million in
1900 to about 500 million today, and at this moment is
growing twice as fast as any other major religious group."[4]
However, at the same time, we have seen an even larger
(massively larger) increase in the world's population.
Hence, the proportion of Christian witness in the world is

smaller today than in earlier ages. The statistics are perhaps best summarized in a way that we can easily grasp in
the words of the Manila Manifesto: "The world population today is approaching six billion. One third of them
nominally confess Christ. Of the remaining four billion
half have heard of Him and the other half have not."[5]
However, the magnitude of the challenge should not
discourage us. "The harvest is plentiful" indeed, "but the
laborers are few" (Matt. 9:37). It has always been thus.
Nevertheless, the mandate and the invitation stands:
"Pray therefore the Lord of the harvest to send out
laborers into his harvest." It was the Protestant theologian and the prior of the Taizé community, Roger
Schultz, who said that "statistics are signs from God."
Like all signs, they need interpretation within the context
of God's promises and supremely against the overwhelm-
ing contradiction of the resurrection: For we must be constantly reminded that it is in weakness that we find true
strength and that it is little people who by God's grace
become the great people of history. Christians must not
speak of success but rather of fruitfulness, and we do not
seek the approbation of the crowd or the mercurial evidence of pollsters.

Yet if we place the call by the Episcopal Church—or,
indeed, the resolution of the worldwide Anglican Communion to evangelization in the 1990s—in this somewhat
daunting worldwide context, we shall almost certainly be
tempted to shrug our shoulders in despair, at worst, or
approach the Decade of Evangelism with, at best, a cautious indifference. The Episcopal Church is a very little
church—a weak and fragile church numbering in America
now approximately 2.5 million members. Compare this
with the 78.9 million Roman Catholics in America or the
estimated 30 million Baptists. The situation is not much
more impressive or reassuring if we look at the so-called
worldwide Anglican Communion, which claims to rep-

resent 70 million Christians—and that is certainly a very generous estimate! Compare these figures with the numerical strength of the Great Western Church of Rome, which has throughout the world over 700 million members, or the Orthodox churches of the East, which constitute today something like 850 million. In what realistic sense, therefore, can Anglicanism take up the challenge of the Great Commission once we begin to see it—as see it we must—on a truly worldwide, intercultural, and international scale?

It would seem there are at least two necessary presuppositions if Anglicanism is ever to take its appropriate place in the front line of world mission today. Or, in the challenging words of the manifesto from Manila in 1989: "calling the whole Church to take the whole gospel to the whole world."

THE RENEWAL FACTOR

"The church [of England] as it now stands," wrote the phlegmatic and urbane Thomas Arnold in 1832, "no human power can save." Look at the situation through spectacles with lenses ground for worldly perspective only and you have to admit that the whole prospect of world evangelization is absurd: absurd, that is, in just the same way as any real match between Goliath the warrior and David the shepherd boy must have been viewed as absurd through the spectacles of common sense by both the Philistines and the Israelites in the days of the Old Testament. Yet what worldly eyes do *not* see, and what only eyes of faith can *really* see, is that the scales are already tipped, not in favor of Goliath, but, on the contrary, that they are well tipped from the outset in favor of David the shepherd boy. So it is with the date of Thomas Arnold's lugubrious projection. The year 1832 in the history of the Church of England with hindsight is not seen as the year of the ultimate demise of the Church of England. Rather, *au contraire*, it is seen as the very year that marked the beginning of wonderful revival, that in turn ultimately burgeoned by the end of that century into several decades of the greatest missionary expansion in the history of the Church of England. But notice—it was renewal that issued in mission and evangelism, church growth and social witness. Notice also that things had to get bad before they could get better. The chances are that Saul permitted David to represent the Israelites against Goliath as a kind of last ditch stand: there was no hope anyway, and frankly David stood as good a chance as anybody. It was an outside chance. Of course, in reality, David stood the only chance there was, and he was certain to succeed in overthrowing the Philistines precisely because he did not rely upon earthly power but upon the true power of God, as always manifested in apparent human weakness. For the boy David had already been anointed by Samuel and therefore came to Goliath, not "with a sword and a spear," but "in the name" (and therefore in the power, for the two are the same in Scripture) "of the Lord of hosts."

Only a Church anointed, renewed, and in the name of Jesus can realistically take its place in the armies of the Lord for confrontation with evil and with the powers of darkness. Let no one be deceived or labor under any illusions: a Decade of Evangelism will necessarily involve a decade of confrontation, not simply with flesh and blood, but with "principalities and powers" and the rulers of darkness. For as St. Paul knew only too well and as he hastens to remind us, "We are not contending against flesh and blood, but against the principalities, against the powers, against the world rulers of this present darkness, against the spiritual hosts of wickedness in the heavenly places" (Eph. 6:12). Things are no different, basically, whether it is in the age of the Roman Empire or the age of the empires of our own day.

Last time Christianity took serious issue with Islam, for example (in the Crusades of the Middle Ages), it was with "a sword and a spear" in our hands. This time we must come to them (and to others) anointed and in the name and in the power of the Lord of hosts. I am not calling for a mindless war between one fundamentalism and another. A plague on both of those houses. But I am saying that the call to win Islam for Christ is on the agenda, along with other great powers who at the moment reject the claims of Christ. Any notion of world evangelism simply has to take such a confrontation seriously. The equivalent of Paul standing on the Acropolis and addressing the Athenians with their entrenched religions would be paralleled in our own day with a similar address to the people in Tokyo, Istanbul, or Jerusalem. It takes, of course, conviction and courage, but no conviction in the world without Emmanuel (God with us) is going to achieve anything. Only a Church renewed in faith, prayer, love, and the power of God's own spirit can go forth and take its place in this battle. Education, apologetics, keen minds, and patient dialogue will all have their part to play in this overall vision and in a new obedience to the call of Christ to world evangelization. Yet education must be subsumed into evangelization, and dialogue alone will not be sufficient to win souls to Christ. The message must be anointed at every turn with the power of the Holy Spirit through the earnest prayer of the faithful if the contemporary walls of Jericho are to come tumbling down. We should never forget that the devil has long ago also passed a resolution calling for worldwide evangelization of his program and has doubtless reaffirmed that resolution and doubled his efforts in readiness for the 1990s!

Happily, often the very commitment to evangelism itself brings in its turn renewal: what Dr. Visser't Hooft calls the "boomerang effect" of evangelism and mission.

The church which would call the world to order is suddenly called to order itself. The question which it would throw into the world: "Do you know that you belong to Christ?" comes back as an echo. The church discovers that it cannot truly evangelize, that its message is unconvincing unless it lets itself be transformed and renewed, unless it becomes what it believes it is.[6]

So renewal must be part and parcel of the call to evangelism. Every diocese, every parish, and every Christian must seek increasingly to constitute the kind of Christian presence that we already believe we should be. For renewal is not a party manifesto for some Christians who happen to like that sort of thing. Renewal is for the whole Church, and the secret of the renewal is an ever-deepening dependency on him upon whom all things depend. That conviction—often reached in pain, defeat, and despair—that apart from him we "can do nothing," gives power to our message. Conversely, only his Church together *with* him—and he with us—gives us that fresh gospel confidence that "nothing will be impossible" (Luke 1:37). The Church frequently has to be brought first to its Waterloo or to its 1832 before it can reach out for that kind of anointing and empowerment. An individual or a nation first has to be brought to its knees in weakness and need before it can be raised up again in power and fruitfulness: put another way, we need to know and to embody first the defeat of crucifixion before we can subsequently know the victory of resurrection. It is precisely when we are cast down that God can raise us up: it is at times of break*down* that God can at last break*through*.

Happily, renewal is with us. In our day, God is renewing his people in a springtime of new love and new compassion. Of course, the devil will have a hand in this as in everything else while it is still "meantime": for that is the time of his hour and the hour of "the power of darkness" (Luke 22:53). A renewed church (like the Corinthian church in the New Testament) is always in a mess, and perhaps the only saving difference is that it knows that it is in a mess! New churches and renewed churches, as new Christians and renewed Christians, have many problems and difficulties—sometimes it would seem more problems and more difficulties than just nice quiet, dead churches, or well-trained and well-tamed churchgoers. A grave-yard, after all, is, on the whole, more orderly and peaceful than a party, let alone than a banquet! We should thank God that he is faithful and continues to bring new life out of death, new strength out of weakness, and an Easter people out of the disarray and defeat of Good Friday. So we need to affirm with determination that evangelizing the Church for mission is a necessary part of the Decade for Evangelism and will play a significant and, hopefully, a helpful part in this book. Renewal in faith, in prayer, in Bible study, in preaching, worship, and ministry are all necessary concomitants of evangelism and all of these must touch and effect the life of the Church in the diocese, the parish and the pew.

EVANGELISM—THE TASK OF THE WHOLE CHURCH

If the renewal factor is the first presupposition to a Decade of Evangelism, the second presupposition must surely be the realization that the task of proclaiming the whole gospel for the whole world is essentially a challenge to the whole people of God and not just the clergy or evangelists. For it is only when the whole people of God come alive in the life of the Spirit, that the spiritual temperature reaches what I call, and shall continue to call throughout this book, *apostolic point*. When water reaches boiling point, two things begin to happen: It takes on new chemical properties that dramatically affect everything with which it comes in contact. And, as we say, it "boils over" and simply cannot be contained by the vessel in which it is boiling. It overflows. It is then chemically converted to steam with new properties that can be harnessed as power. So with the Church that is renewed to apostolic point: It inevitably overflows into evangelism affecting the lives of the surrounding community. For we cannot and we must not go for evangelism for its own sake in a flush of new and self-conscious enthusiasm. That is to make an idol of it. If the call for the Decade of Evangelism is seen along these lines—"now we've got to go all out to get them"—it will be crude, cruel, and ineffective. Evangelism is not a thing in itself: rather it is the by-product of the Church being the Church. Such a Church, renewed to apostolic point, inevitably witnesses to what is already happening in its corporate life: "we cannot but speak of what we have seen and heard" (Acts 4:20) is always the apostolic constraint. Evangelism becomes, in such a faith community, inevitable. It is no use, in the name of common sense, caution, or any other worldly attitude, asking renewed Christians *not* to evangelize! Like water when it reaches a certain temperature, it boils out of the pot and invades the surrounding area. Or put another way, water that has reached a certain temperature gives off steam and that steam, properly directed, harnesses a powerful force that moves people. Boiling water is the basic ingredient and component for power and transport. So renewed faith is the essential component for an apostolic Church and for evangelism.

Evangelists have their place in this larger enterprise. They are called out of the Church for a particular ministry of evangelism. Even in the New Testament, evangelism and evangelists are named along with other ministries and are seen as constituting the whole body of ministry and witness in the Church. For example, Philip is titled as an evangelist in the Book of the Acts of the Apostles (21:8). In the fourth chapter of the Epistle to the Ephesians, the evangelists are listed along with prophets, apostles, pastors, and teachers as having a gifted and specific ministry within the whole body (Ephesians 4). Timothy is urged along with all his other duties to "do the work of an evangelist" (2 Tim. 4:5). Evangelism in New Testament terms, we can safely believe, was a recognized and specific ministry within the whole body of the Church and took its place alongside all the other ministries that are necessary in a healthy and apostolic Church. Certainly the apostles were strongly evangelistic in their ministries. We are told in the Book of the Acts of the Apostles how they very soon found their lives filled with administration and how soon they needed to delegate that aspect of their apostolic ministry in order to devote themselves "to prayer and to the ministry of the Word" (Acts 6:4). Incidentally, it is perhaps worth noting that evangelist was not a job description in the New Testament. The job description of the seven deacons in the Book of Acts was to "serve tables" (Acts 6:2). The diaconate was an order in the early Church: deacons were men and women under orders. Nevertheless, Stephen was conspicuous *within* that job description as a preacher (not only to apostolic point but to martrydom point). Philip, called as one of those same seven deacons, was also specifically named as an evangelist (chap. 21). Both Stephen and Philip were faithful to their work as deacons while also being committed to preaching the gospel as evangelists. Truth to tell, witnessing and evangelizing were an inevitable part of being a Christian, while, of course, some Christians in New Testament times were conspicuous specifically as evangelists and preachers and clearly received the specific graces to empower them for these tasks. All baptized Christians are called by their baptism to witness through deed and word to the life of Christ at work within them.

Eusebius, the fourth-century historian, speaks most eloquently of the work of evangelists and the place evangelism held in the life of the apostles and their successors.

Nevertheless, evangelists are not the same necessarily as apostles, though every apostle is also an evangelist. Lay people, according to Eusebius, were conspicuous for their part in evangelism. "Very many of the disciples of that age," he writes,   .

> whose hearts had been ravished by the divine Word with a burning love of Christianity, first fulfilled the command of the Saviour and divided their goods among the needy. Then they set out on long journeys, doing the work of evangelists, eagerly striving to preach Christ to those who have never heard the Word of faith, and to deliver to them the holy gospels. In foreign lands they simply laid the foundations of the faith. That done, they appointed others as shepherds, entrusting them with the care of the new growth, while they themselves proceeded with the grace and cooperation of God to other countries and other places.[7]

For in another place the same Eusebius tells us that there were "many evangelists of the Word who sought earnestly to use their inspired zeal after the example of the apostles, for the increase and building up of the Divine Word."[8] What a glorious picture that conjures up! How we need in our day to be "ravished" by the good news of the gospel! Then there would not even be a need for a Decade of Evangelism: the enemies of Christianity would find themselves compelled to speak of the disease (not simply the decade) of evangelism! In all this, evangelists had and must continue to have a particular part to play in evangelism, though evangelism is certainly not confined to them. For in a renewed Church, as in the New Testament, witnessing and evangelism are the property and responsibility of the whole people of God.

Clearly, as we have said, the apostles and their successors were specifically anointed for evangelism in the service of proclamation and missionary outreach. "In accordance with the divine scriptures," continues Eusebius, "the voice of its inspired evangelists and apostles 'went forth to the whole earth.' " He goes on to record the rumor, related in the *Acts of Thomas* that the apostles drew lots in order to decide their destinations to different parts of the world. So he tells us that "Thomas obtained by lot Parthia, Andrew Scythia, John Asia . . . but Peter seems to have preached to the Jews and the dispersion in Pontus and Galatia, Bithynia, Cappadocia and Asia and at the end he came to Rome."[9] The same apocryphal book (the *Acts of Thomas*) asserts that Thomas himself went to India and there is much contemporary evidence to support this claim. In any event, Jesus saw the principal task of the apostolic college as one of evangelism in the specific sense of proclamation. Yet as we have seen, we must not stop there. Evangelism, "is clearly not a responsiblity only of the clergy or only of the laity, but of all persons baptized into the death and resurrection of Christ. Evangelism is to be incorporated," insists John Coburn, "into the mutual practice of Christian living for us all, while certain persons may be called for a special role as 'evangelists' they do so only to express a common function belonging to the whole body of Christian people."[10] So at one and the same time we must speak not only of evangelism as a particular ministry but rather of evangelism as a characteristic of the whole people of God. We see this particularity within the generality in many other aspects of the Church's life. For example, in the same way that we speak of apostles as specific people in the Church yet in the same breath we necessarily speak of the whole Church as being apostolic. Apostles are there to make sure that the whole Church is apostolic in its nature. So with the priesthood. The ordained ministry of the priesthood exists to make sure that the whole Church is priestly in its character. You do not get a priesthood of all believers (which incidentally is not the same thing as the priesthood of every believer) from a generality but rather from a particularity. A priesthood of some specifically ordained priests is the source from which the whole Church derives its general, priestly character. In turn, of course, the ordained priesthood derives its particular gift from Jesus, the one great high priest. So with evangelism. The evangelization of the world by all believers is derived from the evangelism of some believers whom we call evangelists, yet who in turn derive their evangelism from Jesus, the great evangelist, apostle, and bearer of the good news of the kingdom.

Proclamation and the verbalization of that good news, as we shall see later, have a conspicuous place in evangelism as in the overall ministry of Jesus. But verbal proclamation is not the whole story. Jesus embodies the message of evangelism and expresses that message in all that he does and says and is. So with the Body of Christ, the Church: it is strongly evangelistic in all its characteristics and in all that it does and in all that it says and all that it is. That message is embodied within the whole Body of Christ—the Church—and in all the baptized. Yet in saying that, hopefully we are not making either of two errors. We are not, on the one hand, saying that, because evangelism is a characteristic of the whole people of God, it does not at the same time belong to particular people within the Body. On the other hand, in saying that evangelism is everything that Jesus does and says and is, we are not saying that verbal proclamation is not a very important, distinctive, and indispensable activity of an evangelistic Church as it was in the overall life and ministry of Jesus.

EVANGELISM AND THE WHOLE WITNESS OF THE CHURCH

So in all this we must surely affirm the statement about evangelism as set out in the Lausanne I covenant: namely, that "in the church's mission of sacrificial service evangel-

ism is primary."[11] Furthermore, as John Stott so rightly
points out, "because evangelism is fundamentally an an-
nouncement, some verbalization is necessary if the content and the good news is to be communicated with any
precision."[12]

At this stage some working definition of evangelism is
clearly necessary. The Greek word *evangelizomai* means
quite simply "to announce the *evangelion*"—namely, the
good news. Good news, as in contemporary speech, can
mean something quite straightforward: almost, we might
say, secular in its meaning. We see such a use of the word
in the New Testament when the angel Gabriel in St. Luke's
Gospel tells Zechariah "the good news" that his wife,
Elizabeth, is to bear him a son (Luke 1:19). Indeed, the
famous preacher Leslie Weatherhead recalls the Church in
its gospel preaching to precisely that kind of announce-
ment. He suggests that the gospel is the kind of thing that
can be shouted across the street or over the garden fence:
"It's all right, she's had her baby!" "He's out of the
hospital, and it's all right!" Gospel proclamation should
be so to the point that it demands the exclamation mark at
the end of its short sentences. It defies discussion by the
very nature of its presentation. It defies discussion because
it demands a decision. It is the sort of statement that is so
presented that you simply cannot shrug your shoulders
and say, "So what?" For such a proclamation then
necessarily goes on to lead the hearer to say something
like, "Is there anything *I can do*?" Yet in saying this, there
is a further subtlety. The proclamation of exclamation is
such that it is putting a question to the hearers: not even
just a question but rather supremely *the* question and
challenge, the ultimate question that can only be put rhe-
torically via unequivocal proclamation and exclamation.
A sufficiently big statement automatically raises big questions. "We are destroying our environment by the minute!"
Such a message—proclamation—demands an exclamation

mark at the end of such a headline, for in many ways the good news is headline, banner line material.

Yet the minute we make this kind of statement in this kind of way, not only does it elicit a question from the recipients, but the very content of the proclamation also implicitly puts a challenge and question to the hearers. "We are destroying our environment by the minute!" implies at one and the same time that I want to suggest a challenge. "And what are you going to do about it now—this minute?" It does not suggest setting up a committee or forming a discussion group. Immediate decision, not infinite discussion, is the appropriate response to such proclamation. Good news proclamation, therefore, in the specific sense of the good news of the New Testament, is not so much God's answers to the questions that we are asking but rather points to the question that God is asking us in the same breath as he is telling us what is really happening. So, Dr. Visser't Hooft writes,

> I do not believe that evangelism is adequately described as answering the questions which men are asking, however deep those questions may be. For evangelism is in the first place the transmission of God's question to man. And that question is and remains whether we are willing to accept Jesus Christ as the one and only Lord of life.[13]

In one sense there is such an objectivity in the New Testament about the terms *evangelize* and *evangelization* that our first interest is not in the response of the people who hear the message but rather with the adequacy of the proclamation of the message itself. In the Book of the Acts of the Apostles (14:7) we are simply told the apostles evangelized in such and such an area. For example, the apostles "evangelized in many villages of the Samaritans" while "Philip" (the evangelist) "evangelized all the towns along the Palestinian coastline" (Acts 8:25–40). (It seems that Philip was forever at the beck and call of the Holy Spirit

and as an evangelist was forever being sent at very little
notice on rather extraordinary errands.) However, the
narrative is not concerned at this point to tell us whether
or not the inhabitants of those towns received the Word,
believed in Jesus, or were baptized. Properly understood,
the evangelist is not concerned with success, numbers, or
the opinion polls in the papers the next morning. That
was surely one of the implied errors in the definition in
1919 of the archbishops' (Canterbury and York) *Inquiry
into the Evangelistic Work of the Church* when it defined
evangelism as "so to present Christ Jesus in the power of
the Holy Spirit that men should put their trust in God
through Him. . . . " There was a dangerous and misleading consequence clause implied in such a statement. For
you could equally (wrongly) define evangelism by saying
that to evangelize is so to present Christ Jesus in the
power of the Holy Spirit that men will *reject* Jesus. Neither
rejection nor acceptance are the primary concerns of the
evangelist. In the parable of the sower, no market research
is done on the ground before sowing the seed. Rather,
there is a ruthless, almost prodigal, single-mindedness
about the sower: he sows literally "in season and out of
season" (2 Tim. 4:2) whether the ground is good or bad or
indifferent. His only concern is to get the Word out, and
so his work can be summed up with the injunction, "Take
heed only to right sowing."

For too long the Church has sought to trim and tailor
its message to make it easily acceptable: first to this vogue
and then to that fad. There is an objectivity about the
Word of God, for in the end, God is the only real evangelist, and the Holy Spirit is both in the heart of the evangelist as well as out there in the crowd, preparing the soil
of the human heart to hear and receive the Word and so to
make the connection between what is said and what is
heard and received.

However, the helpful point in that same definition of

1919 is to see evangelism not only as exclusively verbal. It is rather the presentation of Jesus Christ in all his fullness —making Jesus present by the power of the Holy Spirit. Hence the need to set evangelism within the larger concept of mission. Therefore, in Acts 8:12, we read that Philip evangelized "concerning the kingdom of God and the name of Jesus Christ." In other words, Philip went through those towns doing what Jesus did and saying what Jesus said, with the signs of the kingdom following: healing, casting out devils, etc. If a reporter had gone from Jerusalem asking Philip what he had been doing in his evangelistic program, he could have sent back exactly the same report to the elders at Jerusalem as Jesus sent back to John the Baptist, who had made a similar inquiry from prison: namely, "go and tell what" is happening (Matt. 11:4).

For it is as true for the Church today as it was for the Church in Philip's day: namely, that there is promise attached to the Great Commission. Jesus promises the disciples and apostles that he will be with them "to the close of the age" (Matt. 28:20). That is, in a sense, a further echo of earlier promises made by Jesus to his disciples and apostles in their work of evangelism: "If they kept my word, they will keep yours also" (John 15:20). Furthermore, the disciples are promised that, if they truly believe in Jesus, then they will do the same works as he did in his earthly ministry "and greater works" because Jesus has gone "to the Father" (John 14:12). What a promise! What confidence that promise gave to the timid Church. They would not have spoken of the problems of evanglization but rather of the promises of evangelization. For them, world evangelization was not a problem to be solved so much as a promise to be celebrated and vindicated in their daily experience out in the mission field of God's world.

They knew now that the ministry of Christ would be no less powerful because of his earthly and apparent

absence but if anything, rather more powerful and more
effective because of his continuing, spiritual presence.
Nothing was beyond their capability, eternally aided as
they were by the Holy Spirit. Jesus has gone to the Father,
and so he has sent the Holy Spirit to be with his Church in
order that the Church may be Jesus Christ for the world
today.

EVANGELISM AND MISSION

So in its totality, the Church is nothing less than the
mission of God. God so loves that he sends Jesus. Jesus,
in turn, so loves that he also sends the apostles in the same
way as the Father had originally sent him. "As the Father
has sent me, even so I send you" (John 20:21). The agenda
is the same for both Jesus and the apostles. The apostolic
mission in all its fullness is the work of the Church in
every age. The agenda of that mission is the same as Jesus
gave in his charge to the twelve and to the seventy in the
Gospel. (Luke 10). So then the impetus for all mission
originates in the heart of God.

"I send you out. . . . Carry no purse, no bag, no
sandals. . . ." So we learn from the outset that quality of
complete dependence upon God that is essential for
fruitful mission. "Whom he calls, he empowers," says St.
Anselm. In other words, God will provide everything
necessary for mission right down to food, drink, and
salaries. "Whenever you enter a town and they receive
you, eat what is set before you." Put another way: Live
the apostolic life and then you will be better placed to
deliver the apostolic message. "Heal the sick." Healing
and mission go hand in hand. Furthermore, we know that
they also cast out demons in the course of that first
mission, because they could hardly wait to tell Jesus all
about this on their return (vs. 17). The authority of his
name was sufficient, and that authority is a gift that Jesus

was given by the Father and that Jesus in turn then gives to the seventy (vs. 19). Notice how Jesus prefaces the Great Commission in St. Matthew: "All authority in heaven and on earth has been given to me. Go therefore . . . " (Matt. 28:19). We must not set out on a Decade of Evangelization nor, indeed, undertake any corner of mission without first reclaiming these promises, celebrating them, and being empowered by them. Only foolishness or blatant arrogance could possibly tempt us to do so.

Then and then only, in this context, does Jesus tell those timid disciples what kind of verbal proclamation their message must be. "Say to them" (the inhabitants of the towns) "the kingdom of God has come near to you" (Luke 10:9). The evangelistic content of the mission is to preach the kingdom of God in just the same way as Jesus did when he came into Galilee (Mark 1:14ff).

Such is the relation of evangelism to mission. Yet it has to be said that in recent years the word *mission* has been distorted and generalized out of existence to mean everything that God is doing in the world. We are not here to play semantics. We are here to seek obedience to the Word of God revealed to us in the teaching of Jesus. Mission means specifically what Jesus was sent out to do and, in its turn, what Jesus sent his Church out to do from the time of Pentecost to the end of time. Social concern, care for the world, the poor, the homeless are all surely part of God's love and concern for his world—the love that he felt to such an extent that he sent Jesus into the world to express and manifest it. As such it embraces all that Jesus said and did and was. Yet we need to know from the outset that social action is no substitute for evangelism and mission. Neither is it a means to evangelism, for love needs no justification. We should love the poor because Jesus does and because in loving and serving them we are also loving and serving Jesus. We should love them, furthermore, whether they become Christians or not.

"While we were yet sinners, Christ died for us" (Rom. 5:8).

Yet there are further confusions in much talk today about mission, social action, and evangelism. Social action and justice do not need to be seen as icing on the cake. They stand in their own right as a proper concern for the people of God who worship a God of love, compassion, truth, and freedom. So we should do all this—caring and loving and serving—and at the same time not neglect the other, the specific evangelism to which the New Testament refers constantly. Such concerns of social action, if you like, are the concerns of the "first mile" of mission (Matt. 5:41). We are still "unprofitable servants" when we have done all these things and even when we have gone that "second mile," or given that "coat as well as the cloak."

Yet we might still ask, If social action is not a means of evangelism, is it in some sense a manifestation of evangelism? Yes, in some sense it can be. John Stott suggests that it is a kind of a sacrament of evangelism, that education and medicine are outward and visible signs of an inward message and an inward conviction. However, they do not replace the need to evangelize and to make the love of God quite explicit. When Mother Teresa cares for the sick and the poor and the dying, medically and physically, she also takes them in her arms and tells them in so many words that "Jesus loves" them. In other words, she makes the connection. Do we?

So John Stott writes,

> Social action is a *partner of evangelism*. As partners the two belong to each other and yet are independent of each other. Neither is a means to the other, or even a manifestation of the other. For each is an end in itself. Both are expressions of unfeigned love.[14]

John the apostle writes, "We love, because He first loved" (1 John 4:19). Again he writes, "In this is love, not that we loved God but that he loved us and sent his Son to be the

expiation for our sins" (1 John 4:10). Then follows the
mandate for mission in the very next verse, as surely as
marriage follows upon courtship: "Beloved, if God so
loved us, we also ought to love one another" (vs. 11). Or
as the National Evangelical Congress at Keele put it in
1967: "Evangelism and compassionate service belong
together in the mission of God."
  Or again:

> Although reconciliation with man is not reconcilia-
> tion with God, nor is social action evangelism, nor
> is political liberation salvation, nevertheless we af-
> firm that evangelism and socio-political involve-
> ment are both part of our Christian duty. For both
> are necessary expressions of our doctrines of God
> and man, our love of our neighbor and our obedi-
> ence to Jesus Christ.[15]

EVANGELISM AND THE ECUMENICAL SPIRIT

If evangelism is the total expression of the whole gospel
by the whole people of God, then there is a sense in which
a Decade of Evangelism should necessarily bring a new
passion for the spirit of ecumenism. "The problem of the
Church's mission is the crisis of the ecumenical movement," wrote Bishop Stephen Neill after the Second World
War. "If an ecumenical movement is not primarily a
strategy of worldwide evangelism, then it is nothing but
an interesting academic exercise."[16]
  Sadly, the demise of the ecumenical movement in the
1980s marked a time when ecumenism had in deed become largely "an academic exercise." It suffered from two
misunderstandings. The first was the replacement of our
understanding of unity by the concept of joinery. That is
to say, we saw the work of the ecumenical movement as
trying to join together large institutional blocks of Christian bodies. The primary task behind the planners' desks

was to draw up and to carpenter doctrinal formulae in a way that would permit one church to join up with another church at the level of the doctrinal drawing board. They became known (appropriately enough) as "schemes" for reunion—e.g,. the Anglican Methodist scheme.

The second cul-de-sac of this pilgrimage was a false, or rather, an inadequate view of the concept of unity. It was a largely static concept working again primarily at the level of statements of belief and intent. Such work is helpful and important to a certain extent—that is to say, it is valuable and important homework and must continue at all levels, in what have come, frequently nowadays, to be called "dialogues." Hopefully, it is a step forward that schemes have now been superceded by dialogues.

However, the way forward is not along either of these roads. The way forward is in fact the way forward that we almost stumbled upon at the Lambeth Conference in 1988. We need to replace the abstract word *unity* and the static concept of *joinery* with the more theological and dynamic word *communion*. In turn, we need to spell out how we derive the word *communion* from nothing less than our trinitarian theology, as we seek nothing less than the unity that we see revealed in the communion, life, and unity of the blessed Trinity. Anglicans are deeply divided over many doctrinal issues (some very deep and far reaching in their implications). Nevertheless, bishops left Lambeth 1988 committed to remain in communion (albeit an impaired communion) with each other. Communion is a result of a single intent that transcends particular positions and calls Christians from beyond their traditions to reach out beyond those traditions to what J.I. Packer calls "the convergence of the saints." Put another way, communion is fellowship between people and not the chanting of slogans and ideologies. However much you seek to harmonize the latter, you will not achieve communion.

Communion is a single-minded, transcendent passion

experienced in a personal relationship with God in the ascended and glorified Christ. It must be this single-minded, transcendent passion that also expels the Church beyond its present barriers for the sake of the conversion of the world. It will be within this endeavor that we shall find ourselves drawn together. It is the very opposite of what we used to say: We used to say that we sought a unity that would then enable us best to go on and evangelize the world. Now I think we have been compelled to see it the other way around. With a new sense of urgency for world evangelism, we are finding our selves increasingly drawing closer together at a point of convergence *beyond* where any of our traditions are at the present time. For we are coming to see that our traditions do not go far enough and are not sufficiently rich in their divided self-sufficiency to commend the gospel of Jesus Christ in all its fullness and with all its power—a power that alone can change lives and change the world.

There is simply no way that the churches of the Reformation can evangelize the world unless they are ready to reach out and enhance the gospel with the power of the sacraments. Similarly, there is no way that the Roman Catholic Church or the Orthodox churches of the East can evangelize the world unless they reach out to a richer doctrine of the Scriptures, the power of the preached Word, and that fuller understanding of ministry that we find among many Pentecostals and Anglicans. In their turn, Anglicans need to recover some of the insights of John Wesley and a passion for prayer and worship that we find in the nineteenth-century catholic revival. The charismatic breakthrough of the twentieth century has much to offer the rigidity and formalism of Anglicanism.

But notice this is not the drawing board or the smor-gasbord approach to ecumenism—a little bit of this and a little bit of that, all adding to variety and the spice of life! Rather, it is what I frequently call "the casserole ap-

proach": throwing into the powerful chemical mix of the
Church all the gospel ingredients necessary to bring the
people of God to the apostolic boiling point and to equip
them for ministry and mission in confrontation with evil
and the forces of darkness, sinfulness, and ignorance.
Every insight of every tradition that has been validated by
the missionary and evangelistic experience of any of the
churches over the centuries needs now to be *added*. We
need, like the wise scribe, to bring out from the treasures
of two thousand years of witness "things new and old."
This we can do largely without the doctrinal architects
getting in the way too much. We need them, but their
place is behind the lines, keeping us in touch with the
baseline of theology. Yet at the same time we need to be
released for single-minded combat, not among ourselves,
but with the common enemy of error and tyranny. It is a
truism that nothing draws a country of differing political
persuasions together better than a war with a common
foe. Indeed, as England saw in World War II, the government was necessarily a coalition simply because you could
not afford to keep out from powerful government the
talents, gifts, insights, and energies of anyone—irrespec-
tive of their political colorings.

The coalition government, drawn from all parties, led
by Winston Churchill in 1939 was not the lowest common
denominator but the richest possible "casserole" into
which all the energies and powers of people of varying
political persuasions was poured with passion.

Providing we see the task of world evangelism in a
Decade of Evangelism in sufficiently large and cosmic
terms, then we can be certain that the ecumenical spirit
will take over and, in turn, overtake all our divisions to
empower all the churches with the fullness of the gospel
for the immense task that God is longing to do with us
and through us. It is no use going into this battle with the
spirit of denominationalism. I truly believe that a decade

spent with the spirit of ecumenism forged by the common combat of world evangelism will bring us to "a larger place" in the ecumenical field. Hopefully, the theologians will then not be conscripted in order to tailor theology but rather to express theologically what has happened and is already happening in the field of Christian unity, witness, and evangelism. The prospect is electrifying—electrifying in precisely the same sense as Jesus meant when he said to the seventy after their first program of mission and evangelism and on their return to him: "I saw Satan fall like lightning from heaven" (Luke 10:18).

Denominationalism does not have within it the necessary powers and resources for this particular exercise of world evangelism; surely it is nothing less than such an exercise in which we are engaged at the outset of the so-called Decade of Evangelism. In such a decade, by the grace of God, we may find that a gospel, sufficiently powerful and rich in its very diversity, will reunite us rather than divide us.

We shall discover after all, perhaps, that many of our divisions belonged to the privileges and indulgences of a closeted ecclesiasticism and that they simply have no place (or have been transcended) on the frontiers and battle lines of evangelism. Those are the real battle lines, and there we shall discover that the great divide is no longer between Christians of differing colors and persuasions but rather between those who are for him and those who are against him. The chances are that such lines and frontiers will coincide precisely with those very same lines where true and full-blooded witness is met with bloody martyrdom.

For at the end of the day (or "kingdom come," as we say), evangelism is essentially the compulsion and the content of what I am driven to share with a fellow prisoner about Jesus Christ as we wait together on death row to be shot at dawn the following morning. All of us—laity, clergy, evangelists, men and women alike—need to ask this of ourselves almost daily: If I were waiting to be shot tomorrow morning in prison, what would it be that I simply had to tell my neighboring prisoner about Jesus Christ and about the gospel that meant so much to me?

Notes

1. William J. Abraham, *The Logic of Evangelism* (Grand Rapids: Wm. B. Eerdmans, 1989), 12.
2. *The Truth Shall Make You Free, The Lambeth Conference 1988*, resolutions 43 and 42 (published by the Anglican Consultative Council, 1989), 231.
3. Robert E. Coleman, ed., *Evangelism on the Cutting Edge* (Old Tappau, NJ: Power Books, Fleming H. Revell, 1986), 7. N.B. These projections are computed from figures of the Lausanne Committee for World Evangelization in 1984. For a further discussion of the decline of Christianity's proportion of members in relation to world population, see the *World Christian Encyclopedia*, David B. Barrett, ed. (New York: Oxford University Press, 1982), 3–19.
4. Manila Manifesto 1989, 10, sec. 11.
5. Ibid.
6. Quoted by John R.W. Stott, *Christian Mission in the Modern World: What the Church Should be Doing Now!*(Downers Grove, IL: Intervarsity Press, 1975), 56.
7. Eusebius, *Ecclesiastical History* 3:37 2.
8. Ibid., 5:10 2.
9. Ibid., 3:1 1.
10. John B. Coburn, *Evangelism: The Task of the Whole Church* (Cincinnati: Forward Movement Publications 1982), 4.
11. *Lausanne Covenant*, "The Church and Evangelism," paragraph 6.
12. Stott, *Christian Mission in the Modern World*, 40.
13. Visser't Hooft, *"Evangelism in the Neo-Pagan Situation," International Review of Mission* 63 (January 1974): 84.
14. Stott, *Christian Mission in the Modern World*, 27.
15. Lausanne Covenant, 25.
16. Quoted by Stott, *Christian Mission in the Modern World*, 36.

TWO

Have We a Gospel to Proclaim?

RIFT BETWEEN THEOLOGY AND EVANGELISM

"I consider it nothing short of a disaster that evangelism has been relegated to the fringes of modern critical theology."[1] Surely, the theologians need the evangelists and the evangelists need the theologians. The theologians most certainly need the evangelists. For too long we have assumed that theology is a specialist branch of philosophy concerned with ideas about God. Hence the reduction of Christianity into yet another ideology. Especially since the invasion into Western theology of the German critical school of scriptural theology, theology has become primarily an activity of the mind tested in the laboratory of the debating chamber, the lecture room, or those interminable discussion groups! Archbishop Anthony Bloom, however, was much more on target when he wrote, "Theology is knowing God, not knowing about God, much less knowing what other people know about God."[2] Right on, as Americans say! Certainly the mainstream of Eastern theology has clung tenaciously to that mandate. For the Orthodox churches of the East, the good theologian is the one who prays well: *lex orandi est lex credendi*. If this is true, a new dialogue between theology and evangelism would demand a massive reorientation for theology and a new climate of theological research in our seminaries. Theology in such a reorientation would become primarily an activity of the whole person—body, mind, spirit, and passions—and it would be tested not so much in the lecture room as in the laboratory of worship and in the front line of evangelism. For there is a sense in which pragmatism has its place in checking and correcting theological ideas. If theology is primarily philosophy, then the first question to ask is, necessarily, whether it is true, rather than, "Does it work?" In theology, the two questions interlock: The experience of a worshiping, praying, and evangelizing church interlocks and interchanges with questions of theological truth.

Yet theology, we must assert, is not primarily a philosophy, and therefore we should "regard Christian experience, not dogmatic propositions as providing its sources. It should begin with the facts of experience of God and ask what hypotheses are required to explain them."[3]

For it was a more traditional understanding of theology before the Age of Reason that employed models akin to scientific models of thought in which the question "Does it work?" had a valid place. So the Lambeth Conference of 1948 can write the following very refreshingly:

> Just as the discipline of the scientific method proceeds from the collection of data to the ordering of these data in formulae, the publishing of results obtained, and their verification by experience, so Catholic Christianity presents us with an organic process of life and thought in which religious experience has been, and is, described intellectually ordered, mediated and verified.[4]

Put perhaps more crisply and in more challenging terms, it is not for theology to call the tune; religious experience is a valid area for theological research.

Religion is primarily an experience, and theology is, therefore, the song of the Church, or as St. Augustine so lyrically says, "To sing is to pray twice!" Yes, religious experience is the song of the Church—a love song—probing evermore profoundly into our knowledge, experience, and love of God. The work of the theologian is to follow close on the heels of the worshiping experience of Christians through the ages, sharing in it himself and then seeking to score the tune, attempting to put into black and white the melody of religious experience and, in so doing, to know (as indeed all the greatest theologians would readily acknowledge) that such a score of limited dimensions is only a rough approximation to the truth and to reality. At best, it is only second best. Put more bluntly still, Christianity is not an ideology, philosophy, or theology, or a set of ideas about God: Christianity is not any THING, it is some BODY—in a word, Jesus and the resurrection. Yet it has to be freely admitted that theologians who are not first committed to Christ and his Church *before* they are committed to their craft and career as theologians have reduced Christianity to an ideology; they have reduced theology to philosophy and Christian discipleship merely to holding opinions about Jesus of Nazareth. Such a theology (if it is worthy of the name) puts reason above experience, opinions above obedience, and Christianity alongside other world religions inviting the selection of an ideological supermarket. To many observers, Christians, especially in the West, appear no longer to believe in anything in particular but rather simply to hold differing opinions in general. Little wonder that they have no faith-story to tell, no faith to share, and, therefore, no gospel to proclaim that would even remotely have any power to change people's lives, let alone to change the world. Contrast that with what was said of Paul and his companions: They were accused of nothing less than "turning the world upside down" (Acts 17:6). Yet this was precisely because they did not simply hold opinions but rather proclaimed deeply held convictions that they were not ashamed to tell "the rulers, and elders and scribes gathered together in Jerusalem." What did they tell them? They told them that "salvation was in no one else" except Jesus and, furthermore, that there was "no other name under heaven given among men by which we must be saved," except precisely that same name of Jesus (Acts 4:5ff.).

"Christianity went out into the world," wrote Bishop Charles Gore, "as a life to be lived . . . rather than as a theory or a theological creed to be believed. It ought always to present itself to the world primarily as the good life to be lived in human brotherhood."[5]

So the writer of the Epistle to Timothy is right on target when he warns us that "in the last days" there will be those who hold the form of godliness but deny the power of it (2 Tim. 3:5). The Greek word *dunamis*, meaning "power," in the sense of authority, gives us the word *dynamic*. What I am pleading for is a new dynamic, therefore, in theology. This will only come when our Church is no longer ashamed to proclaim salvation in the name only of Jesus. We simply cannot avoid the scandal of such particularity or of making such exclusive claims for Jesus of Nazareth. There is no pearl of evangelism without the grit of such theological precision. We might have all sorts of ideas about God, but, in practice, we find to our cost that things do not work that way after all. Such a faith, built on such relative theological premises, does not have the power after all to make a difference, to move people, and to change people's lives—let alone to change the world. The authority of the gospel message is tested in the New Testament by the power that the words of Jesus manifestly displayed. When Jesus spoke, something happened! The centurion in the New Testament, himself a man from within a clearly defined authority structure, was quick to recognize Jesus as a mover and a shaker. Unlike the scribes and the pharisees who seemed to have reduced words to a word game (life as a continuous crossword puzzle) and who, therefore, spoke without authority—among them, Jesus stood out like a sore thumb. He did not replace activity by words and more words. When he spoke, something happened. What especially happened was that evil was put down, demons were displaced, light shone in the darkness, the blind began to see, the deaf began to hear, and the lame began to walk. Put in more theological language, in the New Testament, as we shall see, people experience the kingdom of God at work among them—yet only where Jesus is acknowledged as Lord. Hence the claim of Jesus, when he states with absolute authority, "If I by the finger of God cast out demons, then the kingdom of God has come among you" (Luke 11:20).

So the fact that there has been a rift between theologians and evangelists has certainly been a loss to theology and, in turn, to those issuing forth from our theological colleges and seminaries. They so often do not have a gospel to proclaim but rather vague ideas to be discussed. People are leaving our seminaries for ordination to ministry without any expectation that their theological training will be powerful in producing the goods. They have been tied up in an ideological reduction of Christianity (generally of the somewhat left-wing persuasion) and see the communication of the gospel and the work of the Church primarily in the model of a political campaign: out to win voters, if you like, to a point of view. Little wonder that such a "gospel" has won such a following as it has, that is to say, largely among the articulate and middle class. By contrast, the supreme test in the New Testament is whether or not the gospel is so rooted in reality—the flesh and blood kind of everyday life—that even the poor (presumably largely inarticulate) hear it and receive it gladly (Luke 7:22). Put another way, which will surely upset many and, indeed, should do so, if Christianity does not work in the inner city and in the poor, underprivileged ghettos, then it is not Christianity that is being preached but rather some synthetic semi-academic reduction of the powerful chemistry of the catholic gospel.

In all these ways perhaps we can see the urgent need for a renewed interaction between theology and evangelism that will renew theology and, in turn, bring a theological renewal to our seminaries and our churches and to our evangelistic and ministry programs.

MESSAGE OR MASSAGE?

The same is equally true the other way around. Evangelists need theologians, and evangelism needs to be corrected by the insights of biblical theology as well as church history and doctrine. It is hard to find substantial books on the theology of evangelism. In 1953, George Sweazey (incidentally, later to become a professor at Princeton and certainly no theological or intellectual lightweight) wrote a book entitled *Effective Evangelism.* Two years earlier, in England, Canon Bryan Green (that great campaigner for the gospel, to whom this book is dedicated) wrote his book, *The Practice of Evangelism.* Yet in fairness, it has to be admitted that neither work is strong in its critical, theological reflection. For too long evangelism has been left to evangelists who tend to see themselves out on a wing. They are frequently the soloists if not the prima donnas of the Church. I would want to suggest that such a Christian ministry is in serious spiritual danger. It is not accidental or incidental that in recent times well-known television evangelists have fallen prey to corruption. "There are no Lone Rangers in the kingdom," writes Peter Wagner. Evangelism is the property and responsibility of the whole Church. Because evangelists necessarily work on the frontiers and edges of the Church, it is all the more important that they are securely anchored at the center of the Church, where they are less likely to become prey to the temptations of megalomania, isolation, affluence, loneliness, or just the very human prey of trying to play God. Of course, there are men and women especially anointed to be evangelists. But they need the necessary graces to accompany such a ministry, or, put another way, they need to breathe the clear air of a spirit-filled environment where discernment and loving correction can check excesses and the abuses of their power.

For whatever evangelism may or may not be, it is essentially an activity closely related at all times to the community of faith. The popular revivalist model is really a distortion of evangelism unless the ministry of the evangelist arises out of and relates back to the liturgical, witnessing, and everyday life of a specific, local community of faith. Billy Graham, in his crusades, only goes to those cities where the commitment of the local churches has already been declared. Furthermore, he is always at pains at the conclusion of the mission service to point "converts" back to their local communities of faith where they can subsequently grow in discipleship.

For, rightly understood, evangelism is a powerful chemistry. An evangelistic Church has the power to change people's lives. Power corrupts, and supernaturally powerful power corrupts very powerfully! In those very chapters of church history most conspicuous as times of renewal, evangelism, and church growth, we see the Church at its most corrupt. We see such corruption right at the outset of the evangelistic work of the Book of the Acts of the Apostles. Simon Magus realizes only too well what power the apostles are discharging. He wants that power for himself not in order to serve a living Lord, but rather in order to boost his own ego (Acts 8:9ff.). The

alternative to good evangelism is not just bad evangelism
but rather something little short of demonic magic and
irresponsible manipulation.

It is not incidental that popular mass evangelism
thrives so well in America. Surely, it is in America and in
the West generally that individualism has risen to such
unquestionable heights. Renewal and evangelism in such
a climate both degenerate into a pious massage. People are
made to feel better with a God who speaks to their
neuroses. Christianity is not an individualistic faith: it is a
personal faith, expressed at its fullest within a community
of faith.

The bishop of the Rio Grande, Terence Kelshaw, speaking at Trinity Episcopal School for Ministry, reminded the
newly graduated class of that year that the "gospel is
about Jesus Christ. The Church was not brought into being
by God to meet the real or felt needs of people," insisted
Bishop Kelshaw. "In many of our churches, what is being
preached in seemingly evangelical language is not a
Christ-centered gospel. It is a man-centered gospel. You
have a need,' it says, and Jesus can meet it . . .'."[6] The
gospel, the bishop continued, is about Jesus Christ, who
comes with the good news that it is possible to be right
with God. In other words, the test of valid evangelism is
not so much whether it makes you feel better but whether
it changes lives. Surely, it is still a question for massive
consideration that a nation such as America with its outstanding and comparatively massive church attendance is
still the nation with one of the highest rates in the world
for divorce, abortion, alcoholism, drug abuse, and AIDS:
these are all symptoms and signs of an ailing society.
Churchgoing seems to have had little power to create a
righteous nation. The piety of an individualistic massage
has replaced the spirituality of a message that is powerful
to change life-styles and to witness to a kingdom of
righteousness, justice, and truth. The time is right for a

serious theological critique of the message, for what I am contending is not that evangelism is bad but rather that evangelism cut loose from the critical and theological environment of the Church can just run amok and leave disaster in its wake. We really do need a theology of evangelism. Such books are beginning to emerge at last, and they are certainly timely.

THE GOSPEL OF JESUS AND THE KINGDOM OF GOD

This book is not intended as (and neither is the author competent to produce) a major work on the theology of evangelism. However, it is my intention to recall the mainstream churches to the primacy of evangelism. In so doing, some attempt must surely be made to discern the gospel. In order to do this, we need to place the gospel call in the context in which we find it so clearly in the gospel narratives of the New Testament—namely, in the context of the message of Jesus about the kingdom of God. Here again, however, we must recognize from the outset that we are beset by loud contradictions. Our theology of the kingdom of God has been distorted to act as proof texts and slogans for ideological positions—liberals to the left and existentialists to the right. On the one hand, there has been a political emphasis on the theology of the kingdom of God with a shifting focus "to social and political action and this radical change of emphasis continues with the move from the secular theologies of the sixties to the liberation theologies of the seventies and eighties," writes William J. Abraham.[7] On the other hand, there has been a distortion of kingdom theology in a highly subjective and existentialist emphasis that makes the mistake of the early New Testament Church by limiting the God of history to the destiny of an individual, an individual nation, and a particular point in time. Far from holding up a vision of God in history as Lord of history and of creation, we reduce him to an interfering God capable of manipulation to serve the limited ends of "my" faith and "my" health or perhaps worse still, my nation's faith and my nation's health.

This is especially true in the recently recovered emphasis upon the healing ministry of Jesus. Let nothing be said here that in any way detracts from such a wonderful ministry as the healing ministry in the Church today. I would certainly wish to thank God both for what he does and continues to do through the healing ministry in the Church today and not least among Christians who have experienced the power of renewal and healing through the work of the Holy Spirit. However, distortion and faulty theology in this area lead alike to disaster when we see such events as healing miracles purely in therapeutic terms. Rather, in the Gospels,

> the medically curative and philanthropic aspects of Jesus's healings were secondary to His main intention, which was to signify that the Reign of God had begun. Such signs were not only "symbols" of what was happening or about to happen, but also at the same time they were actually *component parts* of these happenings. They are symbolic or sacramental acts that point beyond themselves to some further meaning and not only announce but also help to effect what they symbolize: effectual signs which cause what they signify. And so Jesus' cures, too, were not only symbolic seals of his mission, but at the same time actual victories in the battle that had already been joined against the forces of evil.[8]

So neither the political nor the therapeutic model are adequate. Both of them, in fact, are serious and grievous distortions of that full-blooded theology of the gospel of Jesus and the call of the kingdom that we find in the Gospels. So our task is quite clear. It is a task laid upon the whole Church today: namely, to discern afresh the gospel and then to test that gospel in the environment of lively proclamation by the whole Church from the parish upward and outward. To do this, we must begin where the gospel records begin.

St. Mark tells us, plainly and tersely, "Jesus came into Galilee, preaching the gospel of God, and saying, 'The time is fulfilled, and the kingdom of God is at hand: repent, and believe in the gospel' " (Mark 1:14–15).

THE MESSAGE AND THE MESSENGER

Surely this formula at the outset of Mark's Gospel is, in its compressed form, the essential gospel—the evangel. If this is so, we shall do well to meditate upon these verses at length in our attempt to focus the content of evangelism before we go on to seek in what ways we can minister that gospel and communicate it to the world at large.

The first thing we need to discover is that there is no *thing* to discover. There is no such *thing* as the gospel. For the gospel is not a thing—it is a person: in a word, it is Jesus and his resurrection. For the gospel is not a formula or a text or a code; otherwise, it could have been communicated without getting involved in the whole messy business of the incarnation. An angel or a telegram would have sufficed! The message and the messenger are one. Jesus is the gospel: the gospel is Jesus. At Easter, the deacon at the vigil eucharist on Holy Saturday proclaims the Easter *praeconium*—the proclamation of Easter, which is traditionally sung by the deacon at the opening of that liturgy. It is significant that the Latin word *praeconium* means both the message and the messenger who brings the message.

So with Jesus and the gospel. We have no gospel statement to issue: we have only Jesus to share. And therefore when we (viz., William J. Abraham) ask the question whether or not evangelism is primarily procla-

mation, we have got off on the wrong foot from the start.
This is equally so when we seek to split hairs between our
practice of evangelism, mission, and social action. Such
abstractions lead us into departmentalizing. So we begin
to ask such irrelevant questions as, Is evangelism primarily the message of the evangelist or is it the works of love
and compassion among the needy? Which should come
first? We cut the Gordian knot of this kind of arbitrary
selection if we begin, as we intend to go on, with the simple statement that the gospel is Jesus and Jesus is the gospel.

Start any other way around and you will reduce the
gospel to a message, Christianity to a few rules and
regulations, and worship to some high-flown ideas of
escapists. In that way, Christianity becomes an ideology
and just another religion.* It will then proceed to do all
those dreadful things that religions always have, of course,
done over the centuries and always in the name of "a
matter of principle," with its carefully coded maxims and
slogans for living. Such life becomes a death and such a
religious environment a prison house as we "lace ourselves up in formulas." For "the man of maxims" chooses
to be guided "by general rules, thinking that these will
lead them to justice by a ready made patent method
without . . . a life fitted and intense enough to have created
a wide fellow feeling with all that is human."[9] Our truly
"fellow feeling with all that is human" is to be found in a
person, not a program, and a relationship with Jesus in the

---

*It is perhaps worth reflecting that the word *religion* occurs only in two
places in the whole of the Bible (Acts 26:5 and James 1:26ff). Similarly,
the word *religious* (James 1:25 and Acts 13:43). The word *religion* in the
dictionary is derived from *religio* in Latin and means "that which binds
us." So religion is essentially a matter of principle and the rule of the
law. As such, it is not an appropriate word for Christianity, and in this
way the Christian faith is unique among all world religions. Then it
would seem that the Bible, in this sense, is not a particularly religious
book!

humanity of his incarnation. For the Christian, the rules of religion are replaced by a relationship. It is a relationship of love and faith with Jesus—the divinely human figure of history. Hence, we are rescued from that most damaging exercise of seeking to compress and force our personal lives into anything less than what they are—they are at least personal.

When personality has only the grid of rules, regulations, principles, and abstract religion through which to work out its authentic self-expression, it becomes inevitably maimed. For such a religion, no matter how high-minded and high-principled, is in reality alien to the experience of fullblooded humanity.

Such religion seeks to make men and women smaller, less generous, and less human; they are cramped by such a religion and dwarfed by it, like "a bed too short to stretch oneself on it, and the covering too narrow to wrap oneself in it" (Isa. 28:20). Such an environment does not make either for a good night's sleep or a full life the following day.

So Jesus himself rightly resists the impatient request of Thomas in the gospels: "Lord, show us the way." Here is Thomas longing for a formula for the kingdom so that we can all get on with the business of the kingdom and leave all the other stuff, like worship and prayer and relationships, to those who like that sort of mysticism and those kind of exotic exercises. "No," replies Jesus, and with one of the most revolutionary statements of the gospel he retorts, "*I* am the way and the truth, and the life" (John 14:6). I have no maxims and principles to give you, Jesus is saying. Otherwise, you will rush away and lock yourself up in all kinds of rules, regulations, and religious attitudes. That is a very serious distortion of Christianity, and yet it is the religion of many parts of the Church in our own day, as it has been the religion of many Christians throughout the centuries.

So we must start, rather, where the gospel starts—
"Jesus came into Galilee." Wherever Jesus comes and
wherever he is made present, he carries with him the
gospel of God. He is himself the walking sacrament in
time and throughout time, before time and beyond time,
of the kingdom of God. He is the door of that kingdom.
He is the key to that door; he is the road to that door; and
he is the map for the road! And in a word, that is
supremely the work of the Church as an evangelistic
Church: namely, to make Jesus present "at all times and in
all places." Put another way, the task of evangelism is to
make sure that Jesus in all the fullness of his incarnation
enters the door of every town (beginning in Galilee), in
every community, in every home, "in Jerusalem and in all
Judea and Samaria and to the end of the earth" (Acts 1:8).
That is why Jesus is not ashamed to spell out the mission
of his Church in precise and even geographical terms.
There is nothing abstract about mission: it is always
undertaken *in* time, *in* space, and *in*-carnate.

So we then go on to ask, How is Jesus made present?
In the New Testament, it is always the same. The gift of
the Holy Spirit, brooding and overshadowing, forms Jesus
in the flesh and blood of the here and now just as surely as
by the overshadowing of the Holy Spirit he was formed at
first in the womb of the Virgin Mary (Luke 1:35). It
happened first and foremost in Nazareth and for Mary.
"How shall this be since I have no husband?" she asks.
"The Holy Spirit will come upon you and the power of the
Most High will overshadow you and that which is formed
in your flesh and blood, Mary, here and now, will be Jesus
—Emmanuel, God with us." So before any kind of discussion about the content of the gospel or the techniques
of evangelism or, indeed, discussion of what evangelism is
and what it is not, who evangelists are and who evangelists are not, what evangelists do and what they say—
before all of this, must come our proper understanding of

God as the supreme evangelist and the prime missioner and mover in sending Jesus to be the be-all and end-all of everything to do with us and our salvation.

Jesus came: Jesus comes: Jesus will come again. Once upon a time Jesus came. He always comes when it is "high time"—in God's time (*kairos*). He comes and many of us feel it is about "high time" he came again, not only in the fullness of his incarnation but in the fullness of his glory to fill all things, to judge the living and the dead, and finally to issue in that kingdom that has no end.

Yet, in the *meantime*, the Church is constantly concerned to make Jesus in the fullness of his gospel present, real, and focused in time and space, in flesh and blood. This is always the work of the Holy Spirit. In the words of the Manila Manifesto of Lausanne II: "We affirm that the Holy Spirit's witness to Christ is indispensable to evangelism and that without his supernatural work neither new birth nor new life is possible." For catholic Christians there are many ways in which the Holy Spirit is called down (*epiclesis*) to form Jesus and to incarnate the gospel in our midst so that in our turn we can raise him up (*anaphora*) and be raised up in him.

It is worth noting that in the Book of the Acts of the Apostles, the preacher is frequently spoken of as being filled with Holy Spirit (Acts 4:8). Furthermore, in Acts 10 we are specifically and explicitly reminded that in such apostolic preaching "the Holy Spirit fell on all who heard the word" (vs. 44). In all these ways we must begin to speak more and more of the real presence of Jesus wherever the Word of God is opened up and wherever minds are opened to that Word. Always this is the activity of the Holy Spirit, who formed Jesus in the womb of Mary and who brings Jesus into the present from the shadows of our individual and collective remembrance.

The Holy Spirit brings all the things of Jesus to our remembrance and effectively makes Jesus present for us

(John 14:26). When the Holy Spirit comes down in this way upon a crowd or a community of faith to form Jesus, he knocks at the door of the human heart and, in the words of George Herbert, "No door can keep him out!"

Yet for Anglicans and catholic Christians there is also the way of the sacraments whereby the Holy Spirit is called down, Jesus is formed (in bread and wine at the eucharist, in the bride and groom at a marriage, but always in flesh and blood), and the kingdom comes. Once again, we can sing as the first Christians: "The dark night wakes, the glory breaks," and in a real sense, "Christmas comes once more." Yes, the kingdom is here.

There is also a third way. The word used for the overshadowing of the Holy Spirit is used on only three occasions in the New Testament, and all three occasions occur in the writings of St. Luke. It is first used on the occasion of the Annunciation. The Holy Spirit came down and *overshadowed* (*episkiadzo*) Mary so that the body of Christ was formed in her womb. Second, the same word is used at the Transfiguration in St. Luke's Gospel where the trio of the apostolic circle, we are told, was *overshadowed* by the cloud (the *shekinah*) of the Holy Spirit and the Body of Christ (the Church) was conceived in history and born at Pentecost. Finally, the same word is used to speak of the apostolic mission of Peter and John. On this occasion, in the Book of Acts, the sick are brought out into the streets on stretchers, and we are told that they are *overshadowed* by the shadows of Peter and John (Acts 5:15). Jesus is made present, and, faithful to his promises, the work of the disciples is blessed in the same way that the ministry and work of Jesus was blessed—the sick are healed, the blind see, the lame walk, etc. In other words, the promise of Jesus to his disciples is fulfilled in the apostolic mission and ministry of the Church. "He who believes in me will also do the works that I do," promises Jesus, "and greater works than these will he do, because I go to the Father" (John 14:12). All these events are evangelistic events and signs of the kingdom—and all are part and parcel of Jesus, who embodies the message in all its fullness.

So evangelism, in its fullness, is *all* that Jesus is in relationship to the kingdom. It is speech, sign, sacrament, and service—all done in the power and overshadowing of the Holy Spirit and therefore in the real presence of Jesus, who is formed in all the participants of the evangelistic drama. Any full evangelistic program in a parish or a diocese will contain at least these four essential ingredients because they all belong together: speech, sign, sacrament, and service. They were all aspects of Jesus' earthly ministry in proclaiming the gospel and in heralding the kingdom. The real presence of Jesus in the Church today, *overshadowed* by the same Holy Spirit, extends and continues the same works of Jesus so clearly manifested in his earthly ministry as signs of the kingdom.

Now we see how such rather pathetic questions as, Do we need to mention his name? or, In what ways do we refer to the particularity of Jesus in evangelistic, gospel presentations?—all these questions surely now find their level. If we believe that *the* essential ingredient in all evangelism in all its forms is the real presence of Jesus, then surely we behave with the same courteous, warm, and loving attention that we show when we take anyone with us to a party or to a place. We do not ignore them. We do not call him or her "it," but rather we call them by their name. We introduce them and tell people enough about them to enable such a connection to be formed that a relationship may begin. Admittedly, much of this presentation is verbal, though it generally involves touch and shaking of hands, hospitality (food and drink), and generally sharing our friends with other friends and acquaintances.

If we are truly at home with that friend in an easy,

natural friendship (John 15:15), then there will be nothing unreal, unnatural, pompous, or pretentious about the tones in which we speak of some of our friends to other of our friends. On the contrary, there is something *real* in what we say because Jesus is *really* present by the Holy Spirit, and, according to his promise, "where two or three are gathered in my name, there am I in the midst of them" (Matt. 18:20).

WHAT HAPPENS IN THE PRESENCE OF JESUS?

But back now to our text. "Jesus came into Galilee, preaching the gospel of God." The word *gospel* simply means "good news." Now we ask what is that good news? Mark gives us a short sentence outlining the good news.

The first thing is that like all good news, it is an event. Jesus did not come preaching a good idea. "Look, chaps, I've had a bright idea! Would you like to hear about it and then go away and discuss it?"

No. Jesus comes to tell us what God is doing. We can be forgiven for supposing from the newspapers that history is just one damned thing after another and that God, if he exists, has either fallen asleep, got bored, or is just simply indifferent or incompetent. History, however, through the eyes of faith is not one damned thing after another. It has a shape and a purpose, and so, rather than just "killing time," I can tell you that now it is about "high time." This is the breakthrough for which history is but a preparation. At last, something is *really* happening.

What is happening? God's kingdom and rule are breaking into history. As Bishop John Robinson used to put it so well, "The end is in the middle." The purpose of all things is showing up in the middle of all things by the working of the God of the end of all things. So not unnaturally, insofar as history is largely bad news, you will find the good news of the kingdom all among the bad news. Insofar as the bad news has an address and a telephone number, so does the good news. You need to know where and when to look for that good news.

For, frankly, you are in for a shock! The shape of things to come is far from what you might expect if you took only an evolutionary view of history rather than a revolutionary view of history. So far in the chronicles of history it has been a question of the survival of the fittest, every man for himself, and new life has been achieved by the overpowering and suppression of the poor and the weak. In the coming kingdom, however, everything will be in reverse. Everything will be upside down, inside out, and back to front. In God's kingdom, we shall discover ultimate power in the heart of weakness; it will be every man for others and not every man for himself, and new life will be given wherever life is voluntarily laid down. The first will be last, and the last will be first; the barren will be fruitful; old men will dream dreams, and young men will see visions. It's all most confusing! Kingship in this kingdom is most obvious when it is displayed in loving service. Authority is discovered through obedience and power voluntarily given away while all new life comes *through* death. But again notice that in all references to the kingdom of God we are not given abstractions, codes, or mere rules and regulations. We are pointed to events and teased by them to unravel the implications of such bewildering signs. So when John sent from prison to inquire of Jesus and to ask him if he really was all that he claimed to be, Jesus did not send back to John a *curriculum vitae* or an essay on Christology. Rather, he said quite simply, "Go and tell John what is happening." When you tell him what is happening, he will recognize these events for what they are—signs of the great event, the coming of the kingdom, foretold by the prophets of old (Isaiah 61): the blind are seeing; the deaf are hearing; the lame are walking, etc. (Luke 7:22).

But back now to our prime text. There we find that two of the ingredients of the message point to what God is doing: "The time is fulfilled: the kingdom of God is at hand." The next two involve our response. But note, yet again, how God always retains the initiative. (He is the truly effective evangelist.) Nevertheless, a response from us is necessary and required if the work of the kingdom is to go forward. St. Augustine sums it up in his marvelous syllogism: "Without God, we cannot; without us, he will not."

REPENTANCE

The first task of an evangelistic Church must be to point to God and what he is doing. Put another way, we must hold up Jesus: "Lift high the cross," as we so often sing. Put another way, the Church must become the sort of Church that points men and women to the kingdom, and, therefore, the Church must itself be an effective sign of that kingdom and of the end of all things stuck in the middle of all things and, therefore, sticking out a little bit like a sore thumb. In the West and in Christendom generally, the Church is no longer inextricably so tied up with the state. The Church must not be conditioned by the culture of the kingdoms of this world, but rather it must challenge the culture of the kingdoms of this world by holding up for all to see the conditions of the kingdom of God.

Once again, as before the Peace of Constantine in A.D. 313, there is a real chance that Christians can begin to point again to that other kingdom rather than to reflect the kingdoms of this world. Dr. Robert Webber reminded the students at Trinity Episcopal School that "the mainline churches have moved from mainline to sideline." We are "now in a position to recover" our biblical identity because our decline has forced us to find out what the Church really is and therefore who Jesus is. The Church should be "the sign of Christ," Dr. Webber reminds us, first through its worship and evangelism and then through its ministries of healing and servanthood. "We are now the disestablished church. And we are in a position therefore to recover the gospel because the gospel is not now being defined by the political and social agenda of the world."[10] Our response to this, insofar as it is true, must surely be, "Alleluia!" For the Church is most evangelistic when it is most a sign of contradiction. It must not fit so comfortably into the presuppositions of a worldly view of history that people stop asking questions about Christians, their lifestyle, and their behavior. The world should be genuinely puzzled by Christian behavior, Christian brotherhood, and Christian belief. We should display a freedom that the world longs for and that all the religions and ideologies of the world are apparently impotent to give. The world should feel that somehow it doesn't quite all add up! The Christian, essentially, is a sign of contradiction to those who see history and life through purely secular lenses. So, it is of paramount importance that the Church is not conformed and tailored to the life-style and secular humanism of the world. We need to heed the words of St. Paul to the early Church surrounded by pagan culture: "Do not be conformed to this world but be transformed by the renewal of your mind" (Rom. 12:2). The world will be challenged to ask about the contradictory behavior of Christians as the jailer was compelled to ask in Acts 16: "Why had the unfettered prisoners not escaped? Surely they would run away as quickly as possible after the earthquake had thrown open all the doors of the prison. But no—they really seemed to care more than that, and furthermore they seemed to have a freedom that no prison could inhibit. It simply does not add up."

"So," inquires the jailer, "what must I do to be like you—free, released, healed, and saved?"

In other words, the evangelistic Church should demand

that people have second thoughts about us and about everything that we stand for. Only then will the message (embodied in the Body of Christ) evoke repentance.

Yet beware! Repentance has very little to do with guilt. Guilt is wounded pride, and wounded pride is worthless in the kingdom. *Metanoia*—a change of heart and outlook, a second thought—is probably most lyrically expounded in the words of the song by the wicked Fagan in the musical *Oliver Twist*: "I am reviewing the situation," he sings. In other words, I am going to have to begin to think it all out again. Everything is back in the melting pot once more or up in the air again—depending on how you see it!

Repentance, in a word, is a most unnerving experience. It is, of course, primarily the result of vision. When Jesus is held up or moves into any situation, he demands that we take a second look. Vision leads to repentance. Such repentance happens wherever there is some new insight, and insights are frequently given at times of breakthrough, and times of breakthrough frequently presuppose a breakdown of some kind. Presumably, that is what people said about Abraham when he set out at seventy-five, leaving behind all security, not even knowing where he was going. "Old Abe's having a breakdown," they said. So also with Zacchaeus—"He's having a midlife crisis," they gossiped as he stood outside his house with the front door of the living room wide open, babbling something about giving all of his ill-gotten earnings away.

Truth to tell, both Abraham and Zacchaeus and millions of people before and since have found that, when Jesus comes into their lives and into their towns (when the kingdom breaks in), they are unsettled, confused, "unglued," and pentitent. They are compelled to "review the situation." Call it what you will: it's what happens that matters much more than the vocabulary that we use. For there are many today who are using all the proper vocabulary of evangelism, yet nothing is happening!

All preaching (wherever and whenever Jesus is ministered by word or by deed) challenges men and women to take a stand—one way or the other. In that sense Jesus comes bearing the sword of the Word that sorts out "the men from the boys." In a sense, you cannot be indifferent about the presentation and presence of Jesus of Nazareth. Whether he comes into Galilee, Jericho, or Eureka Springs, by his words, his deeds, and, supremely, his presence, people are moved, divided, and challenged. In a word, repentance occurs. Many people begin to see things from a new position.

So repentance is much more than simply an attitude of mind, though it will certainly involve the mind and also our attitudes. It is at least as all-consuming as "a change of life": It is even more of a crisis than the midlife crisis, though it can feel a bit like the end of all life as we have hitherto known it at any point in life itself. It might happen to a little child or to an octogenarian. It is never too early, but it might be sometimes just that bit too late.

Certainly, it is all-consuming. That is why it frequently involves the whole body and the whole person. We see things and, indeed, life itself from a particular perspective, and that perspective is related to direction and location. For example, we see the services in church very differently if we are facing west than if we turn to face the east. So in the early liturgies of baptism, the new Christians were asked, as indeed they are still asked to this day in many liturgies; "Do you turn to Christ?" Repentance involves turning our backs upon some things in order to face up to others. Hence we see things in a totally new light. As C.S. Lewis says, "I believe in the sunrise not only because I can see it, but because now I can see everything else in the light of it."

When Jesus in the New Testament evokes repentance,

again and again he invites people to make a move (physically). He tells Zacchaeus to "come off it" and come down from the tree. He tells Peter to walk away from those nets, in which he has himself become netted most of his working life. (It is as though he spends all his time working and mending them, rather than fishing with them, and when he does he cannot even catch anything with them. Means have become ends for Peter: he has lost his way [Luke 5:1ff.]). For Matthew, repentance means just simply having to walk away from it all: If you stop to count the small change, you will never get free from it again! The altar call or the invitation to come forward at the end of an evangelistic presentation is scripturally authentic and at the same time sacramental, as an outward and visible sign of an inward motivation. You simply cannot stay in your seat. The altar call is wholly in keeping with the New Testament understanding of the impact of the gospel and the priority and acting out of our repentance. We are visibly moved either to our feet to confess our faith or to our knees to confess our sins.

THE PARABLES, JUDGMENT, AND REPENTANCE

It was to this end that the preaching of Jesus in the gospels was addressed. He wanted people to change their position—to face up to the kingdom—before following in his footsteps. Such is the important place of the parables of the kingdom in the New Testament.

For the parable is not just a story with a moral but rather a drama demanding decision on the part of those who hear it, observe it, and get caught up in it. We see such a parable in the Old Testament on the lips of Nathan the prophet. King David has not only committed adultery but has also been responsible for the death of the husband of his mistress. Nathan is determined that King David should see his life and deeds in a new light—the way God sees them. He tells the dramatic story of the ewe lamb and tells it so succinctly and so well that King David not only hears the words but enters into the passion of the narrative "David's anger was greatly kindled," we are told. The parable ends in such a way that it evokes a judgment from King David: "As the Lord lives, the man who has done this thing deserves to die" (2 Sam. 12:5). "You are that man," responds Samuel.

So the place of the parable in preaching and presentation of the kingdom is crucial. Each little parable draws the crowd into the dynamic of the parable. They are compelled to become emotionally and even passionately involved. They begin to take sides, and then Jesus springs the catch as in the parable of the vineyard: "What shall the Lord of the vineyard do to these wicked laborers?" You can hear the crowd shouting back, "Kill them and give the vineyard to someone else to care for it." Right on! Amen! Yes to that!

Then Jesus leaves them to make the connection, and they frequently do—possibly very painfully. "The Pharisees perceived that he had told this against them." For there are only two responses to the challenge of the gospel—either paranoia or metanoia. Those who repent begin to have second thoughts: to see things from a different perspective and to face up to reality from a new position. That is metanoia. Those who resist this begin to blame the universe, the stars, their genes, or their parents and to claim that the dice are loaded against them and that it is not fair anyway. That is paranoia. Paranoia and metanoia belong to the same world: the only difference is that metanoia makes all the difference in the world! You see the same world very differently! That's all, but it is everything.

St. Mark's gospel is quite explicit in all of this. Those who responded with such a change of heart and became disciples were then further instructed quite plainly "in

private" about the kingdom and all the implications of its
impact upon their everyday lives (Mark 4:10ff.). For those
who repented, the ultimate then became the immediate
and then—and only then—were they ready to hear and
receive all the teaching and further insights Jesus wished
to impart to them. Yet this learning can only take place in
the context of discipleship. It is only to those who have
been moved and who have ceased to hold their original
position that the new life can be made clear. The "old
man" in the "old way" (to use Charles Williams' phrase)
cannot learn anything of the kingdom. Only the "old
man" in the "new way" (following in the Way) can begin
to learn of the new life and so begin slowly to become the
"new man" in the "new way."

Nothing is, in fact, more damaging than for people to
put the new wine and insights of the kingdom into the
prejudices of the old wineskins. Those wineskins need to
be refurbished first (that is what the Greek word literally
means—we do not need new wineskins, but rather we
need the old wineskins made new). If you start to add
knowledge *about* the kingdom to the old outlook on life,
you will get things severely askew. The old ego can be
flattered and "puffed up" by knowledge of that kind, as
St. Paul constantly warns us. First, it is necessary for
repentance and conversion and to begin to see everything
from a completely new point of view: to think as God
thinks and not as the world thinks (Mark: 8:33). For the
kingdom of Jesus, you will remember, is certainly "not of
this world" (John 18:36).

That is why St. Peter fell into such serious difficulties
at Caesarea Philippi. Caesarea Philippi was the place of
Peter's confession, but it was certainly not the place of his
conversion. That comes much later as we know from St.
Luke's gospel: "Simon, Simon, behold, Satan demanded to
have you, that he might sift you like wheat, but I have
prayed for you that your faith may not fail; and when you

have turned again, strengthen your brethren" (Luke 22:31ff.). Rather, the turning again and the conversion of Peter are to be found, in fact, after the resurrection when Peter three times confesses his love for Christ in St. John's gospel in the last chapter. At Caesarea Philippi, Peter attaches the confession of Jesus to the old outlook and to his old ego. The result is that he wants Jesus to be the sort of king that he (Peter) is most flattered by. "That is not the sort of king of the kingdom of God, Peter!" That is the king of the kingdoms of this world: successful, popular, and powerful. Get off on that foot and such a road leads to the demonic and to the perversion of religion. Not surprisingly, therefore, Jesus does not just mildly disagree with Peter's misunderstanding at this point. He roundly turns on Peter and does not say in mild tones, "There, there, that's not quite right; we must look into that later." Jesus sees that, in fact, it is radically and dangerously wrong.

And so Jesus speaks to Simon with a terrifying vocabulary. Simon who was a few moments ago "the rock" is now called nothing less than Satan. And this is so because, in the words of Jesus, he is "not thinking as God thinks," but rather he is thinking as "men think" (J.B. Phillips): that is, according to the latest opinion poll. Hence, the need for what theologians call the *messianic secret*, especially in St. Mark's gospel. The disciples are explicitly requested not to go around telling people that Jesus is the Messiah, otherwise the crowd will get the wrong end of the stick and start to think (as Judas possibly did) that Jesus will soon be leading a revolution against the Romans and the powers of this world. (In fact, the disciples, not yet anointed by the Spirit at Pentecost, were still laboring under precisely this misapprehension as late as the very eve of the ascension [Acts 1:6]. Repentance is essentially the work of the Holy Spirit to lead us into all truth [John 16:13].)

Mere churchgoing can, in fact, be very dangerous. It can be disastrous if it links chatter about the kingdom to an unconverted mind: We start to try to bring in our sort of kingdom (left- or right-wing, it doesn't really matter) and all in our own strength to serve our unconverted presuppositions. Similarly, unconverted religion is about the most dangerous power in the world—as we see in our own day. It blinds men and women; it produces prejudices and in the end fires passions of hatred and division. We only need at the present time to look at the demonic work of religion in Northern Ireland and the Middle East. The bloodiest wars are always religious wars. Unconverted religion is a dreadful and terrible thing. That is why Tillich reminds us again and again that "Jesus came to save us from religion."

So, therefore, "seek ye first the kingdom of God," says Jesus and all these other things and concerns will be added. We must not even seek first for the Church. Church growth is not a substitute for evangelism. No! Ecclesiasticism is a dreadful and terrible thing when the Church seeks a strength and power akin to the strengths and powers of this world and does all this in the name of the kingdom of God.

Therefore, evangelism is primary, not primarily because it will make better citizens, nicer people, fuller churches, or make for clean living. Go for it in that way and the results will be nothing less than demonic, destructive, and counterproductive. (We have frequently been down that road in history, and it is a terrible spectacle.) The history of the American Prohibition is one aspect of this kind of dangerous application of unconverted religion. The potential distortion of Christian, unconverted fervor is as dangerous today as ever. It can lead us to demand (as Judas did), not that we follow Jesus, but that he follows us and links his patronage to our cause, to this or that political ideology. Every age needs protecting from this kind of proselytism because every age has its own idolatries, and our own age probably has more than most. Richard Holloway suggests precisely this kind of inversion and perversion as being at the root of the betrayal of Jesus by Judas—that essentially religious and zealous figure of the gospels.

> Like Judas, we can have Jesus on our terms. We claim to follow him but, in fact, we try to arrange things so that he follows us or at least, keeps out of our life. Judas in other words, is a person who has his own plans, his own policy, his own style, his own way of doing things, yet who claims that they are Christ's plans, Christ's way of doing things. Christ is always the exclusive possession of our club: he is a revolutionary, if that is what you believe in; or he is a conservative . . . whatever it is you believe in, Christ is on your side, backing up your actions, supporting your thing. We all have fears and prejudices, insecurities and resentments; and we use Christ, not to judge them and heal them and burn them up, but to strengthen and confirm them. We don't really follow Christ. Like Judas, we try to get him to follow us.[11]

Perhaps the national anthem of Judas's kingdom would be the words of "Old blue eyes": "I did it my way!"

The first concern, therefore, of evangelism is to bring people to repentance: repentance seen in this fuller sense as we have tried to express it. There is no substitute: it is the *sine qua non* of evangelism. First, we need to call men and women out from the outlook of the crowd and from following in the way of the crowd to following Jesus very closely in the direction that he leads, setting our faces along with his (Luke 9:51). This will demand conversion and the turning around of our lives. Only then shall we see the world from his perspective and from his point of view. Then, and only then, as we walk with him shall we learn of him the things that belong to his kingdom.

The Church is not a one-stop shop for the kingdom. It

requires, rather, that we learn again and again the road
drill of the kingdom of God, which is this: Stop, look both
ways, and then turn round and start walking in the opposite direction.

Jesus does not give us a message or a slogan to hoard
so that we begin to live life as "a matter of principle." Put
another way, Jesus will give us nothing that we can hoard
and then idolize. He will give us nothing; he will only
give us himself. There is no message without a new
commitment to the messenger. We need to become, first of
all, the disciples of Jesus before we can become citizens of
the kingdom. Little wonder that St. Paul can say that
when anyone is in Christ he or she is "a new creation"
(2 Cor. 5:17). Literally, when we are in Christ and he in us,
then there is a new outlook on everything. Or as St.
Augustine puts it so lyrically,

> A new man knows a new song. . . . The man who has
> learned to love a new life has learned to sing a new
> song. Therefore we need to be told the nature of this
> new life, for the sake of the new song. For a new man, a
> new song, and the new testament all belong to the same
> kingdom. So the new man will sing a new song and
> belong to the new testament.[12]

BELIEF AND TRUST

The result and the last words of our text follow inevitably
on all that has gone before. The disciples, so moved from
the entrenched position of principle, rules, regulations,
and the law, begin, slowly and tentatively, to live the new
life. The disciple is now literally "under new management." That was St. Paul's experience: "It is no longer I
who live," he says, "but Christ who lives in me" (Gal.
2:20). Or, as we say in the beautiful Anglican prayer of
humble access, "that we may evermore dwell in Him and
He in us." The consecrated disciple throws his lot in with

Jesus—believing in him and trusting in him. Here is no inflexible rule book for living, no stones on which a law for life is carved. For such a life is in reality a death. It is rigid and frigid. We were not born to be free: such a life that claims freedom becomes of all lives the most predictable. We were born to be possessed—to that extent we are all born with a hole in our hearts, a God-shaped hole that only God can fill. We will fill it with something or somebody. Perhaps the most dangerous thing to fill it with is unredeemed religion. Such religion brings hardness of heart and contempt for God's living Word—and for the words of life. When we are possessed and taken over by Jesus and his Spirit, we are free from principles and rules: We can face each new day knowing that we have all the necessary resources within us to live that day as God would have us live it.

For, in fact, Jesus is God's way of being truly human, and only when he lives in us and we in him do we live a truly human life—and that life is essentially life in the Spirit. Such life is abundant life and real life, and, therefore, it is eternal life. It is that quality of life that Jesus holds out to all creation. It is that quality of life that must possess the Church if that Church is to be truly evangelistic and to be the bearer of the good news of the kingdom rather than the bad news of broken rules and legalism. So Christ calls for nothing less than a total belief in and trust in the gospel: that gospel that he alone embodies. Here again this belief is not a proposition to be filed away but rather a person to be followed all the way. We are not asked to believe *that* something is true. Rather we are asked to believe *in* somebody who is the Truth. The new direction of the converted life focuses upon a personal belief and trust in Jesus, who claims to be nothing less than "the Way, the Truth, and the Life."

But now, of course, we have gone full circle. The Church by the overshadowing of the Holy Spirit is anointed with that Spirit to be the Body of Christ. As such, it holds up to the world the person of Christ—Jesus, the God man. So the incarnation of Jesus among people in Galilee goes on, and our text is reproduced endlessly—to the very ends of the earth. For Jesus comes again and again into London, New York, Tokyo, saying what he always said and doing what he always did: "The time is fulfilled; the kingdom of God is here; repent and believe in the gospel."

Augustine pushes this point even further, for he asks us to spell out what we mean by Jesus going or coming anywhere. "What does it mean, Lord, that you go or that you come?" "If I understand you correctly, Lord," he writes in one of his prayers, "you withdraw neither from the place from which you depart from us, nor from the place from which you come to us. You go by concealing and come by revealing yourself."[13] That is it. The work of the Church is, by the power of the Holy Spirit, to make Jesus present and to reveal him (to represent and to re-present him). He is concealed by the darkness of our minds, the blindness of our eyes, and the hardness of our hearts.

No other message is evangelistic because there is only one messenger. All that is required for the Church to become a truly evangelistic and apostolic Church is for it to be truly anointed and overshadowed by the Holy Spirit. There is no good reason in the world why all of this should not be happening in every parish in the world.

Notes

1. Abraham, *Logic of Evangelism*, 1.
2. Michael Ramsey and Leon-Joseph Cardinal Suenens, *The Future of the Christian Church* (New York: More-house-Barlow, 1970), 5.
3. Paul Avis, *Gore: Construction and Conflict* (Churchman Publishing, 1988), 84.
4. *The Lambeth Conferences* (1867–1968) (London: SPCK, 1948), Paul-II, 85.
5. Charles Gore, *Jesus of Nazareth* (London: Macmillan, 1927), 249ff.
6. Bishop Terence Kelshaw, *Seed and Harvest. A Newsletter for the Friends of Trinity Episcopal School for Ministry*, vol. 11, no. 6. 1989.
7. Abraham, *Logic of Evangelism*, 6.
8. Michael Grant, *Jesus* (New York: Charles Scribner's Sons, 1979), 34.
9. George Eliot, *The Mill on the Floss* (Penguin Classics, 1979), 628.
10. Dr. Robert Webber, *Seed and Harvest. A Newsletter for the Friends of Trinity Episcopal School for Ministry* vol. 11, no. 6.
11. Richard Holloway, *The Killing: Meditations on the Death of Christ* (Darton, Longman & Todd, 1984), 9ff.
12. St. Augustine, sermon 34.
13. St. Augustine, *On the Gospel of St. John 68:3*.

THREE

The Pentecost Event and the Gospel Connection

EVANGELISM AS EVENT

By the end of that first day of Pentecost, Peter was worn out! He had spent his first working day for the Church and in the employment of the kingdom. He had sat on no committees and had spent his working hours in none of those concerns that seem to occupy the successors of the apostles so much in our own day. It had been a day of prayer, preaching, baptism. Prayer and waiting upon God had occupied the early hours of the day with amazing results. Preaching, teaching, and expounding the Scriptures had occupied the central part of the day from nine o'clock onward. The result was a crowd of people visibly moved and, in response to that preaching, asking what *they* should now do as many of them found themselves caught up in the implications of Peter's message.

The result was that the closing hours of the day were spent baptizing something like three thousand men, women, and children (Acts 2:41). Peter, who had begun the day turned *in*, ended that first day of Pentecost thoroughly worn *out*. The gospel message clearly was beginning to turn his own life inside out. Is it too fanciful to suppose that at least St. Luke would like us to make a connection with the account of the call of Simon Peter in the first volume of his writings, when he had "let down his nets" at the word of Jesus and "enclosed a great shoal of fish" so that "their nets were breaking" (Luke 5:1ff.)? Their nets were breaking in the water in those days when Simon was just a straightforward fisherman catching (or not catching) fish. Now his arms and his back were breaking when, as a fisher of men, at the same word of Jesus, thousands were "hooked" on the gospel and brought to the waters of baptism. Surely there is some connection between the word of Jesus by the waters of Galilee ("the people pressed upon him to hear the word of God") with Simon as the fisherman and the same word of Jesus and the waters of baptism with Peter the apostle and fisher of men. Here is apostolic enterprise in the springtime of its mission. So we need to look carefully and at some length at this first evangelistic event to see if we can learn essential ingredients and discern something of a model for evangelism in the Church today. We shall examine this prime evangelistic event under six headings: expectation, experience, explosion, explanation, expansion, and expression.

GREAT EXPECTATIONS

The laws of the universe have been overtaken by the promises of God. When weary theologians speak with disparagement of a God of interference and then proceed to edit out all miraculous events that would contradict the laws of the universe, they have not at all begun to see the shape of things to come. They are blind, which is bad enough, but it is even worse because they think that they can see (John 9:18ff.).

Of course, we need to assert at the outset that God the Creator is a consistent God and not a capricious God meddling and interfering in the laws of his own universe. It is important to speak of the laws of the universe as it has evolved and as they have evolved. In the Scriptures, however, there is an overriding law that slowly emerges in the story of humanity's evolution—it is the "law" of promise. God holds out certain promises, and he is, for his part, faithful and consistent in those promises and covenants that he establishes with his people. The promises all belong to a covenant between himself and his people. Humankind without grace since the Fall is locked into the predictable laws of a prison house. Timetables, the menus, and the agenda of that prison house are all predictable to the point of death. That is the bad news, indeed! However, in these last days, a new dispensation is being worked out. God has made a promise. God and humanity in cooperation will make all things possible. In the new order—the kingdom, as opposed to the old order (before the Fall) in the garden—it will not be God over and above human kind doing it all with humanity as the slaves of God, like cogs in a wheel going through the motions with angels on the connecting rods! No, in the kingdom it will be quite different. In the kingdom we are no longer servants but friends (John 15:15). As friends, we work in close cooperation with God, in willing trust and obedience in partnership with the Creator, and so new things are now possible. "Behold I do a new thing," says God (Isa. 43:19), and even more so in the New Testament: "Behold, I make all things new" (Rev. 21:5).

So when Simon walked away from those nets and boats on the day of his call long since in Galilee, the old sign perhaps on a stone (rather faded) had read (we might suppose), "Zebedee & Sons Limited"—very limited—by company law! Is it too fanciful to see scratched in the sand, as Jesus, Simon, and his brother walk into the sunset at the end of that day, some new words: "Simon Peter & Partners Unlimited"? For in the kingdom it will be partnership. And then, as we are reminded significantly in the opening of St. Luke's gospel, it is (because in the end it will be) no longer God *over and against* us. Now it is Emmanuel (and it will be forever), God *with us*—or, put another way, in the words of the angel of the Annunciation, "with God nothing is impossible" (Luke 1:37). The promises of the covenant can only override the laws and the Law, because the new chemistry of partnership has a greater power. When God and humanity are in partner-ship, anything is possible. The kingdom overrides and supercedes the weary and predictable story of evolution and the kingdoms of this world. So the shape of things to come (which has already come in some sense) is a different shape from what we have known and is only possible because God and humankind in Christ are workers together to finish off, perfect, and finally accomplish a creation that had lost its way. God the Redeemer is the same as God the Creator. But in these last days, there is a new recipe. He did not complete his creation as Plan A and then start Plan B—redemption. God is the continuous and consistent creator. The pattern of creation in redemption is just a little more intricate and includes the cooperation of humankind to complete the ultimate design we call heaven, where we live in communion and cooperation with God and where the central word of the human vocabulary is always *AMEN*, Yes—all right. Hence, Jesus can say, "My Father is working still, and I am working" (John 5:17).

So this is no capricious, interfering God but rather an interfacing God. He is a God who is faithful to his promises even more than he has submitted himself to his own laws of creation. So from now on (A.D.) all things are indeed possible so long as by grace (in these years of grace) we can say that simple word that Mary said—yes, amen, *fiat mihi*, OK, right on—and, of course, mean it. Mary had learned that lesson in the first good-news encounter with the angel of the Annunciation. She interfaces with the God of Annunciation. "I am the Lord's servant," Mary answers, "may it be to me as you have said" (Luke 1:38). "The mood of the verb expresses not reluctant compliance, but willing eagerness, as if to say, `Yes, Yes, please let it happen as you have said.' The gift of the Spirit is in no sense imposed upon her but is gladly received by her."[1] Little wonder that when Mary saw the need to override the natural laws of exhaustion and fatigue at the wedding feast of Cana of Galilee as the wine was running out before her very eyes, she realized the essential ingredients for any new thing to happen would be that same willing cooperation between those servants and Jesus. So she was quite explicit when she said, "Do whatever he tells you" (John 2:5). Mary is the prime witness in the Church to the power that flows from a willing obedience to God's Word, for obedience to the Word alone can herald the kind of authority that makes all things possible. Water can become wine (even better wine than the original wine—as redemption is even more wonderful than creation). Mountains can be moved, along with large stones from entrances to tombs, whether it is the tomb of the revitalization of Lazarus or the tomb of the resurrection of Jesus. All things are possible.

The evangelism event belongs within this scenario. It does not have to be a case of emotionalism or manipulation. It is essentially the Lord's doing in the sense that it is all at his initiative. But perhaps the most difficult hurdle for twentieth-century, logical, and largely voyeuristic people is to believe that anything at all is going to happen. A theology of the God of event—that is what we need today. We need to recapture a sense of expectation that wherever the Word is preached with power (that is to say, where it is anointed), it is effective. Wherever God and humanity in faith and loving obedience cooperate, things begin to happen. People are moved: stones are moved

and lives are changed. What was true before eleven
o'clock last Sunday morning is no longer true after eleven
o'clock on the same Sunday morning, onward and forever.
Part of the good news is precisely that things do not
always have to be like this. Things can change. People
can change. And that is always good news!

So at the end of Luke's first volume—his gospel—
Jesus gave instructions about how they should spend this
difficult time we call "meantime." They should spend the
meantime waiting until it is high time (God's time): until
the *kronos* becomes the *kairos*. So Jesus says to the
downhearted disciples on the eve of the ascension as he is
taking leave of them, "Stay in the city until you are clothed
with power from on high" (Luke 24:49). Again, in the
opening chapter of Acts, Jesus urges the disciples to "wait
for the promise of the Father" (Acts 1:4), and he reassures
them at the same time that they will "receive power" to be
his "witnesses" (vs. 8). Great expectations indeed! Waiting
upon God with a sense of great expectation that this
faithful God will do what he promises, is the necessary
prelude to all evangelism in any shape or form, whether it
be preparing to preach next Sunday morning's sermon or
in readiness for an evangelistic crusade in three years'
time.

The challenge is always the same: do we expect anything to happen or anything to be changed? Prayerful
expectation must accompany all evangelistic enterprise in
the Church as we wait in expectation for a faithful God of
power and authority and as we wait to be clothed with
that same power and same authority that clothed the
apostolic Church in New Testament times. For the word
of power issues out of silence; the word of motivation
issues out of stillness; and the word of change issues
straight out of stability that requires that special staying
power, in season and out of season. Do not think that "a
double-minded man, unstable in all his ways, will receive

anything from the Lord" (James 1:8). So with the Church
at large or the local parish and congregation.

We need to stir up again a new sense of expecation in a
God who acts, not by capricious intervention as we have
seen, but according rather to his promises and according
to a plan in which each of us has a place and purpose. Yet
now we are no longer servants (least of all slaves) but
rather the friends of God and "fellow workers" together
with Christ (2 Cor. 6:1). Whenever and wherever God's
plan is in place, his promises are fulfilled, and the kingdom breaks in. Our predictable universe, locked into the
laws of predictability and death, will be set free to be the
sort of place where fruitfulness will replace what is barren
or worn out, where water will irrigate the desert, where
wine will replace water and life will break out of death.
All this is possible *now* because it already has *been*: Everything is imminently possible everywhere because it has
once happened somewhere. It is happening all the time,
in God's good time, because it happened once upon a time
when it was high time!

EXPERIENCE

Something happened in that upper room! What happened
was so real that it could not easily be put into words.

Now, it has to be freely admitted from the outset that
Anglicanism has a rather short suit as far as religious
experience is concerned. Precisely because of our history
(at least, that part rooted in European history), Anglicans
have played down religious experience or "enthusiasm"
as it was technically called after the frightful wars arising
from passionate religion in the sixteenth and seventeenth
centuries. After such bloody wars, Anglicans were determined to play the next movement of their theological sym-
phony with the use of soft pedal and dampers throughout. Never again, we resolved, would we get into those

kinds of squabbles or allow our gospel enthusiasm to
reach such dizzy decibels. Better to be accused of half-
heartedness than to reap the harvest of such a passionate
sowing. This attitude, accompanied by the ground base of
rationalism in the eighteenth century and the so-called
Age of Enlightenment, was not likely to produce the
passionate music of religious revolution, revival, or renewal. We thought it better to keep Christianity locked in
the mental and cerebral processes and within our con-
trolling power. Christian faith and life would in the future, they thought, be kept well away from the combus-
tible chemistry of emotions, the heart, or the passions.
Religion that affects those areas of the human psyche is
inevitably a religion out of control. When such a religion
gets out of hand, it has frequently been the cause of division, hatred, strife, and the bloodiest of wars. That is what
St. Paul had to face with that new and renewed church in
Corinth. We have only to read those two epistles to know
something of the troubles he faced with such intoxicating
Christianity.

Yet, something happened and continues to happen
wherever new Christians are made and wherever and
whenever Christians are made new. It has always been
the case since the beginning of all things—since Abraham
and Sarah. It is well worth taking a biblical concordance
and tracing back the use of the word translated by the
English of the Revised Standard Version as "troubled."
You will find it at the heart of all profound religious
experience (which by definition is very different from a
few religious ideas off the top of our heads). For there is a
sense in which the whole human fabric is deeply disturbed by religious experience—troubled, thrown off balance, or, as the French say so symbolically, *bouleversé*.
Again and again in the Scriptures—and especially in Luke
—whenever there is a learning situation (particularly for
the disciples), we are told that they "wondered greatly" or

that they were "amazed." Not unnaturally, therefore, on
the day of Pentecost, Luke follows this through by telling
us that the crowds were "bewildered" (Acts 2:6) and (in
the following verse) that they were "amazed and
wondered." Then only a few verses later (v. 12) he tells us
yet again that the observers of the Pentecost event were
"all amazed and perplexed." At the heart of the conversion experience must always be the ability to be surprised constantly. Therefore, the title of C.S. Lewis's
spiritual biography is right on target when he speaks of
his conversion experience as being "surprised by joy."

This is essentially the kind of language we use in connection with the experience of falling in love. "He's head
over heels," we say, and we generally say it with some
suspicion or certainly with a questioning twinkle in our
eyes. Such experiences have several classical manifestations in the Scriptures. Abraham was so *troubled* when he
was told of his role in the great design of God that he fell
flat on his face (Gen. 17:3). The barren Sarah was so completely unhinged by the tidings of the birth of a child that
she doubled up with laughter (Gen. 18:12). Hannah was
so nonplussed by the news of her pregnancy that she was
reduced to gibberish and appeared to be drunk (1 Sam.
1:12ff.). Jeremiah seeks to convey religious experience by
speaking of troubled bowels (Jer. 31:20), as does the author
of the Lamentations, who is afflicted in the bowels, the
heart, and the liver (Lam. 1:20; 2:11). Jesus yearns and
groans in his troubled spirit and weeps tears and sweats
blood in the garden of Gethsemane (Luke 22:44). St. Paul
tells us how his pastoral ministry brings him to yearn for
people in what he calls the "bowels of Jesus Christ." In
the Scriptures, there is little if any talk of headaches but
much talk of heartache and even of bellyache.

Put in more twentieth-century language, religious
experience is not just cerebral, it is inevitably psychosomatic. It takes over the whole range of human expression

and fires on all the cylinders of the five senses. Furthermore, it cuts both ways: to be locked in sin is also to suffer physical and psychomatic symptoms. The Psalms are eloquently teeming with allusions to unpleasant physical symptoms caused by alienation from God. So alienation and reconciliation alike play out a theme on the keyboard of our five senses.

It is interesting that two very different Christians, Richard Rolle (1300–49) and John Wesley (1703–91), both speak of a warming of the heart as they seek to describe their particular religious experiences. Richard Rolle, that fourteenth-century English Oxford student, speaks of the way a burning love for Christ overtook and stayed with him.

> I was more astonished than I showed the first time I felt my heart burn with fire. The sensation was not imaginary: I felt real warmth. I was amazed at the way the fire burst up in my soul and gave me unexpected comfort, and I kept touching my breast to see if there was some physical cause. Once I knew that the fire had been spiritually kindled within me and was nothing to do with earthly love or material cause, then I was assured that it was the gift of my Maker. And so I am glad to melt into a desire of greater love; and especially I rejoice at the wonderful delight and spiritual sweetness of this holy flame which so comforts my mind. Before this moment I had no idea that we exiles could know such comfortable and sweet devotion: for truly my heart was enflamed as if a real fire were burning there.[2]

Four hundred years later, John Wesley tells us of that "strange warming of the heart" that coincided with the moment when he knew that his sins, even *his* sins, had been forgiven. Shakers and Quakers both testify to the impact of the Holy Spirit on the human framework. Writers on Christian spirituality through the ages also speak of these frequently embarrassing manifestations and the expression of the deep impression the Holy Spirit of God made upon them by impacting our humanity. From as early as Tertullian, masters of the spiritual life have frequently referred to "the baptism of tears": Tongues, groanings, and dancing all have had their part in the physical and psychosomatic experiences of conversion and release in the Spirit. In her novel *The Mill on the Floss*, George Eliot writes of the nineteenth-century Church of England in the parish of St. Ogg's: "One aged person remembered how a rude multitude had been swayed when John Wesley preached in the cattle-market, but for a long while it had not been expected of preachers that they should shake the souls of men." No indeed! Preaching in the Church of England has seldom been expected to "shake the souls of men."

Things do not seem to have changed much. Certainly this is true today also: Not for a long time has it been expected that preachers in the Episcopal Church "should shake the souls of men." Certainly, there are no new Christians and no Christians are made new whenever the message and the good news have been reduced to an impotent message addressed *solely* to the mind: *souls* need to be shaken before they can be healed. For whatever happened in that upper room at the first Pentecost addressed those waiting and expectant apostles at the very fount of their being, impacting their hearts, souls, minds, and passions with such a multidimensional power that their senses were no longer able to cope. They gave the appearance, we are told, of intoxication; they spoke in many languages all at the same time, and all this in a highly charged atmosphere of wind and fire.

So the anointed preaching of Jesus in the New Testament does more than leave people with something to go away and think about! It disturbs them; it frequently upsets them and even makes them angry. It repels them, and they walk away, or it causes such a religious experience of

the numinous that they are "beckoned" to leave everything behind, come forward, and follow Jesus. People are
actually and physically moved by the teaching and
preaching of Jesus—moved to leave home, security, occu-
pations, tables or nets, and old patterns of behavior.
Whole villages are disturbed and troubled by the whirl-
wind of Jesus' mission as it passes through their locality
like a hurricane, leaving nothing quite like it was before he
arrived.

> The three characteristically biblical symbols for the Spirit
> —wind (John 3:8), water (John 7:37–39), and fire (Matt.
> 3:11, Acts 2:3–4)—all point to a mysterious, dynamic
> energy that destroys one kind of life and gives birth to
> another. It is only by involvement in these powerful
> relationships that we can know the Holy Spirit.[3]

Now, this is not to plead for hysteria, neither is it to
excuse the place hysteria has often had in evangelism. We
need to get the equation the right way around. We should
not be surprised when people experience quite traumatic
physical manifestations when the full-blooded, catholic
gospel is preached, heard, and received. In fact, the history
of religious experience would suggest that such manifestations are the norm. However, the reverse is not true: All
psychosomatic manifestations are not necessarily signs of
authentic religious experience. They can be manifestations of plain, old-fashioned hysteria. It is John Wesley
who writes, perhaps somewhat surprisingly,

> Beware of that daughter of pride, enthusiasm. Oh, keep
> at the utmost distance from it. . . . You are in danger of
> enthusiasm every hour if you depart ever so little from
> scripture; yea, or from the plain, literal meaning of any
> text, taken in connection with the context. And so you
> are, if you despise, or lightly esteem reason, knowledge,
> or human learning, every one of which is an excellent
> gift of God, and may serve the noblest purposes.[4]

However, neither the Church of England nor the Episcopal

Church in America could be described (at least yet) as being "in danger of enthusiasm every hour." When we get there, we will deal with the problem. Rather, we have the opposite problem of apathy to correct in our own day: that disease of God's frozen people.

Yet we must be quite clear that the point of preaching is not to achieve for their own sakes any or all of these experiences: rather, it is to change the heart and will and lives of those who so receive the message. The chances are, however, that in so being changed the hearers will manifest an outward, visible, and even audible experience that is largely beyond the description of words or that has to borrow a description with which we are familiar in a totally different key, such as hysteria.

C.S. Lewis as usual hits the theological nail on the logical head. He relates a strange experience from the diaries of Samuel Pepys.

> With my wife to the King's House to see *The Virgin Martyr*, and it is mighty pleasant. . . . But that which did please me beyond anything in the whole world was the wind musick when the angel comes down, which is so sweet that it ravished me and, indeed, in a word, did wrap up my soul so that it made me really sick, just as I have formerly been when first in love with my wife . . . and makes me resolve to practice wind musick and to make my wife do the like. (27th February, 1668)

Lewis points out how only one physical manifestation (nausea) expressed very different experiences. "Intense aesthetic delight," comments Lewis, "was indistinguishable from the sensation accompanying two other experiences, that of being in love and that of being, say, in a rough channel crossing." Notice how Pepys tells us that the flute music "ravished" him—significantly, the same expression that Eusebius uses of the impact of the Word of the gospel on the early apostles: ravished, not merely edified. When music, art, drama, or preaching ravishes us, it is, it would seem, almost always expressed physically. However, we have only a limited number of sensual expressions to express an infinite range of ravishing experiences. Little wonder that the senses have to "double up": the same sensual expression manifests two or more very different experiences. "The important point is this," concludes Lewis. "I find that this kick or flutter is exactly the same sensation which, in me, accompanies great and sudden anguish. Introspection can discover no difference at all between my neural response to very bad news and my neural response to the overture of *The Magic Flute*."[5]

For our purposes, an important consequence follows upon this analogy. The experience of hysteria and the experience of being ravished by preaching, while being two essentially different and profoundly moving experiences, are nevertheless expressed in virtually the same way. Perhaps we can now see why religious experience requires careful and detailed discernment in order to distinguish between very different experiences manifested in virtually the same way.

All this is true, of course. Yet we should not be surprised that whenever and wherever the connection is made—especially the gospel connection—"when the penny drops," as we say (or when that cosmic disclosure of which Bishop Ian Ramsey spoke so eloquently occurs), that all sorts of bells begin to ring: goose pimples, cold shivers, tears, giggles . . . The list is embarrassingly imprecise and the language necessarily somewhat colloquial. A false argument of reductionism would argue, as Sargent does in his widely read book *Battle for the Mind*, that all phenomena of religious experience are purely and merely hysteria. Many of them may be and undoubtedly are. The lie is given of course in the very title of Sargent's book. The battle is not just for the mind—it is rather for the whole person, bringing in its wake new and reinforced motivations of the will and of the passions. Strangely enough, the eighteenth-century philosopher David Hume, who was certainly no anti-intellectual, nevertheless made the following corrective claim about the place of reason and its proper relation to the total human personality: "Reason is, and ought only to be, the slave of the passions, and can never pretend to any other office than to serve and obey them."[6] Yet it is essentially and ultimately the will that the passions should drive rather than permitting some kind of schizophrenic force to intervene, making only reason the arbiter of all real and authentic experiences. That is the test of real religious experience: it must point to a new direction in people's lives.

On the road to Emmaus, Cleopas and his friend claim to have had an encounter with the risen Christ. Was it a vision and a genuine, full-blooded experience of the risen Lord, or was it an illusion, a fantasy, a hallucination, or just plain hysteria? The acid test is what they did next and not so much what they claimed to feel. However, we need to note in passing that they also (along with Richard Rolle, John Wesley, and millions of others who have experienced the power of Christ's resurrection in their lives) did not fail to record that, when they were "ravished" with the Word, they felt their "hearts burned within them" as Jesus opened the Scriptures to them. They did not continue to stay out at Emmaus, escaping from the conflicts of the city they had left behind. No! They returned, we are told, "that selfsame hour" to Jerusalem—to the scene of conflict and to the place where far-reaching decisions needed to be made. Their religious experience (heart-warming, in this case) was no escape mechanism: it had turned them and their lives around—quite literally (Luke 24:13ff.). A genuine religious experience turns people's lives around. They are truly converted, and a new direction is given to their lives. That is the test of all religious experience worthy of the name. We need to ask again and again, Does it turn people around and give new direction, or does it push them even further down the unreal road of fantasy, illusion, and escapism? If the latter, it is not genuine religious experience. Rather, it merely gives the appearance of a religious experience: it is hysteria conterfeiting as religious experience. This is the way we need to respond to the New Testament injunction to "test the spirits" to see whether they are of God and all this at the same time as we seek to obey that other complimentary New Testament injunction: "Resist not the Spirit" (1 Thess. 5:19).

EXPLOSION

So "that selfsame hour" being only, in fact, nine o'clock in the morning, fearful and disillusioned disciples still locked behind doors with fear and apprehension in their hearts suddenly become apostles, flinging wide open the selfsame doors of that upper room, tumbling down the stairs into the turmoil of the streets outside. Faith has replaced fear and displaced it. The result is inevitably an explosion. Boldness has replaced apprehension; activity has replaced acquiescence and apathy—they are new men with a new song to sing.

The impact of the Holy Spirit has displaced these men as surely as an explosion creates displacement in the world of physics. So it has always been. When the God of the Old Testament takes hold of people's lives, it is not in order to cuddle them or to give them a massage. Rather, he takes them by the scruff of the neck and sends them on the most absurd errands to the most out-of-the-way places to address the most unprepossessing people with the most ridiculous of messages! We call it the mission of the Church. For mission originates in the very heart of God himself. Since the dawn of religious history, God has been sending people on these errands, but in these "last days" he has sent his Son—his only Son—on the errand of love. Put another way, we can deduce that mission is a characteristic of the godhead of love: that sort of love which *always goes out of its way*. Wherever we see love going out of its way, there we are seeing mission.

So at the baptism of Jesus. Immediately, Jesus receives the anointing of the Holy Spirit. He is expelled and propelled into the desert. The word used in the Greek (*ekballo*) is a powerful word giving us in English the word *ballistic* for a ballistic missile! It is the same word used significantly in the gospel account of the laborers in the vineyard. "Pray therefore the Lord of the harvest to *send out* laborers into his harvest" (Luke 10:2). Both the words *pray* and *send out* are, in fact, rather poor and tame translations in the English. The word for *pray*, at root, is the word for *beggar*. So it would be better translated, "Beg or badger the Lord of the harvest." Then with the second word: it needs strengthening also to get the full impact of the Greek. The sentence should now read, "Beg or badger the Lord of the harvest to take the laborers by the scruff of the neck and *thrust them out* into the harvest!" The whole of God's people by their baptism are anointed for mission and not for a spiritual picnic. Jesus was exploded out into the desert for confrontation with evil, error, and the powers of darkness. We are baptized not simply to get our own miserable souls to heaven but to be truly apostolic—men and women who are "sent out." Disciples are baptized to become apostles for mission and ministry. We are baptized and anointed with the oil of chrism to be Jesus Christ for those outside the Church. Inevitably, therefore, the explosion of the Spirit must expel the Church into the desert of the world to empower it for mission and ministry. This will inevitably involve us in confrontation with evil.

The renewal movements of the last few decades were not intended to be lovely, sweet, and sugary experiences for those in the Church. Rather, the decades of renewal were intended by God to prepare the Church for this

Decade of Evangelism: that is "the reason" we came to this hour, "for such a time as this" (Esther 4:14). Spiritual renewal equips the saints of God for the sort of mission and ministry that is involved in the material world—a mission and ministry that will change the architectural shape of history. Such a ministry will witness in the field of economics, sociology, medicine, genetics, and in all those "corners of the earth" where the mind of Christ is needed most: wherever there are ghettos of any kind, whether racial, sociological, intellectual, or moral. It will empower such anointed Christians for their confrontations with, and for a new assault upon, the powers that be: the powers of darkness and ignorance; the powers of spiritual wickedness; the principalities and the powers of this age. (Eph. 6:12).

And the first weapon in that confrontation, as with Jesus in his tempations in the wilderness, is to have a true knowledge of the Scriptures. Three times, like three claps of thunder, Jesus refutes the devil and unmasks his masquerade with the phrase "It is written. . . . It is written. . . . It is written. . . ." (Incidentally, it is worth noting how the devil is duplistic, fraudulent, and masquerading when in the third temptation he perverts the use of Scripture itself and seeks to turn the tables on Jesus by the use of the very same phrase—"It is written"! The Antichrist can also use Scripture and quote texts. As we come nearer the heart of the conflict, we need to pray ever more intensively for discernment to distinguish between things that differ.)

So we need to ask ourselves as Episcopalians whether our knowledge of Scripture is sufficiently deep and whether the vocabulary of Scripture belongs sufficiently to the vocabulary of our everyday life to enable us in times of crisis to say immediately from the heart and from the passions, "It is written. . . . It is written. . . . It is written. . . ." Only those who have read the Scriptures, marked them, learned them, and "inwardly digested" them will be sufficiently well equipped for such a confrontation. Only so will our church become truly apostolic as it witnesses "at all times and in all places" to Jesus and the resurrection.

EXPLANATION

Notice the character of the first Christian evangelistic crusade. The preaching or the messages of the apostles are godly answers to the questions derived from a secular outlook evoked in the minds of the spectators and all this by the ambivalent events that they are observing. So William Abraham can write in his book *The Logic of Evangelism*, "The gospel spread and the church grew because the sovereign hand of God was in the midst of the community that found itself surrounded by people who were puzzled and intrigued by what they saw happening."[7] In the Church today, are we surrounded by people who are "puzzled and intrigued" by what they see happening among us? Or is our gossip and our backbiting all too predictable? The evangelistic event evokes the questions that are answered by a scriptural explanation, best summarized in the phrase "Jesus and the resurrection." It is supremely that event, foreshadowed in the scriptures of the Old Testament and made explicit in the New, which is the best explanation of the extraordinary life-style of Spirit-filled Christians. In other words, the scriptural explanation makes the best sense of the actual event that is so evidently happening in their midst. With their limited secular agenda, those people on the first day of Pentecost naturally supposed that the apostles were drunk. No, on further reflection, they had to admit that they could not be so drunk after all, as it was still only "nine o'clock in the morning." Their questioning so far is purely rational and purely secular. So what on earth is really happening? "I'll tell you," says Peter in effect.

"Don't you have to agree that this is surely that event foretold in the prophecy of Joel: that topsy-turvy event from the landscape of the new world foretold by the prophet in which old men dream dreams and young men see visions. Look out! It's here in your very midst, in all its fullness for those with eyes to see and ears to hear. And, supremely, it is most obviously here—and wait for it—in that completely overturned and recent event you all know about—Jesus and his death and resurrection, all of which have just occurred in this very city. This is where it is at (as Americans say), and we have found ourselves caught up in all of this. Now, we want you to see the connection between all these "happenings." When you do so, you will likewise be overtaken by the Spirit of this same Jesus and his resurrection. What is happening to us will then begin to happen to you."

Here is the convergence of three stories, or three testimonies, if you like: the story of the Old Testament (Joel in this instance); the story of what is happening to the disciples before the very eyes of the crowd (their story); and the story of Jesus and his death and resurrection (the Jesus story). All three stories are very disturbing and upsetting. In fact, they turn all sensible worldviews upside down and inside out. It is hard to make sense of any one of the stories without reference at least to one of the other two stories. The job of the preacher, the messenger, and the apostle is always the same: to bring all three evidences together; to make the gospel connection; and to say, in effect, the time is now, the place is here, and the person is you. "Look out! This is your life!" The evidence of all three stories and testimonies converges in the here and now—so, "Here am I. Send me" (Isa. 6:8). The objective reality (the shape of things to come, which is the shape of things as they should be and eventually will be) is appropriated subjectively and evokes the ultimate question from the crowd: "So what should we be doing?"

All preaching (worthy of the name) must have this dynamic about it. It must disturb people to the point where they will begin to ask themselves disturbing questions.

Yet notice that the only real qualification for Peter to take the initiative is that he, along with all the other apostles jumping up and down in the street like drunken men yelling their heads off and praising God, can claim to be a *witness* of these things. Jesus had given to his apostles their apostolic identity before his ascension when he had told them in so many words, "You are witnesses of these things" (Luke 24:48). That is to say, they are witnesses both of the written record of the suffering, death, and resurrection that you find in the Scriptures (history) and in the contemporary Jesus event of the past few weeks (Luke 24:44–48). "But now in these last moments you have had the same experience and a similar breakdown and breakthrough in your own lives. The same outpouring of the Holy Spirit has fallen upon *you* and has made the Jesus event real for you, in your own breakdown and your own breakthrough—your own death and your own resurrection."

At Pentecost, Peter is therefore able to say in words that carry real weight, "We are witnesses of these things." In fact, this phrase becomes the refrain of the apostolic preaching and proclamation and occurs several times (Acts 2:32; 3:15; 5:32). It is indeed the gospel connection that St. Luke wants us to see between the end of his first volume (the gospel) and the beginning of his second volume (Acts). In the closing chapter of his gospel, he tells us of Jesus' admonition to his anxious disciples that will be his witnesses (Luke 24:48). Then in the opening of the Book of Acts, when the apostles are selecting someone to replace Judas, we are told that the only qualification necessary for this office was that the candidate had witnessed all the essential events of Christ's death and resurrection.

The theme is taken up again when we find that apostolic preaching is essentially witnessing to Jesus in his death and resurrection and witnessing to the place that his death and resurrection have in our own lives. In all these instances, "witness to the resurrection" is the heart of the matter. We can only be truly and fully apostolic when we have witnessed the power of the resurrection of Jesus at work in our own lives. That is the supreme way in which worried disciples become witnessing apostles.

That is the only way we can explain such absurd evidence and happenings both in our own lives, in the torn lives of those around us, and in the disasters of the world. Only when we are witnesses of resurrection (breakdown and breakthrough) can we discuss good news in the very last place on earth that you would ever expect to find it—namely, among the bad news. To put all of this in a word, it is Jesus and the resurrection—or simply Jesus. That is the content of apostolic preaching. For truly evangelistic and apostolic preaching is essentially the same as it has always been. Peter begins the main part of his apostolic, explanatory preaching with the two simple words *this Jesus*. We have suggested that there are three witnesses—history, my story, and the Jesus story. In one sense it does not matter which story you start with so long as you bring all three to a point of convergence so that people can make the gospel connection for themselves. More accurately, that work of making the gospel connection is the work of the Holy Spirit.

We are told in one of Peter's subsequent sermons that "while Peter was still saying this" (and invariably it seems that he would always say the same old thing!) "the Holy Spirit fell on all who heard the word" (Acts 10:44). They made the connection and responded accordingly. For them, it was a crisis moment and, in a real sense, judgment was occurring. They had to make a decision, for all preaching needs to bring the hearers to a point of decision.

Either they must go for it (literally forward and be baptized) or walk away from it, like the rich young ruler (and generally that leaves people rather sad, mad, bad, or even angry).

So apostolic preaching is essentially an explanation or exposition of an event that is already happening or has already happened—either in history, the Jesus story, or in our story or in the story of the nation or the community of faith. It is not just some idea (however holy and religious that idea may be) about God. It embodies and articulates nothing less than an encounter with Jesus and the resurrection.

EXPANSION

We are told on that first day of Pentecost that "three thousand souls were added" to the Church. In one sense, the numbers game is not the concern of the clergy or of the Church. We should not be counting heads or becoming neurotic about falling numbers or increasing numbers. This is the work of the Lord of the harvest, and we are only the sowers. St. Luke is quite clear that it is God's harvest not ours (Luke 10:2). Nevertheless, wherever the Word is preached faithfully (not even eloquently or impressively), God anoints that faithfulness, and lives are changed and people are moved.

It is interesting to watch Billy Graham, the master evangelist of our own age, at work. He is not particularly eloquent nowadays nor even is he charismatic as a person, in the limited sense of that word. There is nothing particularly magnetic about Billy Graham as such. He is now seventy, but he has spent nearly half a century faithfully preaching the Word. He preaches from a full script and only preaches for about eighteen or twenty minutes at most of his rallies. Nevertheless, people come forward in their hundreds and thousands.

The cynic may well say that most of these will fall
away afterward. They probably will. I doubt very much
whether more than three hundred of the three thousand
converts on the first day of Pentecost were still "regularly
attending church" three months later! How many of them
would be sufficiently deep in their faith to be ready to die
for Jesus in the months and years following that event? Yet
it is interesting to reflect that the present Archbishop of
Canterbury was converted at a mission by Billy Graham
many years ago. It is also interesting to note that
Augustine was converted by the faithful preaching and
teaching of Bishop Ambrose in Milan in A.D. 396. In both
cases we are talking about a single life being touched by
faithful preaching, but surely such lives represent in
history something of a hinge on which many other lives
turn. The joy and thrill and awe of preaching is that you
never quite know what you are doing or where it will all
end! You never quite know what the response will be—
and neither should you.

Integrity for the preacher is simply a faithfulness to
preaching the Word in season or out of season and leaving
the rest to God. It is true, as we shall see later in this book,
that another part of the work of the Church, which is also
evangelism in its fullest sense, is to nurture these new
Christians in their new-found faith. However, we should
be confident that, wherever the Word is preached with
faithfulness and in the power of the Spirit, it will make a
difference and that difference will be recorded on some
scale—numbers, intensity, quality of life, or whatever is
the appropriate barometer or thermometer with which to
examine an increase in Christian mission and evangelism.
Success is not a New Testament word, but *fruitfulness* most
certainly is. Wherever the Spirit is at work, it is not long
before there is an increase of some kind. Yet it is not for us
to concern ourselves with market research to see which
ground will be fruitful. Our part in the whole divine

economy of evangelism is simply to get the Word out and to keep casting the seed of his Word like a faithful and persistent sower.

EXPRESSION

The ultimate product of all of this is the catholic Church of Jesus Christ, which is also in its turn inevitably an apostolic Church. Such a body of people have only one requirement in order to become members of the catholic Church. All they need to do is to request baptism for themselves or for those for whom they are responsible —family, children, or even slaves—in a word, for their "whole household" (Acts 16:34). Notice that there is no account that the three thousand or so baptized began to speak in tongues or, indeed had any other religious experience of any kind. They were moved simply to ask what they should do. "They were cut to the heart" (Acts 2:37). Apostolic preaching is a word that goes to the heart of the matter and that cuts through so much verbiage, discussion, and so-called intellectual problems. Peter's message touched them on the raw. It was not just matter for further debate, as Paul's rather disastrous presentation on the Acropolis turned out to be. It is perhaps worth noting that Paul on that occasion only spoke of Jesus anonymously and of the resurrection as an idea up for discussion. The crowd was not moved to *do* anything but only to go on talking and forming discussion groups and then possibly to form a subcommittee to look into the possibility of resurrection!

Apostolic, evangelistic preaching is made of sterner stuff. It cuts people to the heart and moves them to express a question. And for some of them the result is baptism.

The catholic Church of Jesus Christ is not constituted around any one religious experience—whether speaking in tongues, shaking and quaking, being slain in the spirit, laughter, tears, or apparent drunkenness and the like. It is simply and solely the outward, visible, and corporate expression in history, in time and space, in flesh and blood, of those who, for all kinds of reasons and for none at all, have been moved to request baptism.

Of course, that is only just a first step, but it is a decisive step over the only line that God has chosen to draw—namely, the line between the Church and the world. Significantly, in the New Testament as in the Old, that line is the line of water—the Red Sea or the Jordan. For all new life begins the other side of water. You do not even have to be able to swim across: it's all right to go under. In fact, that seems to be the principle expression of this new life—you undergo baptism. You cannot reach out and do it for yourself or, indeed, to yourself. There is no such thing as a do-it-yourself baptism kit!

Yet notice that the Church is the expression of evangelism and not a substitute for it. A Church that is not evangelistic in this generation will not exist in the next. Furthermore, people are not being evangelized if all we say is "come and join us." Church membership through baptism is the *result* of evangelism and may even be the cause of evangelism, but it is no substitute for evangelism. Cardinal Basil Hume says rightly that most Catholics today have been oversacramentalized and underevangelized. He is right. And what he says is equally true of most Episcopalians and Anglicans.

Yet notice that Peter did not set out to increase the congregation from twelve to three thousand. He was impelled (compelled and expelled) to tell others what was really happening in the real world. What was really happening was such good news that he was compelled to gossip it around Asia Minor—compelled, not in the sense even of being mandated to do so, but rather in a real sense, he was *driven* to do so. As he said himself, "We cannot but speak of what we have seen and heard." (Acts 4:20).

So, displaced from the security of that upper room with locked doors and intimate relationships, Peter and the others were driven to go to the ends of the earth to tell others by word and by deed of the core experience of Jesus and the resurrection. Peter was driven to tell what it was doing to his life and the lives of his friends and, therefore, by implication (made quite explicit, however), what it could mean in other lives, other places, and at all times until the end of time. The result has been the extraordinary and ambivalent phenomenon of the catholic apostolic Church in the history books of the nations of the world. The message has gone out from Jerusalem on that first day of Pentecost to Rome, London, New York, San Francisco, and to the ends of the earth on many other days of Pentecost. It has gone wherever successors to Peter and the other apostles have been so filled with the Holy Spirit, anointed, and evangelized for a truly apostolic ministry of witness to Jesus and his resurrection.

NOTES

1. Tom Smail, *The Giving Gift: The Holy Spirit in Person* (London: Hodder & Stoughton, 1988), 26.
2. Richard Rolle, "Prologue to the Fire of Love," quoted in *The English Spirit. The Little Gidding Anthology of English Spirituality*, ed. Paul Handley (Nashville: Abingdon Press, 1987), 27.
3. Smail, *Giving Gift*, 20.
4. John Wesley, *A Plain Account of Christian Perfection*, Question 33.
5. C.S. Lewis, They Asked for a Paper, Geoffrey Bles, London, 1962, p 169
6. David Hume, *A Treatise on Human Nature* (New York: Oxford University Press, 1978), 415.
7. Abraham, *Logic of Evangelism*, 38.

FOUR

The Local Church and Christian Presence: An Environment of Evangelism

To evangelize is to spread the good news that Jesus Christ died for our sins and was raised from the dead according to the Scriptures, and that as the reigning Lord He now offers the forgiveness of sins and the liberating gift of the Spirit to all who repent and believe. Our Christian presence in the world is indispensable to evangelism, and so is that kind of dialogue whose purpose is to listen sensitively in order to understand. But evangelism itself is the proclamation of the historical, biblical Christ as Saviour and Lord, with a view to persuading people to come to Him personally and so be reconciled to God. In issuing the gospel invitation we have no liberty to conceal the cost of discipleship. Jesus still calls all who would follow Him to deny themselves, take up their cross, and identify themselves with His new community. The results of evangelism include obedience to Christ, incorporation into His church and responsible service in the world.[1]

THE LOCAL COMMUNITY OF FAITH

The Church is both the product of evangelism and the producer of evangelism as defined above. Yet only a truly gospelled community can itself communicate the gospel.

For truth to tell, a truly gospelled community cannot but gossip the gospel by what it says, by what it does, and what it is. There is no magic formula for Christian evangelism. Thank God there is not, otherwise, human lives would be little more than objects that could be manipulated and moved at the whim of words and magic wands. Simon Magus would have the last word, after all. Yet human motivation (whether emotional, sexual, or intellectual) is not cool and logical, plain and straightforward: like love, it is seldom pure and never simple! It is, in the end, a great and awesome mystery. What does it take to move my life and to change me?

The mystery of election grapples with this very issue. But throughout the ages of the Church, all the doctrines of Christianity derived from the work of grace have been complicated, divisive, and are at the root of most dissensions. On the one hand, we must maintain the sovereignty of God in all things in his divine initiative. "You did not choose me," says Jesus emphatically, "but I chose you" (John 15:16). On the other hand, at one and the same time as we emphasize God's sovereignty and initiative in all things in general and in evangelism in particular, we must also stress the place of choice, decision, and the human response in the working out of our salvation. Without his prevenient grace (which is always at least one step ahead of our yearnings), we could not even choose to follow him. Yet there is also the indispensable need to respond to the call of God and personally to make it my own.

The whole theology of the church throughout the ages concerning the massive doctrine of grace has always, at its best, sought to express a paradox. Perhaps that paradox is best preserved in all its fullness by a formula that might go something like this: "We must indeed answer *for* ourselves, but we do not and cannot answer *by* ourselves. The ability to respond freely to the promise of Christ's coming is the work of the Spirit in us."[2] Or again, we may need to turn to the familiar words of St. Augustine already quoted in this book: "Without God, we cannot; without us, he will not."

Yet it is the local church and the environment of grace that we can find there, which is the natural setting for evangelism. The danger in calling for a Decade of Evangelism is that we shall try to set up a whole new superstructure in the churches geared to a thing called evangelism. If that is our vision for the Decade of Evangelism, the building up of the Church will elude us, and this decade will fail to produce the results for which many of us are praying at the outset. The first converts gathered around the disciples and met together in the Temple and in their houses for teaching, for prayer, praise, fellowship, mutual care, and the breaking of bread (Acts 2:42). William Abraham reminds us, "In other words, evangelism was rooted in a corporate experience of the rule of God." We best experience, test, and discern the rule of God in the faith communities of the Church, in other words, in parishes. Such parishes, however, are representations of more than mere churchgoing attendance. Rather, they are communities of faith, witnessing by their lives, works, words, and worshiping to the coming of the kingdom while at the same time taking their place alongside and rooted in the wider local community. In a word, we are talking about revitalized parishes becoming communities of faith.

For one of the basic premises of this book is that we do not need to go out and buy for ourselves a do-it-yourself evangelism kit. Already in America there is a whole network of parishes and dioceses. Such churches rightly energized to what we call in this book apostolic point will inevitably be evangelistic—living souls of evangelization.

"I do not believe we need a great network of national or diocesan offices in evangelism which would ignore the rich potential of our parishes," said Dr. Robert Runcie, the Archbishop of Canterbury in the General Synod debate on the Decade of Evangelism in July 1989. "Our officers in evangelism are the bishops and clergy, our missionaries are the laity." True evangelism should be locally focused, Dr. Runcie emphasized in that same speech, and that must mean that it must be rooted in the local church.

MAINTENANCE AND MISSION

Of course, all this is so true. Yet equally true, though perhaps not so easily acceptable by the parish clergy and congregations, is the bald fact that at heart many congregations simply do not want to grow.

There is all the difference in the world between a half-full bottle of water and a half-empty one: though, of course, to all appearances they both look the same. A church that is half full is already full—of expectation to be fuller. Its purposes, its goals, programs, finances, its whole dynamic throughout its parish policy, and its outlook in general are all geared to look beyond the church itself. It probably has a building project involving money that it has no immediate prospect of obtaining! It is a parish that is always overspending and overspent in every way, yet refuses to submit a balanced budget at the outset of each year. It projects growth always and expects growth always. Like the Christian doctrine of hope, it lives by a self-fulfilling prediction. "Faith is the assurance of things hoped for, the conviction of things not seen" (Heb. 11:1). It sees every year of its life not so much as a year in which the budget should be balanced but as a year of grace that is infinitely rich in its resources and promises. So in every way, such a parish relies upon the grace and power of the Holy Spirit, deeply trusting in the promises of Christ—promises that nevertheless are addresssed only to a missionary church and not to a church of maintenance. The food at the feeding of the multitudes is only multiplied as it is given away: it does not grow in order to be stored away in the deep freeze! You cannot hoard the manna of God's grace and life. If you could, you would become self-sufficient and independent of his daily, life-giving grace, and that is death.

A half-empty church, on the other hand, while still giving the appearance of success, is programmed always for retreat and reduction. It hoards what funds it has, keeping a careful balance in the bank, and lives by that dangerous maxim of cutting its cloth according to its means. The maintenance mentality can always be defended as being the sensible, prudent policy that is "realistic" and that makes sense in the present uncertain climate! After all, they will argue, "you always need to put something away for a rainy day!"

Yet, an even more disastrous state of affairs than the state of mere maintenance is that attitude of mind in a congregation that actually does not want to grow. It confuses remnant theology with the oddment mentality. The priest in such a parish is frequently hijacked by the shrinking congregation and pampered to become a private chaplain to a small, inward-looking community. If at the same time the particular parish can be wedded to a particular doctrinal stance or liturgical whim, so much the better—there is something to fight for, a position to be maintained, and, therefore, lines to be ever more clearly and closely drawn. Furthermore, if it has a large endowment fund, then its death is almost certain!

Yet to reverse the situation of a half-empty church or the kind of parish that we have been describing above and to turn it into a half-full parish demands nothing less than the working out of the miracle of the resurrection in all its fullness. The dynamic has to be reversed. It demands nothing less than the resurrection reversal such as we find at Cana of Galilee or in the prophet Joel. In both sources of the Scriptures, we find the process of resurrection reversal at work. So at Cana of Galilee the bewildered and

confused ruler of the feast says, "Every man sets forth at
the beginning good wine and when men have well drunk,
that which is not so good." That's the natural dynamic,
program, or shape of things at most parties, in most
human relationships, and in the ways of the world. We
put our best foot forward first, and then that which
follows is not quite so good and so on into steady decline.
But in our relationship with God in the resurrection of
Jesus, everything is reversed. "But you have kept the
good wine until now" (John 2:10). In the kingdom,
everything is back to front, inside out, and upside down as
in the picture given to us by the prophet Joel. "Young
men" normally dream the dreams, and visions are left to
old men. But in the new shape of things to come (in the
kingdom), here again everything is in reverse: "Young
men are seeing visions and old men are dreaming dreams"
(Joel 2:28).

In a half-empty church, the preaching, the worship,
and the life in the Spirit must all be aimed and directed to
go over the heads of those present in the church. So unless
the existing congregation turns round and begins to look
beyond where they are, they simply cannot see the point
of it all and what the preacher is trying to get at. The pace
must quicken, and expectations and projections be raised.
It is not the job of the preacher to unchurch anyone or to
throw anyone out. It is his or her task, however, to point
and direct in such a way that pastoral pampering simply
cannot be promoted or tolerated any longer. As with a
good trainer in a gymnasium or a good school teacher, the
pupils need to be stretched beyond their immediate attain-
ments. "Ah, but a man's reach should exceed his grasp, or
what's a heaven for?"[4]

COMMITMENT OR COUNSELING

However, it has to be admitted that much training in

seminaries since the Second World War has actually aided and fostered the maintenance mentality. In my seminary, nobody seemed to mind too much whether you read the Bible from cover to cover as long as you read all the right books about the Bible—the books that were required to pass the examinations. Most of these books told you what it was no longer necessary for you to believe in the Scriptures! It is probably true that no generation has sought to understand the Bible so much as this generation, and yet no generation has known the Bible less than this generation. For, truth to tell, the Bible is not there primarily to be understood only in a purely intellectual way; it is primarily intended to haunt you and so to make you go beyond mere reading and intellectual competence into the realm of the imagination and the firing of the will. It is directed to the subconscious, to precisely the same place as subliminal tapes in our own age are directed. It is directed to the place of images and dreams, only to be released into the conscious in the form of "comfortable words" (to use Cranmer's phrase) in times of crisis, breakdown, sleeplessness, and, supremely of course (as with Jesus on the cross), when we are *in extremis*.

However, one very large book on all our seminary shelves was required reading. It was a huge, yellow-covered *magnum opus* by Dr. Frank Lake entitled *Clinical Theology*. This book had to be read, learned, marked, and inwardly digested! Preaching, in the age of television, we were told, was finished. Counseling now was the model for the maintenance of each parish, and the pastor was essentially to model his or her ministry on that of the counselor. So the main work of the parish priest was not preaching, Bible study, or even prayer, we were told, but rather counseling.

Dr. Lake had cobbled together a somewhat questionable thesis (later to be totally disproved by the professionals). The drug mescalin, we were assured, reproduced birth trauma, and it was in our birth trauma that all our future behavior patterns were to be discerned. So it was that a whole decade of seminarians (at least in England) were subjected to this (at best) marginal requirement in the curriculum of a ministerial pastor. Such seminarians let loose in parishes in the sixties, seventies, and eighties filled their calendars, not with visiting, Bible study, sermon preparation, and prayer primarily, but with semiprofessional appointments to receive counseling at the hands of the self-appointed counselor of the parish—who was often the rector. It was not too long before, in fact, you could fill a whole working week with a few mentally or emotionally disturbed people. I would suggest that such pastoral strategy can only result in a maintenance mentality—and maintenance minus mission surely equals, in the end, mausoleum.

What, in fact, we were being subjected to in our seminaries is now much clearer to many of us than it was at the time. Alastair Campbell in his remarkably timely book *Rediscovering Pastoral Care* says these terrifying words: "Our age is far from unique in having divergent theological opinions, as even a cursory study of church history will show, but there is now an increasing tendency *to welcome* pluralism and imprecision in doctrine rather than to deplore it."[5] (All this in spite of the fact that both statistics and common sense would tell anyone since the time of St. Paul that "if the bugle gives an indistinct sound, who will get ready for battle?" [1 Cor. 14:8]) Notwithstanding, Alastair Campbell continues:

> Appreciation of the complexity of truth, tolerance of ambiguity, and awareness that all theoretical formulations are only approximate to the reality they attempt to descibe are regarded as marks of the educated intellect. Faith is experienced as a *quest* for understanding, requiring a constant renewal of theological categories to do it justice.[6]

Surely, in such a theological outlook, sin, repentance, forgiveness, and grace have very little part to play. Yet, although "sin is really no stranger to us," Alastair Campbell continues, nevertheless, "we need to learn its name afresh and to recognize its many manifestations in our age. Thus the rediscovery of pastoral care must include a fresh understanding of both guilt and grace."[7]

If it does not do so, then the only model to which the pastor can revert is the model we were given in our seminaries—namely, the model of counseling. "Recent pastoral counseling," writes Thomas C. Oden,

> has incurred a fixated dependency and indebtedness to modern psychology and to modern consciousness generally that has prevented it from even looking at premodern wisdoms of most kinds including classical pastoral care. . . . We have bet all our chips on the assumption that modern consciousness will lead us into vaster freedom, while our specific freedom to be attentive to the Christian pastoral tradition has been plundered, polemicized and despoiled.[8]

THE CHALLENGE OF CHANGE

For if we go all the way with the counseling model, we shall find that there is no place in pastoral ministry either through the preached Word or through the pastoral sacraments of the Church to challenge or to change people in their lives. The exciting prospect of the gospel of Jesus Christ faithfully preached and taught is that it preaches directly for such a change of lives. The problem for all of us to the extent that we are emotionally or mentally damaged is that, of course, we do not particularly want to change. The New Testament gives us that terrifying text, "We shall not all sleep, but we shall all be changed" (1 Cor. 15:51). Truth to tell, most of us would probably prefer to die and certainly to sleep rather than to change. Yet here

St. Paul is working out the implications of resurrection
and sees the capacity to be changed (rather than to
change) as integral to such theology. We need to ask ourselves whether God's resurrection people have lost this
expectation of resurrection in the community of the
Church. Or has it been taken from them by a clergy who
have forgotten the centrality of the doctrine of the
resurrection? Have we been too busy arguing about the
mechanics of Jesus's resurrection to recall the mighty
promises of God for resurrection in our lives NOW?

The contemporary English novelist who is much read
in the United States at the present time—Iris Murdoch—in
all her novels is concerned with the ability to change and
to break free from old patterns of behavior: degrees of
freedom. In her novel *The Good Apprentice*, we find a dialogue involving Stewart, whose father has been having an
affair with Midge. Midge has come to see Stewart in the
hope that they might endlessly discuss the situation.
Stewart, however, refuses to act in the role of a counselor
and to listen to all of this. The following dialogue ensues:

Midge says, somewhat full of anguish, to Stewart,

> "What I want is to understand what I've done— that's
> what I want to talk to you about—and about it all, and
> what such things mean anyway. How can I judge? I
> need your help, I beg you to help me, I want to confess,
> I want to pour it all out in front of you—"
>
> "I understand, but pouring it out is just what won't
> help. It's no use telling me. That's just a diversion,
> another emotional experience, a way of experiencing
> —of continuing—that relationship. Go to Thomas [her
> husband]. Telling *him* is what will make everything
> clearer and real. You've been living in some sort of
> dream—that's how I see it anyway—until you tell
> Thomas, you won't know what you are doing. Once
> you have told him you will be a different person."
>
> "That's what I'm afraid of."[9]

Yes, that's the point! That is what we are all afraid of! Do we want to be different, or is it, in fact, being different that is the basis of so much fear? Dare we face change? The counseling model does not demand that we change. Yet the gospel message is not primarily based upon a counseling model but on a model of challenge, confrontation, and crisis—with the eternal possibility that we can and, indeed, that we must change and become different. Only grace can perfect nature without annihilating it. That is the glorious truth about grace. Naturally, we are afraid of the kind of change that would annihilate. I believe much counseling does create a synthetic person and that much of the "kick" in the old faults and failings is lost in the pursuit of health and wholeness. If we were clinically whole, we would probably be irredeemable! The work of grace is more subtle and always full of surprises. The leopard's spots don't need to be removed after all: just reordered in a more intriguing design.

So natural humanity (unaided by grace and unchallenged by the gospel invitation to new life) actually fears change and, not unnaturally, does not want to be healed: like the man by the pool of Siloam. When Jesus asked him the leading question, "Do you want to be healed?" he does not even reply to that question. Rather he puts back the record on the record player and reproduces what he has been saying for the past thirty-eight years: "Sir, I have no man to put me into the pool when the water is troubled, and while I am going down another steps down before me" (John 5:7). He had been saying that for thirty-eight years, we are told. So Jesus cuts through all that protective armor and issues the challenge and the command, "Rise, take up your pallet and walk" (vs. 8). (I have always wondered secretly if the man was rather afraid of the water and that the last thing in the world he ever wanted was for anyone to throw him in!) In any event, life (handicapped or paralyzed or less than it could be) can so easily become a life that is pampered, and, of course, that is no life at all. Yet it is in some strange way (like sin itself) in the end rather comfortable and even comforting. Life becomes like an old pair of worn-out slippers that are no longer any use—nevertheless, it's the way we've always known things to be, and their very familiarity that has the incredible capacity to be both comforting and imprisoning. As Emily Dickinson so rightly says, "A prison gets to be a friend."

Add to all this some verbal misunderstanding about the Holy Spirit and you can see how a pastor and the pastoral ministry become caricatured into a gentle, semi-absent-minded, old professorial figure who just goes around gently tapping people on the back and encouraging them. For too long the Church has spoken of the Holy Spirit as the Comforter, little realizing that the word *comfort* as used in the Prayer Book is a Middle English word and means something very different from *comforting* and *comfortable*. In Middle English, it does not conjure up at all the concept of carpet slippers and teddy bears. Look at the Bayeux tapestry. There you will see King Harold ordering his troops to battle. And yet in the Middle English in which the tapestry is subtitled, King Harold is portrayed as "comforting his troops." Ghostly counsel and advice is much more correctly portrayed by that picture of the king than the picture of the average parish priest sitting with a parishioner undergoing counseling. For, in fact, the word translated in Middle English as *comforting* means "goading, exhorting, egging on." The work of the Holy Spirit, therefore, is to exhort us and to challenge us to change and to become different—to break loose from the prison house of habit and of our past.

Likewise, the pastoral ministry: In its classical form, it is made of sterner stuff than counseling. It is, in fact, what we like to call nowadays tough loving and tough caring. It holds out the possibility of new life—the *vita nova*—and

new possibilities. It holds out the possibility that the
windows can be thrown open and the prison bars broken
down and, indeed, that all the fetters can be loosed, as we
see so graphically described in the activity of the Holy
Spirit with Paul and Silas in prison at Philippi (Acts 16).
Tough loving and the caring of Jesus long to bring us into
the larger space of God's love and the light of the kingdom. It tells us that things do not always have to be this
way. Change is a real possibility, providing we seek the
way of grace and not simply the way of selfism or counseling. All that has been predictable can now be reversed,
and the degrees of freedom can be extended. Such a
model for pastoral care refuses to collude with the casualty—whether it is the casualty of sociological, psycho-
logical, or medical causes. It is not afraid to speak of judgment because it can just as readily speak of mercy and
forgiveness. Pastoral care modeled on that of the Good
Shepherd is neither paternalistic nor patronizing but
rather exhibits that tough love, which also points to the
truth—that truth which alone can set us free. The writer
of the Epistle to the Ephesians has got to the heart of it in
that marvelous combination when he exhorts us to speak
"the truth in love" (Eph. 4:15).

Parishes that have a strong program of counseling are,
generally speaking, not parishes of growth, evangelism,
and mission.

THE PLACE OF THE TEACHING MINISTRY

Earlier we spoke of shooting over the heads of the inward-
facing congregation, demanding that they turn around,
look outward, upward and beyond to see the point of it
all. The pastoral demands the prophetic, and the two are
in tandem in a healthy parish, if such a parish is not to degenerate into a cozy club for the protection of the delicate.
Parishes where there is a strong teaching program and

especially a lively Bible study program seem best able to snap out of the maintenance mentality. Again and again I have found as I have gone around the United States that it is in parishes where the pastor spends most of his or her time in teaching that we find growth and the mission mentality.

One parish in one of the weakest and smallest dioceses of the United States has grown in the years between 1979 and 1989 from a dismal budget of only $236,760 to $1,117,772. Furthermore, the congregational list has grown from only 1488 baptized (1153 confirmed) to 2557 baptized (2298 confirmed). In that parish, the parish priest spends 80 percent of his working week teaching or preparing to teach, and nearly always the programs are focused upon Bible study.

One of the most urgent things in the Decade for Evangelism will be the replacing of the counseling model by the teaching model if the Church is to be reversed from the maintenance mentality to a fresh and lively mission mentality. Presumably it was precisely this discussion that lay behind the resolution at Lambeth '88:

> This conference called for a shift to a dynamic mission-ary emphasis going beyond care and nurture to procla-mation and service: and therefore accepts the challenge this presents to diocesan and local church structures and patterns of worship and ministry, and looks to God for a fresh movement of the Spirit in prayer, outgoing love and evangelism in obedience to our Lord's command.[10]

For only richly energized churches can become the bearers of the good news and begin to be agents of evangelism and mission.

CONVERTING THE CHURCH

Put another way—and perhaps more theologically—you cannot heap good works on top of an unconverted, inward

-looking, nice person. The converted Christian is essentially the "man for others." In the world and in evolution, it is every man for himself. Take a bunch of such people and persuade them to come to church, motivated largely by the personality of the parson or as part of the respectable life of the community, and you will naturally end up with an inward-looking club. Clubs exist essentially for their own members and are naturally inward-looking and territorially minded. The converted church is not such a club. It exists for the sake of those who are not members—or to use Archbishop William Temple's famous phrase, "The Church is the only society that exists for the sake of those who are not members of it." Such a Church is, essentially, outward-looking and sees the world as its parish and its purpose for existing as focused in God and his kingdom. Good works, witness by word and deed, care for the poor, and a passion for justice—all these flow out of a Church that has reached what I have come to call apostolic point—as naturally as water overflows its container once it has reached boiling point.

This kind of local church, converted, energized, and empowered, will forward not only a Decade of Evangelism but evangelism, period.

In the next chapter, we shall see how such churches, in every aspect of their life, worship, and witness, become such vehicles of the gospel. However, I want to suggest that much of the break-through comes at that very point I have tried to focus upon in this chapter—namely, the conversion of the existing Church. The Church of England needs to be converted so that it may become the Church of God in England. So with the Episcopal Church. Necessarily, much of this starts with the parish priest and, indeed, with the bishops whose representative the local parish priest is. For many of us that will mean frankly admitting that after seminary we got off on the wrong foot. I am not suggesting that we tear Mr. Lake's book from our shelves. There must be many things in it from which we can profit with careful and selective reading. What I am suggesting, however, is that in all seminaries the clergy of whatever churchmanship need to go back to a new love of the Scriptures and to the lively faith of tradition interpreted through reason and human experience. "Nothing hinders evangelism today," writes John Stott, "more than the widespread loss of confidence in the truth, relevance and power of the gospel."[11] For many clergy, that loss of confidence came at the very outset of their ministry—back in the days of the seminary. C.K. Barrett, in his book *Luke the Historian*, is at pains to point out how St. Luke in both his gospel and also in the Book of Acts sees the Word of God as that which goes out breaking new ground in the vanguard of the evangelistic thrust of the early Church. "The prime agency by which the Spirit extends the sovereignty is the Word of God."[12] In fact, as Barrett points out so tellingly, "preaching or receiving God's Word comes as many as thirty-two times in the Book of the Acts of the Apostles." Expanding on this primacy of God's Word, Michael Green writes,

> For eighteen months and more at Corinth it was the Word which gripped Paul (18:5). It was the same at Ephesus during the two years of his mission. . . . When Luke wants to indicate the success of the mission, he says that the Word of the Lord grew and prevailed. The Word makes its own impact on Theophilus (Luke 1:1, Acts 1:1), the centurion Cornelius (10:44), the proconsul of Cyprus (13:7), the citizens of Antioch (13:44). No wonder the Twelve made it their priority (6:4).[13]

Contrast this with the heroic, romantic, and splendid words of Bishop Charles Gore, the remarkable Anglican bishop of the nineteenth and early twentieth centuries. Remarkable and estimable he certainly was, yet notice how his estimate of the impact of the early Church's message is empty of its essential ingredient. He writes,

> We see the spectacle of a widespreading community
> gradually winning its way over enormous obstacles in
> the power of an unconquerable hope and vigorously
> reforming the life of men in this world while the secret
> of its confidence lay in the world beyond. Nothing
> could daunt it . . . they stood before the world as the
> brotherhood of the redeemed.[14]

Great high-sounding words, yet they have sadly emptied out the specific grit of the gospel pearl. Their "secret" was not to be found in "the world beyond." Otherwise Marx and other critics of Christianity are right. It is just blatant escapism after all and the "opium of the masses." Rather, the secret of their confidence was that God had and continues to have a Word for this world—a living and converting Word. In a word, it was Jesus and the resurrection.

RECOVERING THE AUTHORITY OF SCRIPTURE IN THE LIFE OF THE CHURCH

Do we make this Word of God our priority? Has Bible study, work on commentaries, and sermon preparation the top priority in our weekly timetable as clergy? Only as and when such items come to the top of our list of priorities in ministry shall we begin to see church growth, let alone be ready to undertake a Decade of Evangelism. "The sheep look up and are no longer fed," wrote John Milton. To which one is tempted to retort in the second half of the twentieth century, "The sheep are fed up and are no longer looking!"

Yet note that I am not saying that we should become fundamentalists about the Scripture. But I am saying that it would be wonderful if we so clearly loved the Scriptures to such an extent that people thought we were fundamentalists! Wouldn't that be marvelous? We would become a truly scriptural Church, which is what Anglicanism was refashioned to be at the Reformation. For if in order to love the Scriptures you have to leave the Episcopal Church and join one of the fundamentalist sects, then that, in turn, is a negative judgment upon the Episcopal Church. The witness of the history of the Church is always the same: Whenever and wherever men and women have picked up that book and read it (*tolle lege*): wherever they have read it, marked it, learned it, and inwardly digested it—their lives have been changed. After all, sacramentalists have appeared to love the Blessed Sacrament so much that bystanders could be forgiven for supposing that they were committing idolatry and worshiping the sacrament rather than Christ in the sacrament. And frankly, it must be freely admitted that many sacramentalists do become idolaters of this kind. Nevertheless it is not a reason for ignoring the sacraments and hedging them about with such reductionist theology, continually and only speaking of what they are not, so that our lives are no longer enriched by such focused adoration in the Blessed Sacrament or by liberation from the bondage of sin such as we experience in the Sacrament of Reconciliation.

So with the Scriptures. After all, Anglicanism was built firmly at the Reformation on a reaffirmation of the priority of Scripture. The Episcopal Church is a scriptural Church or it is no Church at all. For the first thousand years the bishop's distinctive activity was to teach and preach the Scriptures. Go to Milan in the fourth century or to Hippo in the fifth century and there, each and every day in the cathedral, you would find Ambrose or Augustine as bishops sitting and expounding the Scriptures to the flock of Christ. The bishops of the early Church were the prime ministers of the Word. All bishops today, wherever they meet with their clergy or their laity, should begin with at least thirty minutes of scriptural exposition, whatever other business is on the agenda. Just let's try it, and we shall soon find that it is indispensable. It was the

Bible study at groups at Lambeth '88 that changed the
whole chemistry of that meeting of the worldwide
bishops. Similarly, it was the meeting of the House of
Bishops in Philadelphia in 1989, which was modeled on
the Bible study groups at Lambeth, that experienced a
dramatic sense of new direction and more positive delib-
eration. Just "taste and see" is the lesson we can learn
from these two occasions. Every meeting of the vestry and
of all our committees should begin with Bible study, for
the Bible forms the mind of the Church and reforms it to
become the mind of Christ.

Hopefully, this reaffirmation of the place of the Scriptures in the life of the Church will percolate from the
bishop to the parishes. Of course, there are wrong ways to
read the Bible. We must freely admit that many Christians
are abusing the Scriptures in our day. They are approaching them like a telephone directory. However, if this is so,
then surely the time has come for the clergy to start showing us how to read the Bible properly. (This will require
that they have first been taught in seminary how to read
the Scriptures—both critically and yet affirmatively.)
Nothing would change the chemistry of the local parishes
today more in the direction of evangelism than a new generation of Scripture-loving clergy. The love of Scripture
can become infectious and contagious and can become the
greatest single catalyst in the change of heart so needed in
all our churches today, both corporately and individually,
if they are to forward and not hinder the work of evangelism in the coming decade.

BEYOND BIBLICAL CRITICISM

I am not saying that there is not a proper place for biblical
criticism. There most certainly is, and there always has
been since the days of Jerome and Augustine, since the
schools of Antioch and Alexandria. Yet I am saying that it

must not displace that cherishing and loving of Scripture that has always characterized chapters of renewal throughout the history of the Church. Insofar as scriptural criticism has damaged the Church, it has done so, not because it went too far, but generally because it did not go far enough. A little learning is a dangerous thing. Seminarians have left seminaries in recent decades with just enough knowledge of biblical criticism (generally of the nineteenth-century German school and the Oxford and Cambridge schools of the twentieth century) to unnerve them and to displace the proper use of Scripture in worship, prayer, and preaching.

Where there is a lively, scriptural preacher, there is always a living Church and where there is a living church, there is always a Word from the Lord to people in need, who come to hear it and to receive it. "Receive with meekness the implanted Word, which is able to save your souls," urges the writer of the Epistle of James (James 1:21). Millions of Christians today can attest to the reality of that experience in their lives and to the fact that their lives have been empowered and changed by that living and effective Word. For the experience of Christians down the ages has always been the same. If only we will open the Scriptures and allow the Holy Spirit to open our minds to the Scriptures (and release us from the tyranny of a twentieth-century mind-set), there we shall discover that the Bible is a book of presence and a book of power and a book of promises that no amount of biblical criticism can refute. We need to begin to speak of the real presence of Jesus in the Scriptures in just the same way and with neither more nor less cautions than we speak of the real presence of Jesus in the sacraments. For the real presence of Christ is at the heart of the experience of a truly scriptural Church. What you make of that experience then becomes a theological problem for theologians. It is the work of the theologians to go away and to try to score out the theology of the experience of the Church. However, we must not allow the theologians to rob us of the reality of God, who makes himself known and present to his people *through* the sacraments and *through* the words of Scripture and *through* the fellowship of the Spirit.

"Is there a Word of the Lord for us?" asked Zedekiah to Jeremiah. The answer is the same today as it was yesterday and as it will be forever. Yes, thank God, indeed there *is* a Word of the Lord for us in the twentieth century and even in America! Furthermore, it is a living Word. It is Jesus and the resurrection. The first prerequisite for a scriptural Church is to be "ravished" (to use the word of Eusebius) and possessed by that Word with our whole being. Then, inevitably, we shall strive to get that Word out—in a word, we shall strive to make evangelism a living reality in every parish church in the Episcopal Church today. Anglicans need have no problems in affirming the Manila Manifesto when it expresses not a fundamentalism of Scripture but rather reaffirms the power of the Bible as God's gift to a word-weary world. "We affirm," and so must Episcopalians at the outset of the Decade of Evangelism, "that in the scriptures of the Old and New Testaments God has given us an authoritative disclosure of His character and will, His redemptive acts and their meaning, and His mandate for mission. We affirm that the biblical gospel is God's enduring message to our world and we determine to defend, proclaim and embody it."

Notes

1. *Lausanne Covenant*, "The Nature of Evangelism," paragraph 4.
2. Abraham, *Logic of Evanglism*, 38.
3. Smail, *Giving Gift*, 27.
4. Robert Browning, *Andira del Sarte*, lines 97–98.
5. Alastair V. Campbell, *Rediscovering Pastoral Care*, (London: Darton, Longman & Todd, 1981), 4.
6. Ibid.
7. Ibid, 9.
8. Thomas C. Oden, "Freedom to Learn," (paper delivered at the International Edinburgh conference on Pastoral Care and Counseling, 1979).
9. Iris Murdoch, *The Good Apprentice*, (Penguin Books, 1987), 366.
10. *The Truth Shall Make You Free: the Lambeth Conference 1988*, resolution 44 (report published by the Anglican Consultative Council, 1989), 231.
11. Stott, *Christian Mission in the Modern World*, 40.
12. C.K. Barrett, *Luke the Historian*, (Grand Rapids: Wm. B. Eerdmans), 68.
13. Michael Green, *Evangelism in the Early Church*, (Grand Rapids: Wm. B. Eerdmans, 1970), 149ff.
14. Charles Gore, *Reconstruction of Belief*, (London: John Murray, 1921), 646.

FIVE

Marks of a Renewed Church and a Revitalized Parish

THE REAL PRESENCE OF CHRIST IN THE COMMUNITY OF FAITH

"Our Christian presence in the world is indispensable to evangelism," says the Lausanne statement. Peter Wagner in his book *Frontiers in Missionary Strategy*, has popularized what he calls "3-P Evangelism"—"presence, proclamation, and persuasion."[1] Like all neat formulae this is in danger of being superficial and slick. However, it gives us three useful pegs on which to hang large amounts of material in our discussion of the marks of a renewed Church. We recall that the basic thesis of this particular book is that, when the Church of Jesus Christ is the sort of Church that Jesus intended it to be, it will automatically and inevitably be an evangelistic Church. For the Church is intended to be an incarnate *presence* of Jesus Christ: saying the things he says, doing the things he does, and by the power of the Holy Spirit being the sort of Church that continually makes Jesus Christ present in our world today.

The primary task, therefore, for a Decade of Evangelism is to energize that Church and so help it to become what it is truly intended to be.

A COMMUNITY OF PROMISE

The Church exists, if it exists at all, because God is faithful
to his promises going right back to the days of Abraham.
Old Abraham is the last person on earth you and I would
have chosen to start anything. Clearly, he was past it—he
was past everything. Yet the joke of God is that old
Abraham is precisely the kind of person God does choose
and has continually chosen through the ages to be the
agent of his (God's) promises. God promised Abraham
that he would make of him "a great nation" (Gen. 12:2).
All this will have to be perceived for Abraham, of course,
by faith, since it could clearly not be so by sight or by any
worldly, everyday perception. Any ordinary, matter-of-
fact assessment of Abraham would have written him off
years ago! Yet the point is that the old Israel exists by
promise, and so does the new Israel. In both old Israel
and new Israel alike, in the words of St. Paul, "We walk by
faith, not by sight" (2 Cor. 5:7).

So often today in church councils we are burdened by
problems. The list is endless—the problem of racism, the
problem of manpower, the problem of the physical plant.
The first decisive change in attitude required in all our
churches—local as well as national—is to begin to replace the negative word *problem* with the positive word
promise. Christians are a people of promise, and God is
faithful to his Word of promise. Our charter is a charter
of promise. Those promises become facts by faith and
through prayer.

Abraham's descendents are all descendents of promise. Jesus *promised* to be with his people forever (Matt.
28:20). Jesus *promised* to his anxious disciples the gift of
the Holy Spirit to teach them and to lead them "into all
truth" (John 16:13). He *promised* them that in the power of
that same Spirit they would be enabled to do all the works
they had seen him do and even greater works than he had

done, because he was going to the Father (John 14:12). He *promised* them that as people had listened to his words and to his preaching and teaching, people would also listen to theirs (John 15:20). Above all and beyond everything—beyond every conceivable problem—Jesus *promised* the gift of the Holy Spirit (John 14:16 and Acts 1:8) and the presence of himself and his Father in the hearts and lives of all who believed and obeyed him (John 14:23). What more can God give us, for heaven's sake? (Incidentally, it is worth noticing perhaps that the word *problem* does not occur in a biblical concordance, while there are several columns listed for God's promises.) So then,—for God's sake let us stop talking about problems and let us start celebrating promises. And notice further that in the New Testament economy of faith the "joke" is that we believe we have received something before we even receive it, for that is part of the process by which we, in fact, receive it (Mark 11:24).

For Christians are a resurrection people and "alleluia" is our song. In that sense, we are a J-shaped people: always being put down by life yet raised up by God. So St. Paul can celebrate the contradiction of the Christian experience in such lyrical words as these:

> We are afflicted in every way, but not crushed; perplexed, but not driven to despair; persecuted, but not forsaken; struck down, but not destroyed; always carrying in the body the death of Jesus, so that the life of Jesus may also be manifested in our bodies. (2 Cor. 4:8ff).

This is what the resurrection is all about. As J-shaped people, Christians belong to that long line of other J-shaped people who have gone before us: such people as Jeremiah, Joseph, Joel, Job, Jonah, the Jews, and supremely in the end as in the beginning, Jesus. All God's people are a J-shaped people. They have the same profile and family

likeness of promise and can make sense of their lives and
their experiences only in the context of that ultimately
J-shaped event—namely, the death and resurrection of
Jesus.

St. Paul is determined to put all his confidence in that
one determinative event—which for him is the hinge of
history—and the center of his own story: namely, the
death and resurrection of Jesus. This is the secret of his
dynamic power and preaching. He will not be deflected,
he reassures the Corinthians, by anything—any problem
of any kind—but has set the course of his life and his message on "Jesus Christ and him crucified" (1 Cor. 2:2).
Hence, Christian communities throughout the world
located in the most unpromising places, like the slums of
Calcutta or the horrors of Northern Ireland or the poverty
of the ghettos or the difficulties of the large inner-city
areas of the West—Christian communities of faith in such
places are intended to be signs of contradiction to the
local, wider community. They should spell out, celebrate,
and make explicit the death and resurrection of Jesus,
while at the same time doing all in their power (and in the
power of the Holy Spirit) to remove the scars and scandals
of poverty and injustice from our society. Such parishes,
by faith, are the places of hope, where resurrection could
be most gloriously celebrated. After all, Corinth was the
last place in the world that anyone in their right mind
would have chosen to plant one of the early Christian
churches. It was the New York of the ancient world. In
fact, to describe something or somebody as being *corin-
thianized* was a term of the lowest abuse in the world of St.
Paul. Yet Corinth was the very place in which the dying
and rising of Jesus could be most evidently and powerfully discerned. For "problems are solutions in disguise,"
as the paradoxical words of a large advertisement in the
subway of London once read. It could read, problems are
blessings in disguise. After all, from the Christian per-

spective of resurrection faith, we can surely speak even of death as being resurrection in disguise! You find the good news as a Christian among the bad news neither by running away from the bad news to a brighter location nor by ringing your hands over the problems.

The first task, therefore, in a Decade of Evangelism is to raise the expectations of God's people to expect the mighty works, signs, and wonders of God to be at work in their lives and in their community of faith. "The signs and wonders associated with the ministry of Jesus and to which Jesus introduced his disciples continued in the early community."[2]

Such expectations of the signs of the kingdom will, in fact, have some very practical outworkings. At the very mundane level, does your congregation expect outsiders to be at the main service next Sunday morning? Do you? Then why is it that the notice board is so faded that you can hardly read the times of the main services? Why is it that you do not have a clearly printed order of service available for every person—old and new—printed for next Sunday in such a way that a newcomer could find his or her way through the service? (The new Prayer Book is a wonderful resource book but useless as a pew book and potentially a great hindrance to worship.) Everything from the size of the church's parking lot to the presence or absence of greeters at the door to welcome people tells me whether or not you are really, in fact, expecting anything new to happen next Sunday. Or will it be the mixture, much the same as before? Does the priest always welcome newcomers from the chancel step every Sunday in his notices even if he cannot be sure that there are newcomers in the congregation? Is there provision for them after the service to be met and taken care of?

The same should be said about the expectation of the sermon. Do we expect that anything will happen when the Word is preached faithfully and with power? Do we expect signs and wonders in our midst, or have we, in fact, closed all the doors of our perception over the weary years and ceased to expect anything at all? Is there an opportunity for a prayer ministry, with the laying-on-of-hands in the ordinary, everyday, week-by-week ministry and worship of the local parish? If not, we must ask ourselves what we have ceased to expect. Surely, we are ceasing to expect resurrection in any shape or form. We are just like the Sadducees, and our faith is degenerating into a legalistic religion. The Sadducees were the ruling party, in the majority, and the priestly order in charge of running the Temple: They were the sort of "high church" party of Jesus' day. We are told quite explicitly that they did not believe in the resurrection. Their mind-set was closed. The universe was for them a closed system, or, in the words of the writer of the Book of Ecclesiastes, there was "nothing new" for them "under the sun." No wonder they did not believe in the resurrection. They had ceased to expect any surprises in the universe whatever; they had everything buttoned up, packaged up, and neatly labeled. Of course they did not believe in the resurrection: that's the reason the Sadducees were so sad, you see!

Yet, that is also the reason why so many Christian communities are so sad and defeated: They do not really believe in the resurrection, let alone that they could ever be "witnesses" of that resurrection in the life of their own faith community. They think, at best, that the reason Jesus rose from the dead was because of a once-off juggling act with bones! They do not see the shape of Good Friday and Easter Day as the shape of things to come or as the shape of their own destiny in Christ. They do not witness the contradiction of resurrection, and they do not expect, therefore, that some contradiction of resurrection will be at work in their lives and in the life of their community of faith. Such a community cannot begin to be truly apostolic, let alone evangelistic.

The intense celebration of Holy Week and the paschal

mystery of Good Friday and Easter Day, presented in good liturgy accompanied by fine preaching, teaching, vigil, and fasting, can do more toward renewing a parish for "resurrection expectation" than almost anything else that I know. It is significant that the renewal of the Roman Catholic Church can be traced to the years in the 1950s when they took the Holy Week liturgies out of the clerical closet where they had been for several centuries and began to celebrate, with the whole people of God, the paschal mystery. The work of the people of God is to celebrate the mystery of their own identity. We are a people of promise and expectation most clearly understood in the full-blooded reality of the resurrection of Jesus once for all in history, yet continually reproduced and celebrated in the life of his Body on earth—the catholic, apostolic Church.

We cannot explain suffering, and certainly what happens in the world is far from fair. Counseling and pastoral care all have their place in the first aid of compassion for so many people in our parishes, where lives are strangely, and apparently unfairly, scarred and wounded. They all have a story to tell if someone had time to sit down and listen to that story. Yet, just telling it (no matter how many times) will not change things in themselves. I want to suggest that the main question in most people's hearts is not only (indeed, not so much), "*Why* has this happened to me?" but rather, "Who on earth am I and whose am I?" Put another way, the real agony at the heart of most people's lives is what we call nowadays an "identity crisis": something akin perhaps to the identity crisis experienced by an ant in an ant hill.

Yet you do not solve an identity crisis by endless introspection but only by frequent retrospection and by asking yourself the question, "With whom do I identify?" "Does my story make any sense at all?" It only makes sense, of course, when I begin to relate to it and, in turn, relate it to other stories from the history of the Old Testament and the story of God's people through the ages. Look at these stories. Look at the stories from the life of God's people and supremely, of course, the Jesus story. In the Scriptures, you will find all these other stories of people like Job and Jonah who are strangely related to your story. Christians of the new Israel are related to the heroes of faith in their suffering, passion, defeat, and death—and, of course, in their vindication and resurrection. They, like us, are J-shaped people in that sense.

Yet "without us" (and Jesus) they will "not be made perfect" (Heb. 11:40). So, to what does Jesus point on that road to Emmaus when he is trying to help Cleopas and his friend to discover for themselves his own true identity? He does not teach them to rely upon appearances, which are, of course, so often deceptive. He does not invite them to look inward. Rather, he urges them to look backward: not introspectively but retrospectively. (Is that perhaps why so many Americans go to Europe to look for their ancestors? Could it be that such a pilgrimage and quest belong to a larger, national identity crisis: "Who are we?") Jesus begins with Moses and shows how the death and resurrection event is prefigured in the stories of the Old Testament: "And beginning with Moses and all the prophets, he interpreted to them in all the scriptures the things concerning himself" (Luke 24:27).

So a "resurrection faith" begins to come alive when the three evidences and witnesses agree and resonate: his-story, my story, the Jesus story. So it is that the preaching program of a parish, week in and week out, must be preaching that relates the three stories—those three J-shaped stories: my story, his-story, and the Jesus story. It does not matter too much which story you begin with, so long as you go on to make the connection—that gospel connection—between all three of them. Then the Holy Spirit, like lightning, will touch the hearts of your hearers so that they can make the connection for themselves, with their own lives and with their own stories. Essentially, the heart of it all and the point where all three stories converge, is Jesus—Jesus and the resurrection. It is not incidental (nor perhaps accidental) that Harvey Cox, after struggling for so many years to be "relevant" in his lectures and in his writings, finally elected in 1989 to give a course simply entitled "Jesus." More students enrolled for that course than any lecture room on the campus could contain. A lesson is there somewhere for all of us who are called to be ministers of the Word. We need to know that there is a power in that name and that there is "no other name under heaven" whereby we may be "saved" than his most blessed name. And furthermore, we need to know as preachers that salvation is the name of the game: not simply education, edification, or even meditation (though, of course, they all have their place). We must preach, therefore, in the sure and certain conviction that it is salvation that everyone present has come to seek and that for us, as for St. Paul, it is also true to say, "Woe to me if I do not preach the gospel" (1 Cor. 9:16).

It is only in the context of such preaching and proclamation that problems begin to become promises. When we celebrate the complex of events we call the paschal mystery, we celebrate then, not only liturgically, but in our own lives as well. The community of faith, both individually and corporately, incarnates, celebrates, and proclaims the mystery of faith: "Christ has died; Christ is risen: Christ will come again." We begin, if you like, *to do the resurrection* and therefore to become witnesses to resurrection. Then we become truly a community of promise and not of problems, a community of resurrection and new life rather than a community of death. We are living by promise—by faith and not by sight, by faith and not just by weary, good works. We belong to an environment where people can find faith and hope.

THE COMMUNITY OF POWER

For in the Scriptures and the record of faith-history, we find that it is the weak who are given power, the poor who are made rich, the hungry who are fed, and the cast-down who are raised up. So St. Paul could testify with confidence, "When I am weak, then I am strong" (2 Cor. 12:10). Mary, the mother of the Lord, celebrated and embodied this contradiction most eloquently in her reedited version of Hannah's song from the Old Testament, which we call the Magnificat. Interestingly she looks back to the Old Testament record and identifies with Hannah in her unexpected pregnancy. For Hannah first sang the first draft of what the church has now come to call the Magnificat. Clearly, Mary identified with Hannah in the absurd contradiction of being unexpectedly expecting! (What a wonderful description of the Church: a body of people unexpectedly expecting!) So she sings the Magnificat. (Of course, it does not actually say she sang the Magnificat. But you can be fairly certain—with some poetic license—that she did so, because what is certain is that "contradiction—Christians" and all J-shaped people have been singing it ever since. "The church with songs must shout, no door can keep it out!" [George Herbert])

For the first Beatitude of the kingdom is translated in the New English Bible as, "Blessed are those who know their need of God" (Matt. 5:3). So who are the people who best know their need of God? The answer is clear and evident. It is the elderly, the underprivileged, the poor, the barren, and those who have no helper, of course. These people are not fulfilled by the gifts and graces, so that is the reason they can best be filled full by the standards of the kingdom. They can best be gifted and graced because they are frequently least talented and most ungracious. They are empty, waiting to be filled; they are hungry, waiting to be fed; they are poor, so they can easily be enriched; and they are often finished and at the end of their tether so that at last God can begin and make a new beginning for them. They have broken down so that God can break through.

It is such people (and such congregations) who can best receive the gift God has to give—and, of course, the supreme gift is the gift of the Holy Spirit. Furthermore, such people will be the first to "ask," to "seek," and to "knock." And in so doing they receive, they find, and the door to God's treasure house is thrown wide open. In a word, they receive the gift of the Holy Spirit.

It is a theological commonplace, of course, to speak of the central theme in Luke's Book of Acts as the work of the Holy Spirit—sometimes even called the gospel according to the Holy Spirit. For the Holy Spirit writes his testimony to Jesus in the pages of history and in the hearts of everyday lives. However, the Church has tracked through huge wastelands and deserts of its history scarcely referring to the Holy Spirit. In the Book of the Acts of the Apostles, the Holy Spirit of God anoints the preached Word of God with such power that it becomes an effective Word. Furthermore, in the Book of the Acts, St. Paul embodies that same Holy Spirit and so, not surprisingly, undergoes his passion and death, which are strikingly analogous to the passion of Christ as related in the gospel account. Volume 1 and Volume 2 of St. Luke's writing are, thus, very similar in shape and structure: the birth of Jesus is paralleled by the birth of the Church (and both alike are produced by the overshadowing of the Holy Spirit). Then there is the preaching and teaching of Jesus in the gospels paralleled by the chapters in Acts that tell of the apostolic preaching by Peter through to the conversion of St. Paul. The conversion at Caesarea Philippi in the gospel is paralleled in Acts by the Damascus road incident. All of the preachers are anointed with the Holy Spirit. Then that same Holy Spirit expels both Jesus in the gospel of St. Luke, and the apostles (notably Paul) on missionary journeys of teaching and preaching. Finally, in both the gospel of Luke and in Acts, there is a dramatic turning point when both Jesus and then Paul set their faces toward Jerusalem, passion, suffering, and death (viz., the parallel of Luke 18:31 with Acts 20:22). Jesus turns to "go up to Jerusalem" and so does Paul, where a similar phrase is used. They both "go up to Jerusalem" to face up to it all, and both of them are "bound in the Spirit." Redemption in the person of Jesus and redemption in the life of his Body, the Church, have a similar geography, a similar pattern, and a strikingly recognizable shape and direction.

"The Christians," writes Michael Green, "were convinced that the spirit of Jesus had come into their midst and indwelt their very personalities in order to equip them for evangelism, for making Him known to others."[3] Yet we must note carefully the purpose of renewal in the Spirit, or, put another way, we must notice why men and women are given the Spirit. They are given the Spirit as the gift that supremely must be given away: It is not to be kept and hoarded; otherwise, we lose it—possibly forever. "The evangelization of the world was Luke's outstanding interest and concern," writes J.H.E. Hull in his book *The Holy Spirit in the Acts of the Apostles*. "The church received the Spirit not for its selfish secret enjoyment but to enable it to bear witness for Christ."[4]

Surely, we need to thank God for the renewal movement that has swept through all the churches in the last few decades. It has brought a new springtime for believing, a new joy in believing, and a new love in our fellowship and in our worship. Pentecostal renewal has opened the Church again to the power of the Holy Spirit. How on earth did we ever believe that *we* could pray? We need to be reminded again and again that it is not we who pray but rather that it is the Holy Spirit who prays in us and with us (Rom. 8:26). And we need to be reminded constantly to let him have his way with us, in every way.

How could we have forgotten that all ministry (if it is the ministry of Jesus and not just the exercising of our talents, enthusiasms, or guilt) was charismatic ministry in the true sense of that word—namely, that such ministry is a gift of God? After all, in the Prayer Book, the bishop says quite explicitly when he ordains the new priests, "Receive the Holy Spirit for the work and office of a priest in the church of God." That surely is charismatic ministry. We are all charismatics if we are Christians at all, and if we mean all that we should mean by that glorious and much abused word *charismatic*. For all Christians are given the *gift* of grace in order to be what they are—Christians even remotely worthy of the name. St. Luke in the Book of the Acts is at pains to make it quite clear that, whether it is Peter before the Sanhedrin, Stephen in Jerusalem, or Philip with the eunuch, all this is the work of the Holy Spirit and not just well-intentioned, clever chaps doing great things for God. "The greatness of Luke's view lies in his showing more impressively than anyone else that the Church can live only by evangelism and by following whatever new paths the Spirit indicates."[5]

Such has been the experience of many churches and congregations renewed in the Spirit in the renewal movements of the past few decades. Yet something is going wrong with the renewal movement. The reason for this is not hard to discover. Renewed Christians have come to regard the Holy Spirit as their property, to hoard him and to institutionalize him. Writes Jim Packer:

> When churches treat any of their characteristics—their orthodoxy, their separated stance, their loyalty to traditional expressions of faith, their up-to-dateness in worship, their charismatic ethos and routines, their interests in "signs and wonders," or their opposition to cooperative evangelism and Geneva-based ecumenism—as guaranteeing that the Spirit will be with them to bless them, irrespective of whether or not experience

bears them out, they are institutionalizing the Spirit. They are making the same mistake if they look to their own good organization and administration, alluring programs, stockpiled counseling skills, and ecclesiastical expertise in general as constituting sufficient proof that God is with them (Eph. 4:15ff. and Col. 2:19).

He concludes:

Institutionalizing the Spirit in the way described makes for apathy and indifference to spiritual quality so long as the ecclesiastical machine rolls on. This obstructs church growth in Paul's sense of the phrase—that is, corporate advance toward the fullness of Christ (Eph. 4:15-16; Col. 2:19) and thus quenches the Spirit by not taking him seriously. Complacency is the cause, and Laodicean lukewarmness the consequence.[6]

In all these ways we need to see how the Spirit is given in order to be given away. We cannot hoard the Spirit or his gifts. We begin to do this once we begin to talk in abstract terms about grace as though grace is a thing. When we do that, it is not long before we continue by referring to the Holy Spirit as a thing and an abstraction.

THE COMMUNITY OF PRAYER

You will find all this both in renewed and in clearly unrenewed churches. We can only receive the power of the Spirit as we give it away. We cannot hoard yesterday's manna or last year's renewal mission. Tom Smail reminds us in his wonderful book on the Spirit: "What God gives us in him [the Spirit] is less like a fortune to possess and spend and more like a friend to cultivate and love."[7]

The gift of the Spirit is our daily bread, and we need to come before this gracious and generous God of ours daily, in order to receive that bread, to be fed in our hunger, enriched in our poverty, and empowered in our weakness. And always it is the same: to be given away in mission, for however far you go with this Jesus, he always wants to go further. The Spirit and the spirit of scriptural promises point us beyond the Church as it now is to the Church that God wishes it to become in order that one day the gift of the Father to the Son may be given back to the Father, enriched an hundredfold by the outpouring of the life of Jesus in love on the cross. It is in mission that the Church transcends itself and is saved from triumphalism, ecclesiasticism, and self-sufficient independence. The power and the promise belong together, and both are gifts of the Father.

THE COMMUNITY OF PRAYER

So we need daily to pray to the Father and to ask him to send his Holy Spirit on his people to make them powerful in their weakness, wise in their ignorance, and eloquent in their silence.

"If you then, who are evil, know how to give good gifts to your children, how much more will the heavenly Father give the Holy Spirit to those who ask him!" (Luke 11:13). Prayer and fasting must accompany all mission and evangelism if it is to be effective and powerful. Prayer and fasting belong very much together in the Scriptures. We cannot receive anything if we are filled already. If we have our hands full, our stomachs full, our pockets full, and our calendars full, like the rich young ruler we shall not be rich at all, let alone a ruler: we shall just be poor old things. Fasting is an incarnational and sacramental expression of the first Beatitude—poverty of spirit, standing before God with our hands empty and open, waiting to receive all that is necessary for the task that he gives us to do. "Whom he calls, he empowers" (Anselm).

So Jesus commands his apprehensive disciples to stay in the city until they "are clothed with power" (Luke 24:49). We are told by Jesus, in preparation for mission and evangelism, to be still and to be silent until we are given the necessary power so that the spoken word of power will then come out of the silence as all movement is given direction as it issues out of quiet and stillness—and all this as we wait upon God daily in prayer and fasting.

Prayer needs to be the very environment in which the community of faith lives—the air it breathes "at all times and in all places." The daily office of morning and evening prayer, the daily mass can all be prayed by two or three parishioners daily in our parishes—and especially as we come to the close of the twentieth century. For there have never been so many Christians, better fed, with more spare time than there are today in the West. At the Reformation, the daily office was rescued by Cranmer from the closet of the cloister and from the muttering of monks to be the prayer of the whole people of God. Each day God's people were to gather and to read the Scriptures and the Psalms together and to make their prayers. In the seventeenth century, George Herbert, the Anglican divine and poet, renewed his small, insignificant country parish by encouraging the lay people to join him daily in morning and evening prayer. The Protestant community of Taizē in France is most conspicuous for the pride-of-place it affords to the daily office, prayerfully and yet simply sung and offered in the presence of thousands of young people who have trekked halfway across the face of the earth to be present.

In an age (in the West) of early retirement, redundancy, and people living to greater and greater ages, we have a whole army of people bored out of their small minds with nothing to do all day long. *Orate fratres!* For God's sake, get them praying. Morning and evening prayer in the church (opened daily for the purpose) or in homes and houses of the aged and housebound—all this should begin to be part of the day-to-day life of God's people and not just on Sundays. The daily eucharist can be and should be celebrated at all sorts of times and on all sorts of occasions in the course of the week. Invade our community with the power of corporate prayer: that should be the mandate for a Decade of Evangelism.

Then there are the times and places of personal prayer and prayer ministry—making our requests known to God and ministering Jesus and his resurrection to people at their point of need. Why do we wait so often for the deathbed scene to release the ministry of the Church to the place and point of need. We are all sick, most of the time. By the principle of the incarnation, the Church's ministry of prayer (not least for healing) must be peripatetic— meeting in people's houses, sharing our common life, and ministering Jesus at all times and in all places.

Nothing is more needed today in our churches than that quality of ministry that convinces ordinary, everyday sinners that their sins are forgiven, that they are loved by God and always will be, and that health and healing, freedom from guilt and freedom to fail again and again—all of these are the birthright of the baptized and of those who refuse to know any other righteousness except that righteousness which has been appropriated to them through grace and grace alone.

Renewal in all the churches and in the traditions has brought in its wake a personal ministry in which we share Jesus with others and minister him to others—that same Jesus who was first ministered to us. Whatever happened, then, to the Sacrament of Reconciliation? Thank God that is has been brought out of the sacerdotal and somewhat legalist closet of the Anglo-Catholics in recent years by the charismatics and by renewed Christians. Thank God that once again it has been set at the very heart of personal ministry, where it is happily free from party and denom-inational labels to be the glorious, scriptural, and evan-gelical sacrament that it is intended to be.

G.K. Chesterton said that he had become a Roman

Catholic because only the Roman Catholic Church knew
what to do with sin. There is enough truth in that statement to bring the Episcopal Church up with a start. Do
we Episcopalians know what to do with sin and how to
minister to sinners for whom Christ died? Or are we
much more at home with nice, middle-of-the-road people.
The Sacrament of Reconciliation was retained in our
Prayer Book at the Reformation. It is there in our tradition
and in the experience of many of us who would not be
Christians today if we had not known how to avail ourselves of this most remarkable sacrament of reconciliation,
reassurance, forgiveness, and healing. Anglicans do not
need to ape or copy slavishly the form and style of the
Roman Catholic abuse of the confessional that we associate with late medieval decadence. Rather, we need to
bring it out of our closets; we need to stop apologizing for
it, to dust it, and to start to practice it. Come back confession; all is forgiven.

Yet come back now to be used in the wider context of
renewal and personal ministry, in the context of prayer,
anointing, the laying on of hands; come back in the context of the ministry of deliverance and the healing of
memories. For we need to know with reassurance and
certainty that, wherever there has been such a gloriously
gospel ministry of renewal, repentance, and reconciliation,
there God's people have experienced a new power to
witness, a new freedom for service and ministry, and a
new capacity to live out their baptismal vows with joy and
with confidence in a God who went out of his way to
"seek and to save the lost."

There is a new need, as we approach the Decade of
Evangelization, to recover our nerve concerning the well-
tried ways of "bringing people to Jesus." In earlier times,
both evangelicals and Anglo-Catholics knew from experience and from their training programs for ministry the
"how-to-do-it" approach to conversion, renewal, and

reconciliation. For evangelicals, it was often simply a question of saying to the inquirer something along these lines: "Would you like now to give your life (afresh) to Jesus, as your Savior and Lord?" The inquirer or the lapsed would then be invited to pray with the minister (lay or clerical) and to say a simple prayer of oblation and commitment, line by line, after the minister. Equally, the Anglo-Catholic tradition was not ashamed to minister Jesus to the bewildered or the lapsed by inviting them to make their (first) confession. Alec Guiness, in his autobiography *Blessings in Disguise*, tells how a priest in Bristol, England, sheltered him in his rectory during the days and nights of intense bombing by the Germans in the Second World War. One night, when the bombing was particularly intense and all human life was at great risk, over a glass of sherry before dinner, the priest pointed out that neither he nor Alec Guiness might live to see the morning. The priest, in language we perhaps would now find all too rigid, self-conscious, and streamlined, nonetheless invited Guiness, there and then, to kneel down and to confess his sins. For Guiness it was before the days of his discipleship, but nevertheless that clear love of souls, manifested by the priest in a moment of danger and crisis, left a permanent mark in the faith story of Guiness that belonged to the larger design and picture of a full gospel faith later in life.

The Decade of Evangelism needs to be very practical at every point. It needs to teach and to train clergy and laity "how to make a friend; how to be a friend; and how to bring a friend to Christ." Parish visiting in pairs will demand training programs that are not ashamed to be quite detailed in suggesting ways of bringing others across the threshold of faith—in a word, training others to minister Jesus "at all times and in all places."

Just stop and recall the shape and structure of that early, fragile little Church in its first steps of infectious and contagious mission in the Book of the Acts of the Apostles. "Day by day, attending the temple together and breaking bread in their homes, they partook of food with glad and generous hearts, praising God and having favor with all the people. And the Lord added to their number day by day those who were being saved" (Acts 2:46–47). Put another way, we can turn to the words of George Herbert: "Seven whole days, not one in seven" is his mandate—"I will praise thee." Such a community of *daily* prayer will be empowered to confront disease with healing, and the kingdom will break into the life of that community so that the works of Jesus become manifest in the local church. Healing, reconciliation, forgiveness of sins will be daily bread and butter in such a community, not set up as a thing in itself, but as an inevitable by-product of a church living by the promises of Jesus, by the power of the Holy Spirit, and in daily prayer to the Father, from whom "every good endowment and every perfect gift comes" (James 1:17). St. Luke, in his account of such a church in the Book of the Acts of the Apostles, throws in as an aside, almost as an afterthought, the fact that such a church, daily renewed in prayer and power, was bold in ministry and witness and was growing in large numbers, and new Christians were being added daily. With that kind of order of priorities, we should approach a Decade of Evangelism.

COMMUNITY OF PRESENCE

If many nineteenth-century Anglo-Catholics were concerned to reaffirm the real presence of Jesus in the mystery of the eucharist, surely the concern for late twentieth-century Christians must be that even deeper mystery—namely, the real presence of Jesus in the baptized community of the faithful. It is one thing to point to the eucharistic bread and to say the words of

Jesus; "This is my Body." Such an affirmation demands faith and is clearly a profound mystery. Yet we need to go further. We need to plumb this mystery of the real presence of Jesus. Can we, by faith, freely go on to acknowledge that it is clearly a mystery (if not a joke) when we point to next Sunday morning's congregation and say also, "This is my body; this is my blood; this is Jesus in the fullness of flesh and blood in this locality today?"

At a diocesan conference where I was present some years ago, halfway through the morning's proceedings the lay chairperson announced with some sadness that one of the diocesan clergy not present at the conference had just had a severe stroke and had been taken into a hospital. "So," said the well-intentioned chairperson, "we will be praying for Father X at the noontide eucharist today." The diocesan bishop jumped up from the front row and went further. "Yes," he said, "we will most certainly pray for Father X at the noontide mass, but let's also pray for him now. Will you all please stand. Take hold of the hand of the person next to you and so reach out to touch another part of the Body of Christ, and in the Spirit of Christ let us pray together for Father X." Yes, that's got it! That went to the heart of the mystery of prayer in the Body of Christ. For that bishop had gone on and made the connection between the sacramental presence of Jesus on the altar and the mystical presence of Jesus in the flesh and blood of his people. Both of them are surely the Body of Christ. The Church is literally a walking Sacrament. The real presence of Jesus and the Sacrament of the Eucharist is there in order that the real presence of Jesus may be equally effective in the body of his people. "Man is what he eats"—indeed he is and such in spite of himself, were the religious rather than secular words of Feuerbach. So St. Augustine can say, "We eat the Body of Christ in order to become the Body of Christ." Our diet determines our destiny, if you like. And what is our destiny as baptized

Christians? Surely, it is to be the community of presence—
the real presence of Jesus in his Body mystical. "Our
Christian presence in the world is indispensable to evangelism." We need to be more explicit than that. "The real
presence of Jesus in his Body the Church is indispensable
to evangelism."

All those trips to the Holy Land that seek to take us
back to where Jesus was, where Jesus walked and ate and
talked—they all have a place in Christian devotion. However, in a real sense, that kind of nostalgia should pale into
insignificance compared with the awesome and over-
whelming reality of the presence of Jesus in his Body the
Church in this town and this community today, here and
now. The quality of the life of faith of God's people in any
local parish today determines whether Jesus will lurch
around our parishes in a drunken and deformed state or
will walk around those same parishes doing the same
things he used to do, saying the same things he used to
say, healing the sick and caring for those in need. The
Incarnation of Jesus is not some past event. A proper
doctrine of his mystical Body, the Church, should reassure
us that Jesus can be let loose in our parish today, now, in
the flesh and blood of the Body of his people; fed and
sustained with the sacramental Body of Jesus from the
altar; fed by the Word of Jesus from the pulpit; and
sustained minute by minute by the same Spirit of Jesus
given to his people according to the promises of Jesus and
the gracious generosity of the Father, in reconciliation,
forgiveness, and healing.

In all these ways a renewed Church will bring a Christian presence into our world today that will inevitably
result in effective evangelism.

Notes

1. Peter Wagner, *Frontiers in Missionary Strategy* (Chicago: Moody, 1971), 134.
2. Abraham, *Logic of Evangelism*, 38.
3. Green, *Evangelism in the Early Church*, 148.
4. J.H.E. Hull, *The Holy Spirit in the Acts of the Apostles,* World Publishing Co., Cleveland, OH, 198, 178.
5. E. Schweizer, *Church Order in the New Testament* (*Naperville, IL: A.R. Alenson, 1961*), 75.
6. David F. Wells, *God the Evangelist: How the Holy Spirit Brings Men and Women to Faith* (Grand Rapids: Wm. B. Eerdmans, 1987), xii.
7. Smail, *Giving Gift*, 21.

SIX

The Local Church: A Unit of Evangelism

"Evangelism itself is the proclamation of the historical, biblical Christ as Saviour and Lord, with the view to persuading people to come to Him personally and so be reconciled to God" (Lausanne).

A COMMUNITY OF PROCLAMATION

There is necessarily an assertiveness about the concept of proclamation that does not sit well with contemporary ideals of armchair dialogue and two-way communication. In the dictionary, we see *proclamation* as "announcing officially," a declaration (of a war or a peace). Latent within the word is the concept of "making claims." What is quite clear is that the local church as a community of proclamation is no debating society. It is at least assertive enough to be making certain claims about the person of Jesus and therefore the truth of God.

For gospel communication is a communication of truth or it is nothing at all. The Bishop of Lichfield in the debate on evangelism in the English Synod in 1989 was quite right, of course, when he said that the "questions being asked in the Western world were not only whether

Christianity was useful or relevant but whether it was true." There is most certainly a place for Christian apologetics, and it is a place urgently needed in the contemporary climate. We certainly need today as much, if not more than we have always needed, writers and speakers who will make a primarily intellectual case for the claims of Christ. Furthermore, as we shall see in another part of this book, there is an urgent need for apologetics to return to its proper place in theology. In seminaries, we need once again to train ministers of the Word for this particular and crucial aspect of Christian proclamation (the *kerygma*) in the overall commendation of the gospel. Yet just as proclamation is no substitute for apologetics, neither is apologetics any substitute for proclamation. "Apologetics may be important, but its rightful place," as we shall see later in the book, "belongs to a subsequent exercise in Christian growth and understanding and not to evangelism proper."[1]

Jesus came into Galilee making very assertive claims. They were certainly claims for the truth. Surely, the point the Bishop of Lichfield did not go on to make also needs to be made. Truth boldly stated can be indifferent or irrelevant. I can make a true statement that inevitably implies the response, "So what?" Suppose, after all, the moon really is made of green cheese! The only appropriate response would be a shrug of the shoulders and something along the lines of a cry of indifference: "So what?"

The point about the truth Jesus proclaimed is that it makes a double claim. What he is claiming in his proclamation is that God is doing something now that, whether you like it or not, is going to make all the difference in the world to the way things will turn out for you and for me both in the present and in the future. "The true work of art belongs to its own time and to ours, that is to say, to its presence in front of us. Life is only of one time: art is of other times as well. It owes its deep reach to this *double grip*."[2] That is the point. Christian proclamation differs from the presentation of all other truths in that it seeks what the above writer calls "a deep reach," and this is derived from its power to have a "double grip": i.e., it is true once for all, and yet at the same time it is true for me now. That is to say, it is very relevant for me and for you at all times and in all places. Hence, the word *proclamation* is highly appropriate when we come to talk about the communication of the gospel. After all, you proclaim a state of war or of peace. Such a proclamation has precisely what we are calling the double grip: It is true objectively (and in one sense, what you or I think about it is irrelevant). It is—whether you like it or not, believe it or not—a reality. It is the way things are—whether you know it or not, respond to it or not. Neither your attitude nor mine will make any difference. We are at war—like it or not, believe it or not. But the double grip is also true. From now onward, the truth is going to affect my life and yours in the here and now and in the detail of every day so that an appropriate response to this proclamation most certainly could not be the cry of indifference: "So what?" The appropriate reply would be something more like, "Well, what should I be doing about it?"

This kind of message Jesus carried around in his person as he came into Galilee preaching the kingdom. This kind of message Jesus still longs to declare to his people now, in our own day. The work of the Church is to continue that proclamation to the four corners of the earth.

THE DOUBLE GRIP

What is it that gives it this double grip? It is not so much a trimming of vocabulary or even a massaging of the message (as we were urged to do so very much in the fifties and sixties). Rather, the work of the Holy Spirit in the hearts and lives of those who hear the message gives it

this incredible relevance and what we are calling the
double grip. The Holy Spirit can give the ring of truth to
the call of Christ, which is the same call issued by the Jesus
of history when he first came into Galilee preaching and
teaching. This generation in general or any one in particular can hear the same message (the same words) yet be
deaf to their appeal and their inner challenge. The Holy
Spirit alone anoints the words that are spoken and fills the
speaker with that same Spirit. It is also the Holy Spirit, at
work in the lives of those who hear, who makes the gospel
connection and so gives the double grip of which an artist
can also speak or the ring of truth of which a dramatist
might speak or to which a barrister might appeal. As we
say in colloquial English, "the penny drops"—or all those
other cliches that we all use for moments of cosmic disclosure. All our attempts to put into words the experience, existentially, are the same: namely, it is the moment
when the objective truth becomes (generally rather
alarmingly) essentially and subjectively true for me, here
and now. The Bishop of Lichfield was proclaiming (even
if he would not wish that to be his stance) a rather dangerous half-truth. He was right when he implied that so
much evangelistic proclamation has degenerated into a
mere subjective, existential, experiential massage, which
"works" and makes us feel better. To that kind of ap-
praisal I would want to enjoin "amen" and ask the same
basic question: "So what? I want to know if it's true." Yet
we must not replace the distinctive method of proclamation as the means of communicating the truth and substitute discussion groups or an apologetics class or a debating society, for the unqualified and unquestioning proclamation of Jesus and the gospel through the preached
Word. All these other things have their place (even under
the umbrella word of *evangelism*, as we shall see). But they
are no substitute for the sharp-edged, gospel proclamation
initiated by Jesus and with Jesus in Galilee two thousand

years ago. Such proclamation is a vital and necessary ingredient in the life of every church, every Sunday, in every corner of the world, here and now.

For Anglicans, this same proclamation has a double power because, in the catholic tradition, Word and sacrament go together in tandem and, through both media, Jesus is made present by that double grip of the Holy Spirit, who takes the things of Jesus and makes them present, relevant, and urgent for me today. "Today if you will hear his voice . . ." (Ps. 95:8).

Through both the media of Word and sacrament, the message of the gospel is the same. The message does not try to tell us what God is like but rather to declare and proclaim who he is. He is like what he truly is. That is to say, he makes himself known to us by what he does and by what he has done. In the Old Testament, we do not see so much the face of God as the hand of God in the events and in the stories of the old Israel. In that same Old Testament, the people of Israel were taught that they must not try to describe God—he is beyond words and beyond all our most far-reaching images. To speak of God as the ground of my being, however, or as a daddy above the bright blue sky is to be equally guilty of idolatry on both accounts. The former idolatry is perhaps on the whole slightly more dangerous than the more blatant idolatry of the latter example, because it might seduce us into believing that God really can be described essentially in the pseudosophisticated phrase "the ground of my being." We might start taking such a phrase rather too seriously, whereas a daddy above the bright blue sky is an image that is all right as far as it goes (which clearly and obviously is not far enough) and that then does not demand us to take it very seriously any further. It is an image that is useful as far as it goes and that can easily be discarded as it becomes clearly seen to be an inadequate image. Yet in all of this, the truth is too self-evident; namely, "our God is too small" whenever we try to conceive him with our finite minds, and all images are inadequate and in the end bankrupt.

So in the Old Testament, you were forbidden to collect images of God, however "true" or "lifelike" they might be. For there was always the danger of practicing armchair theology as a kind of spectator sport. Theology in the Old Testament was much more demanding than that. God did not show the Israelites his face, as we have said, so that they could put his portrait into the Pantheon or art museum along with all the images of all other gods. Rather, they came to know him, not so much by what he was like, but by their involvement in what he was doing. The God of the Old Testament is the God of event, not showing his face in visions but rather his hand in history.

EXPERIENCING THE EVENT AND
TELLING THE STORY

The people of Israel were not bound together by a common dogmatic theology but rather by continually rehearsing and remembering everything that they had *undergone* together at his hand. It was their common experience related in their common stories that formed the foundations of their community of faith. In that sense, their theology was occasional theology called out and demanded by the events of the day. The events of their history bound them together, not in an armchair spectator theology, but in the painfully glorious memories of the history they delighted to recount again and again to their children and to their grandchildren, frequently reenacting them as they were telling the story.

Zaccheus in the tree in St. Luke's Gospel (today doubtless fully equipped with camera, video camera, and tape recorder) wanted, of course, to see what Jesus was like and then to leave it at that. Then he could just add Jesus to his collection—after all, he was a collector of some sort, albeit a tax collector. Zaccheus remembers that day, however, not so much because of what he saw, but because of what happened. What happened was an extraordinary sign of contradiction, which completely reversed his worldview. Zaccheus, a little man by all accounts, had always been looked down on by others. However, in his first encounter with God, that worldview was turned upside down. Consistently bad news suddenly became surprisingly good news.

The last thing in the world he would ever have expected actually happened: Jesus, we are told, "looked up" to little Zaccheus and made him feel at that point ten feet tall! The destiny of little Zaccheus was, however, not to become a big man (which in his fantasies he had always hoped) but rather to become a great little man: one of the great little men of history.

In Jericho that day, then, it was a saving event that occurred—the kind that could not be recorded on a camera or tape recorder but that could only be recalled by a loving heart and in the annals of the Spirit. So it is with all the saving events of salvation history. They are wonderful tales of the unexpected, and they make for enticing stories and even soap operas! You can imagine Zaccheus telling and retelling that story to his dying day and boring all his dinner guests over the years of grace! As Van der Post so rightly says, "If you have not got a story to tell, you have not got a life to live."

So, with God's people today, "this is our story, this is our song!" We are a people with a life to live because we first have a story to tell. (The community life of the new Israel, like that of the old Israel, is ideally built, not so much upon a common, dogmatic theology, but more upon the relating of common experiences undergone by God's people and continually related and remembered through story and song.) So we sing again and again, "Tell me the old, old story of Jesus and his love." For we do not learn from experience, necessarily (that is an oversimplification). Rather, we learn by evaluating our experiences— turning them over again and again until we completely appropriate them and interiorize them.

Gospel proclamation is not a tedious photographic theology (however accurate or truthful). Rather, it is the telling of the story of what we have all been *through*: what we are as a truly passionate people and, therefore, what we have undergone. It is that Red Sea story told by a Red Sea people. This is history, and this is my story as well as, of course, being the Jesus story.

But notice now what can happen and what frequently happens by the power and overshadowing of the Holy Spirit. *His* story, the Jesus story, and my story can become your story by the double grip of the Holy Spirit, who makes the connection between what happened once for all, what has been happening for many years and many times since, and what is happening already in your life and in the here and now: in the life of the faith community, in our parish, today. In that sense, all gospel proclamation is not problematical nor diagrammatical. Rather, if there is such a word, all gospel proclamation is "pragmatical." To use a word from the language of Alcoholics Anonymous, it is an intervention motivated by nothing less than love. It breaks into what would otherwise be a predictable and weary journey of decline and decadence, reversing it into a slow, ascending course to God.

THE GOD OF EVENT

For the ultimate event of contradiction that Christians love to recall, remember, and celebrate is the event of Jesus and the resurrection. We recall this event as the climax of all those other strange salvation events in our common history as God's people, and by the calling down of the

Holy Spirit (*epiclesis*) that truth and that event are super-imposed upon the profile of the life of the here and now. So, the full-blooded Jesus is made present in the sacrament of his Body mystical (the congregation) and the sacrament of the altar (in the bread and the wine). At the Easter vigil when we celebrate the paschal mystery, the Church delights to tell the whole story. Necessarily, the service is a long service—no longer than perhaps all liturgies should be if they are to meet us where we are and take us where God wants us to go in worship and in adoration. It tells the story of the mighty acts and salvation events of God throughout history beginning with creation; passing through Moses and the Red Sea; through the deliverance of Jerusalem in the days of Isaiah; and so through the ages until we reach the same J-shaped events in the story of Jesus and the resurrection. Then we move from the telling of the story to the celebration of the event in the first eucharist of Easter Day.

In all these ways the connection is then made by Word and by sacrament and by celebration, but always by the same calling down of the Holy Spirit both to anoint the Word that is read and spoken and to overshadow the eucharistic gifts on the altar together with gifted people of God gathered around. In all these different ways, Jesus, the Word of God, is made present to the people of God by the overshadowing of the Spirit of God.

Christian proclamation is an event that needs to take its place along with all these other events. The words that are used, therefore, in the proclamation must be effective words that affect what they symbolize so that what is being related is also an account of what is happening. Here again is this double grip of truth with which we are so concerned. People begin to nod their heads, not because (hopefully) they are falling asleep, but rather because they are waking up to what is really happening— what is really happening in their lives and in their midst at that moment. They are nodding either as an act of affirmation or adoration—for to do the latter it is necessary first to be brought to the former. All gospel preaching should either bring us to our feet to confess our faith or bring us to our knees to confess our sins—or both. We first confess our faith with the word *amen*, and we then move to adoration of the object of our faith—Jesus—with the word *alleluia*. Alleluia is on our lips because amen is first in our hearts.

So it is that both Word and sacrament for Anglicans are means to this end and, in both cases the congregation becomes attentive and responds. In other words, people are moved, displaced, and transported.

In the case of the eucharist, Eastern theology is quite adamant. Not only do people surge forward to receive Jesus afresh into their lives (as surely as Zaccheus moved forward out of the crowd to greet Jesus and "to receive him joyfully"). They also are lifted up (*anaphora*). The Church at some point is itself moved—moved into the kingdom. In the eucharist we are "enkingdomed" as we say (or sing) the prayer of the kingdom—namely, the Lord's Prayer. We then move forward individually to feast at the banquet of the kingdom and partake of our communion.

Put another way, all worship, in order to be effective, must be transcendent as well as imminent. It must meet people where they are in order to take them where he would have them go ("I ascend to my Father and to your Father" [John 20:17]). Worship, like lightning, must have a double dynamic: down to earth, yet heavens above, and both at the same time and almost instantly. And notice that all this has very little to do with that "old chestnut" of whether we use the old Prayer Book or the new Prayer Book. It is essentially the work of the Holy Spirit. It has taken the charismatic movement to remind us of this. The charismatic movement at its best can take our weary words and tongue them with fire—whether it be words of Latin in the Middle Ages, sixteenth-century English, or twentieth-century American.

CELEBRATING THE EVENT

Yet neither preaching nor the sacraments are primarily cerebral. Both speak to the whole person in words but also in actions that speak louder than words. This is not a book on preaching, nor is it a book on worship. Suffice it to say that, at the human level, the clergy in particular need to recover by gesture, vesture, and posture a transcendent credibility "on stage" and "off stage" if the Word and the worship are once again to belong to the environment of proclamation.

The sermon must tell the old, old story and not just tell some people some wonderful ideas about how to run a wonderful church. It must be the story of the love of God, who is committed to loving sinful, stupid, broken, and weak humanity—what happened and what happens in that encounter and therefore what is happening now (or could happen now) in the life of this congregation. The Bible story is only one of the stories. But to be seen as the saving event that it is, it must relate to that second story of Jesus and then make the connection with my story and your story in the here and now. All proclamation, as at the outset in Cana of Galilee, points to vision and leads to repentance: It points to the gap between things as they are and things as God would have them be.

So also with the sacraments. We reenact and record the saving events of history in actions and words and at the same time (or in the fullness of time) the ultimate story of Jesus and the saving events of his passion, death, and resurrection. The congregation completes the action of the eucharist in a word (the great amen at the end of the thanksgiving prayer) so God's people make all this truth their own: The truth overtakes them, and the past begins to stick to them. (It's no longer necessary for them to try to stick to their past!) Then, in the deed and the action of receiving their communion in the fullest sense possible, God's people "swallow" the truth and embody it. Having been overtaken by the truth, truth now incarnates us and possesses us. What leaves the church at the end of the service is a walking sacrament of Jesus truly present for the wider community—especially for those who never darken the doors of a church.

So in both Word and sacrament there is an *epiclesis* and an *anaphora*. The Holy Spirit comes down (*epiclesis*), and God's people are raised up (*anaphora*), and all because Jesus has first been raised up and has sent down the Holy Spirit as he promised he would. Of course, we are not up to this, which is the reason why he had to come down to all of that (the incarnation)! We need as a Church to work out the practical, even the rudimentary, theology in our preaching technique, for technique has its place most assuredly. We need to prepare carefully the music, the drama, the movement, and the worship. For preparation most assuredly has its indispensable place if anything is to be truly spontaneous and open to the response and movement of the Holy Spirit.

Ministers of Word and sacrament need to be strongly encouraged to take more trouble and to give more time to preparing their sermons and to preparing worship that is truly converting. Both alike have fallen on hard times. "There are today many millions of people who hold 'right opinions,' probably more than ever before in the history of the church. Yet I wonder if there was ever a time when true, spiritual worship was at a lower ebb. To great sections of the church, the art of worship has been lost entirely, and in its place has come that strange and foreign thing called 'the program.'"[3] Commenting on this, Dr. Jim Packer has, as usual, a timely word.

Worship . . . has been largely replaced, at least in the West, by a form of entertainment. . . . Neither stylized charismatic exuberance nor Anglican Prayer Book correctness, nor conventional music-sandwich Sunday morning programs provide any magic formula for this rediscovery. It can occur only when the Holy Spirit is taken seriously as the One who through the written word of scripture shows us the love and glory of the Son and the Father and draws us into personal communion with both.[4]

This task of revitalizing the ministry of Word and sacrament and placing both alike on the substantial foundations of Scripture is an urgent one. It is difficult to stress sufficiently how important such a task is, especially for seminaries, for clergy in-service training courses, and clergy diocesan conferences—to say nothing of the need to bring all church musicians on board this refurbished ship.

When, yet only when, all this is in place, the rest of the week flows freely for the common life of the Body of Christ. For the rest of the week and for the whole community of faith, gossiping the gospel will be the name of the game. I want to suggest that Alcoholics Anonymous in this regard, as in so many other ways, is a most helpful model.

We shall need to meet together frequently (as for recovering alcoholics). Then we need to tell our story— our faith-story. I would suggest that in a Decade of Evangelism every bishop needs to call together his clergy in synod and share his faith-story with them. Then the clergy must begin to share their faith-story with their people. In a nutshell, that story is simply in the words of the psalmist: "I will tell you what the Lord has done for my soul" (Ps. 66). Slowly, the evangelism event breaks out in our church like an infection: we are all telling our stories, not so much now as problems but as the vindication of a faithful God who has kept his promises.

THE GOSPEL CONNECTION

You would think from the way we as Episcopalians refuse to talk about our faith that witnessing was really something only certain classes within society undertook. You might suppose that if you belong to a certain class (and, sadly, Episcopalians are predominantly from the upper middle class of society) then you do not witness and talk about your faith to others. So what is it then about Alcoholics Anonymous members (who are certainly drawn from all classes) that enables them to tell their stories so easily and so frequently? The answer is, of course, that their story is the sort of story that demands to be told. Their release from the bondage of drink has released their tongues!

Could it be that there is some necessary pre-evangelism to do in the church and for the church in preparation for a Decade of Evangelism? Are Episcopalians converted churchgoers or just reluctant churchgoers? Where the latter is the case, does this not ask some serious questions about the nature, context, and content of preaching as practiced in so many Episcopal churches today? Does it not at the same time ask many questions about the nature, context, and content of worship and sacramental life in our church today?

For proclamation, Word and sacrament in Bible study classes and in the reading of Scripture publicly and privately—all of these must come under urgent review in a Decade of Evangelism. I want to suggest that, if this is not to become divisive in the renewal of the Church, the bishop is the person to initiate this Decade of Evangelism. The bishop must begin to see once again his apostolic task as the prime minister of evangelism. In the early Church, the apostle was the prime minister of the Word, and the apostle or bishop would spend most of his time telling the "old, old story" from Scriptures, from tradition, and from the corporate experience of the community of faith. Because he stood on the frontiers of faith (or sat, because that was where his teaching chair was located, right on the frontiers of faith) for that kind of encounter with the world of non-faith, he was therefore the minister of the sacraments of initiation. He had the last word because he had had the first word. Christian proclamation, apologetics, evangelism, and the whole business of becoming a Christian focused in one and the same person who was always there for you at the turning points in your Christian pilgrimage and life. That person was the bishop—the prime minister of initiation. The evangelist was not preaching one sort of medicine and the sacramentalist another sort of potion (possibly less potent). There were not two sorts of Christians therefore, not two sorts of Christianity in the early Church. Both the Christianity of Word and of sacrament had a sufficiently powerful chemistry to change people's lives.

There is a crying need today to recover for the episcopal office the apostolic icon we see in the pages of the New Testament. A Decade of Evangelism will need to win the confidence and support of the House of Bishops and the seminaries if it is to bite deeply into the Church and to be owned by the whole Church and not just by those parts of the Church that happen to like this kind of thing. Evangelism is not an option in a living Church, and neither is it an option for some Christians. It is the imperative for the whole Church and for all Christians—and especially for the bishop.

A COMMUNITY OF PERSUASION

The goal of proclamation is "to persuade people to come to [Jesus] personally and so to be reconciled to God." Augustine, the great convert, preacher, evangelist, and bishop, borrowed from his former hero, Cicero (the great communicator of the ancient world), when he wrote these words: "To teach is a necessity, to please is a sweetness,

but to persuade is a victory." He goes on to remind us that
"the eloquence of the discourse pleases in vain unless that
which is learned is implemented in action." A sermon that
does not move people in their will is no earthly use to God
or human. "It is necessary, therefore," he concludes, "for
the ecclesiastical orator when he urges that something be
done not only to teach that he may instruct and to please
that he may hold attention, but also to persuade that he
might be victorious."[5]

So for Augustine, the sermon was an event in which
"one loving heart sets another on fire." The man and his
message were fused in the crucible of God's love to such
an extent that the message spoke from the whole person to
the whole person. So with the study of theology. It is
intended to invade the whole personality or, put another
way, in the words of Philip Brooks the great preacher,
"preaching is a sacrament of the personality."

Traditionally, the word *conversion* is substituted for the
word *persuasion* in Christian proclamation. We need to
look most carefully at this word *conversion* and at its
proper use. Conversion, as a word, is used only once in
the New Testament, (Acts 15:3) though its inner meaning
is implied frequently. The abuse of this word is at the root
of many misunderstandings about evangelism. If we see
it purely in emotional terms, we will be rightly accused of
being mindless, and it will not be long before evangelism
will become synonomous with emotionalism and
manipulation. If, on the other hand, we claim only purely
intellectual content for that word, we miss the powerful
chemistry of conversion as we see it at work in the pages
of the New Testament and in the lives of Christians over
the centuries. To say this is not to say, however, that
apologetics have no place in evangelism. They clearly do.
"Primitive evangelism was by no means mere proclamation and exhortation; it included able intellectual
argument, skillful study of the scriptures, careful, closely

The Local Church: A Unit of Evangelism

reasoned teaching and patient argument."[6] Yet these are
not the whole story, as we have seen earlier. That is why it
is important that we do not see conversion solely in terms
of instant and a total sanctification of life all in a blinding
flash. If we do, then we exclude at the outset many for
whom a Christian discipleship is a long, slow, uneven, and
painful journey into maturity and holiness of life.

WHAT CONVERSION IS AND
WHAT CONVERSION IS NOT

Perhaps we need to tackle the last point first. The jargon
and cliche frequently attributed to evangelists and evangelism as their stock-in-trade phrase is, of course, "Are
you saved?" Such a question, put in such a way, conceives
of salvation as a static, once-for-all moment in time, before
which I am one sort of person doing and believing certain
kinds of things and afterwards a totally different person
doing and believing totally different things. Such a person
is termed both converted and saved.

Surely, this caricature is at the root of much opposition
to evangelism in general and, therefore, potentially to a
Decade of Evangelism in particular.

Yet Cyprian the bishop, speaking of his conversion and
baptism in the fourth century, could write,

> The water of regeneration washed away the stains of my
> past life. A light from above entered and permeated my
> heart, now cleansed from its defilement. The Spirit
> came from heaven, and changed me into a new man by
> the second birth. Almost at once in a marvelous way
> doubt gave way to assurance, what had been shut tight,
> opened; light shone in dark places; and I found what
> had previously seemed difficult had become easy, and
> what I had thought impossible could be done.[7]

Such material, misused or as propaganda, can be
highly misleading, for there is a paradox about conversion

as there is about everything even remotely orthodox. We need to speak quite definitely of a turning point or of turning points in our lives. Essentially, we are speaking of a turning from one attitude and outlook to another attitude and outlook. So in the baptismal liturgy from the earliest of times, the new Christian has always been asked a similar question: "Do you turn to Christ?" However, we need to remember that the word *conversion*, as such, is not an especially New Testament word. It occurs in various forms less than a dozen or so times in the whole of the New Testament. Yet used in the context of Christian initiation, it is an indispensable word and, even more, an indispensable experience. "Once sever the fundamental root of conversion to Christ from the Christian message, and it becomes a broken and a lifeless plant, however beautiful the flowers of Christian concern and social involvement it displays."[8]

There is a real turning away from an old life and a turning to the new life. Furthermore, such a moment is rooted in an experience—even if that experience occured while we were simply screaming babies who apparently did not wish to be baptized (but more of that later). Something happens, after which things are never quite the same, though much is still very much the same. Although such an experience is frequently a once-off moment, it is also frequently a recurring point in our lives. We can only be baptized once, of course, yet we spend the rest of our lives "unpacking" the full implication of that decisive moment—a moment of decision, whether it is the decision of parents and godparents or the decision of the new Christian. The rest of the Christian life is a continuous and continual confirmation in the life of the Spirit, given once for all at baptism.

The analogy that helps the author most is derived from swimming. Until my fiftieth birthday, I was not a swimmer. I could not swim, and I did not swim. On July 4th

(Independence Day) a few years ago at the house of a friend, I was taught to swim by a friend. When I arrived at my friend's house, I was not a swimmer; when I left, I was a swimmer—not a very good one but nevertheless a swimmer. (You cannot be a theoretical swimmer any more than you can be a theoretical Christian.) You can be a bad swimmer: I am. For example, I could not save anyone else's life, and I could scarcely save my own in rough water. However, I am a swimmer now whereas before I was not.

On that day I underwent an experience. For me, learning to swim was mainly an attitude of mind. I was trying too hard to do the wrong things. My instructor who initiated me to the mystery of swimming went at it from the right end and tackled it intellectually—in my case. All my efforts to swim thus far had been an attempt to stay on top of the water and not to go under—and certainly not to let my head go under! So I was taught to swim by first learning to go under (to undergo) and then to know that it was all right to go under and that it would not necessarily mean that I would finally undergo and go under forever! Then I learned how very hard it is to stay under! It is, in fact, very difficult to swim under water. I learned to swim by first learning how to go under the water, rather like I suspect you learn to live by first learning how to die.

Now I am a swimmer (not a very good one, though slowly getting better, I hope). Everywhere I go to stay, I always pack my swimming trunks. July 4 marked for me a very special turning point, but I did not become a life-saving, perfect swimmer overnight, and I have still not arrived at that excellence.

Nevertheless, there was a turning point in my life, and I can tell you the place where it occurred and almost the time of day at which it occurred. There are probably many more points in my swimming career ahead of me: Indeed, there will have to be many more if I am to become a good swimmer, let alone be able to rescue others in distress. I suspect that, like C.S. Lewis, I shall have to learn to dive one day, and that will certainly be a turning point for me as it was for C.S. Lewis. He tells us that he learned to dive the same year he became a Christian and that for him, also, learning both of these arts involved not trying quite so hard (in his case also, intellectually).

So conversion is a reality and is an appropriate expression or turn of phrase—even for Episcopalians. Furthermore, it has its proper and crucial place in any commitment to a ministry of evangelism. Yet if it is not to degenerate into a glib, superficial manipulation, we must see it in the full context of the Christian life and of discipleship and the long process of sanctification. For St. Paul, the experience after his Damascus conversion was summed up in these words: "For I do not do the good I want, but the evil I do not want is what I do" (Rom. 7:19). Definitely saved, Paul is nevertheless still a sinner: Justified and reckoned righteous in the waters of baptism, he is still the man of weakness, still only seeing "in a glass darkly." His knowledge is still "only partial" (1 Cor. 13:9). So he can write toward the end of his life, after many years as a Christian (not a theoretical Christian and by no means a perfect Christian), those amazing words from prison in his letter to the Philippians: I have not "already obtained this or am already perfect; but I press on to make it my own, because Christ Jesus has made me his own. Brethren, I do not consider that I have made it my own" (Phil. 3:12–13).

THE CONFIRMATION OF THE SPIRIT

So the confirmation service in the old Prayer Book rightly prayed that those who would turn to Christ in baptism and confirmation would "daily increase in His Holy Spirit more and more." New Christians experience conversion, but so also do renewed Christians and Christians at every stage of renewal. There is both continuity and discontinuity with the old self in this developing life of discipleship. For grace perfects nature, it does not annihilate it, and the joke is that from the new perspective of repentance even my weaknesses duly confessed can in reality become my greatest strengths. Even the minus marks in my life, by his grace, can become the plus signs: to borrow a phrase of Robert Schuller, "my scars can become my stars!" All this is what we mean by the process of sanctification—becoming more and more the person Christ wants you to become. Proclamation, persuasion, and conversion have a real part to play on that long road of discipleship as we come to turning points and milestones along the pilgrim way. I can rightly look back with thanksgiving to a date and to a place and give thanks at "all times and in all places" for what the "Lord has done for my soul" over many years of grace.

So the Christian Church is the community that is always undergoing conversion. Michael Green reminds us that "the search for truth and the search for deliverance seem to have been the two main paths by which those who have left literary remains [i.e. those whose literature we still have] speak of their conversion."[9] Augustine is the prime example of those who speak of their conversion in terms of deliverance. He had undertaken most of his searching for truth and his intellectual homework long before he was in that garden one summer's afternoon in A.D. 386. He needed deliverance from behavior patterns in which he had become imprisoned. Sin is bondage, and it is compulsive—that is its very nature. Not only alcohol abuse and chemical abuse set up compulsive patterns of behavior. Sin is a chemistry, not just an idea.

So all sorts of things set up a compulsive pattern of behavior. Erotomania is now a recognized behavior pattern afflicting many people in the West. The theological diagnosis of such a human condition (not only in matters sexual, alcoholic, or drug related and in the addiction of acquisition or the more "dramatic" sins, but also in the ordinary weaknesses of everyday life) is summed up in the words of the ancient collect, which certainly has the ring of truth: "O God, you know that we have no power of ourselves to help ourselves." That was Paul's experience; it was Augustine's experience; it is the experience of every recovering alcoholic, expressed so plainly in the words of the first step to recovery: "We admitted we were powerless over alcohol—that our lives had become unmanageable." Nevertheless, that acknowledgment is the first step in recovering sobriety for the alcoholic. There is nothing that you or I can do to stop drinking, if drinking is our problem, except to acknowledge the fact freely and openly: we are powerless. Then (a bit like learning to swim) you will stop trying to do all the wrong things—stop trying to stop drinking and start trying to accept the fact that you are not able to stop drinking in your own strength. Acknowledge that in this realm you are powerless, and then you will find the source of real power—namely, the power that comes alone from accepting that you are powerless. In that confession of powerlessness, you are given power and strength, not to stop drinking as such, but to know your own powerlessness; to be able to accept it and then to live each and everyday as though that reality is true. Live every day drawing on the power you know that you do not possess but can only receive as a gift. Your power to stop drinking and, indeed, everything else, which we call sin, is a gift from that Higher Power beyond yourself, to which Alcoholics Anonymous does not give a specific name.

As Christians, however, we know his name—his name is Jesus. Subsequently (and this has to be a joke), at some point the sober alcoholic is able to thank God even for his alcoholism, for it is through this dreadful illness that he or she has learned what most of us in our delusions never learn, namely, that we are indeed (all of us) powerless in everything to renew ourselves. Only then can we begin to live the new life, the other side of "death"—that kind of death to all self-sufficiency and independence.

THE NEW LIFE—VITA NOVA

The worldly wise get by, more or less, most of the time, until they are struck with a particularly crucifying afflication such as alcoholism. The truth is that we all suffer from the ultimately crucifying affliction of sin. But we are able to delude ourselves most of the time because we are just about able to avoid crime or at least avoid being found out, and so we maintain a more or less respectable front. But what sort of life is that? As such, few people are further from the kingdom of heaven than the respectable and the self-sufficient. For "blessed" indeed—Jesus would remind us—are the people of the first Beatitude, namely, "those who know their need" (New English Bible). The alcoholic in the gutter or the prostitute in the street is nearer the kingdom of heaven, often reflecting more the words of that first Beatitude by approach, than somone who has managed to get through life without doing anyone too much harm or without getting caught! G.K. Chesterton reminds us that the man who knocks on the door of the prostitute's house is probably looking for God. Insofar as that is true, that man is "not far from the kingdom of heaven."

For Christians who have primarily sought deliverance, their conversion is often quite a dramatic point and is certainly a decisive one. They still live only one "drink" from catastrophe and frequently skid and fall into sin and into the ditch. Whenever they do so, they know the road back to the highway. It has a name. They can recognize it and recall it, for they have been there before. The word on

the signpost is *repentance*. In the words of the service of
the reaffirmation of baptismal vows, you cannot promise
that you will not sin again, but you *can* promise that
"whenever you fall into sin" you will "repent and return
to the Lord."[10]

Often intellectuals also seem to have the need for
deliverance from compulsive behavior. The intellectual is
not free from that "thorn in the flesh" of which St. Paul
speaks so honestly. Thank God that they are not! If their
minds have been converted and they are no longer
assailed with intellectual doubts (as indeed was probably
the case with St. Paul), how on earth are they to be kept
humble and close to the Lord except through this door of
need? For the door of sin is the same door through which
grace enters our lives. Given half a chance, such people
would soon begin to try to live without grace and to live
in their own intellectual power, strength, and conviction.
Before long, they would become irredeemable! The door
of sin repented is indeed the same door through which
grace can enter our lives so that that door, even if it is a
grave moral weakness, can itself also be a cause for
thanksgiving. St. Paul was not a great, strong, impressive,
polished Christian. He was a weak man who could not
speak very well. He was a man of frailty, and yet it was in
his very frailty and weakness that the power and strength
of God were most vindicated. For "we have this treasure
in earthen vessels, to show that the transcendent power
belongs to God and not to us" (2 Cor. 4:7).

THE PLACE OF THE INTELLECT

Intellectual conversion is often a slower process. In this
whole process, of course, we must take seriously the place
of Christian apologetics—"prepare to make a defense to
anyone who calls you to account for the hope that is in
you" (1 Pet. 3:15). There was a time when Anglicans could

boast of this ministry with international names drawn from the fields of science, philosophy, and especially literature: C.S. Lewis, Dorothy L. Sayers, T.S. Eliot, William Temple, Charles Williams—to name but a few. A blind leap of faith is not what Christian conversion is all about. The leap should be directional and should lead where the thought processes are pointing. Yet notice the need for the leap. You cannot get all the way on the stepping stones of intellectual propositions. They will take you part of the way, but in order to arrive, you have to go further than it is purely reasonable to go. In order to live the life of faith, you must first make the leap of faith.

Yet there is nothing anti-intellectual about that proposition: the proof of the pudding is in the eating. That is, in reality, a very scientific approach. There is surely an element of obstinacy in much unbelief that masquerades behind so-called intellectual propositions. Part of Christian proclamation must be to challenge such people to come out from behind their intellectual shibboleths and to make the same kind of leap in the area of Christian discipleship and to take up precisely the same kind of pragmatism in their Christian life as they do in every other intellectual discipline and, indeed, in every other walk of life. For in every walk of life you prove that something is true by living and acting as though it is true. The ultimate proof of the hypothesis can only be discovered by acting out the program on the basis of the hypothesis. *Solvitur ambulando* is not only the way to walk by faith, but it is also the way by which the scientist pursues his or her experiments. We walk by faith and not by sight, otherwise we would never walk at all—let alone learn to swim or fall in love, learn to ride a bicycle, get out of bed in the morning, or anything else.

Furthermore, much of our lives as intellectuals is not purely intellectual. We are moved to do things as intellectuals through other motivations—we are moved biologically, psychologically, and through many other forms of logic. Faith is the assumption that a fact is true because it makes the most sense of all the other facts we are seeking to place in the jigsaw puzzle, though each of those facts in isolation could possibly be explained in 1,001 different ways. Hence,

> if someone is looking for a railway station in the village and finds himself in station road, passing the station arms, with people hurrying the same way with cases; if when he asks he is told that the station lies in the direction in which he is going, and he himself sees smoke over the fence at the end of the road—if all this happens it is still possible to explain every separate indication in another way; the road and the public house may be named after a station that was closed years ago, the people may be hurrying to catch a bus and his informant may be a pathological liar and the smoke may come from the chimney of a hidden cottage.[11]

Of course, you can explain any of the phenomena in a thousand different ways. But the fact that makes the most sense of all the other facts is that there is indeed a railway station just out of sight at the end of station road. Of course, you will only prove that it is so if, by faith, you begin to walk down the road and arrive at the station to prove the basis of your hypothesis.

One further point needs to be made. The leap of faith that is required is essentially an identification with the whole faith of the whole Church through the ages. A personal faith is not limited only to those things of which I may have individual experience. I am not free to select some points of Christian belief and practice and reject others. We call that eclecticism. Such eclecticism would be analogous to the behavior of a person who, having obtained from the Automobile Association of America an itinerary for a journey that they wish to make, promptly trusts only in those parts of the itinerary that are already validated from purely personal and individual experience and rejects or selects from the rest.

Yet in all this sifting, speculation, analysis, and reflection, the intellect does play a real part in the whole of our lives' journeyings. The point that we need to make is that it should play neither more nor less a part in the life of discipleship than it does in the rest of our lives. An intellectual person does not commit himself or herself to matrimony purely intellectually. Hopefully, the commitment is an act of faith based on a whole range of evidence gleaned from a short or more lengthy courtship. The leap of faith Christ invites us to make is not, therefore, a crush (to continue the analogy). That is a blind leap and is generally disastrous. Rather, the leap of faith Christ invites us to make is a directional leap, based on previous testing and experience in every aspect of life.

Such is the place for apologetics and for the intellect in the overall process of faith and, indeed, in the proclamation of faith. Preaching for persuasion in a community of faith, therefore, is not necessarily anti-intellectual, though for some the direction of their leap of faith is necessarily more motivated by the mind than by the emotions or by the heart.

Yet through whatever door the message enters, it has only one golden objective. That is essentially to go straight to the will. On that road from head to heart and beyond to the gut—and it is a very long road, perhaps the longest journey in the world and certainly the most important in our quest for maturity—on such a road, there are many roadblocks and inhibitions.

It is the work of the Holy Spirit to bring release and to open up these roadblocks. For however far we have traveled, it is still possible that a further roadblock will inhibit our journey of faith. A lifetime of churchgoing, of prayer, and of Christian witness can still bring us to a further roadblock. Until it is removed, our road of faith has become a dead end. Again and again when we read St. Paul he uses the phrase "I am persuaded." We sometimes feel that we need to ask whether he is finally persuaded or whether he has more roadblocks ahead and whether he will need to say again, as yet another roadblock gives way to further experience and further freedom, "Now at last, I am finally persuaded!" The community of persuasion needs to be persuaded again and again by Word and sacrament, by confession of sin and reconciliation, by hearing the Scriptures read, and by personal, careful, and prayerful reading of them. We need to be persuaded again and again and confirmed in our faith by the anointing of oil and by the laying on of hands; by transcendent worship, by prayer and praise; by service, compassionate care, and much loving. We need to be persuaded early in life "once upon a time" yet many times and "at all times" renewed and refreshed on the long road of faith. We need to be persuaded late in life, for it is never too late, and while there is life there is hope. We need to be persuaded *in extremis* as we are dying, through the ministry and care of the Church and its sacraments, as "food for the journey" (*viaticum*).

At all these points on the long road of faith, the work of the Church is essentially the same. That work is to persuade men and women, in spite of much evidence to the contrary (intellectual and experiential), that there is a God and that God really loves them. Ultimately, there is no other objective evidence for this in history, in time, or in space, except the evidence of Calvary hill. It is not until I know that Jesus died for my sins and that he lives as my Advocate and Savior forever that I can really be certain I am loved from eternity to eternity: that he who knows all is ready to forgive all. And so to persuade wavering souls (to confirm them in faith) is, indeed, the main task of the Church so that joy increasingly replaces despair; faith displaces fear; sight replaces blindness, freedom for service replaces bondage with self; and the worship of God finally and forever displaces obsession with that self. "For I am persuaded," says St. Paul, "that neither death, nor life, nor angels, nor principalities, nor things present, nor things to come, nor powers, nor height, nor depth, nor anything else in all creation, will be able to separate us from the love of God in Christ Jesus our Lord" (Rom. 8:38ff.).

He had been persuaded once upon a time on that road to Damascus and had the first glimpse of that awesome reality of God's love for him. However, he spent a lifetime in the community of persuasion and had to go through many trials and undergo many experiences that, in turn, removed the roadblocks and inhibitions of faith before he could be finally and ultimately persuaded and totally confirmed in that first conversion when Jesus Christ first took hold of him.

Notes

1. Abraham, *Logic of Evangelism*, 63.
2. Bernard Lamarche-Vadel, *Michaelangelo* (London: Chart-well Books, 1986), 5.
3. A.W. Tozer, quoted by J.I. Packer in the introduction to Wells, *God the Evangelist*, xiii.
4. J.I. Packer, in the introduction to Wells, *God the Evangelist*, xiv.
5. St. Augustine: *Epistoli* 21:15.
6. Green, *Evangelism in the Early Church*, 160.
7. St. Cyprian, *Ad Donatum* 3, 4.
8. Green, *Evangelism in the Early Church*, 148.
9. Ibid. 162.
10. *The Book of Common Prayer Book* (New York: Church Hymnal Corporation, 1979), 293.
11. Michael Marshall, *A Pattern of Faith* (London: Hodder & Stoughton, 1967), 114.

SEVEN

The Community of Passion and Compassion

"Jesus still calls all who would follow him to deny themselves, take up their cross, and identify themselves with His new community. The results of evangelism include obedience to Christ, incorporation into His church and responsible service in the world" (*Lausanne Covenant*).

EVANGELIZING THE CHURCH FOR MISSION

The thesis throughout this book has been that a church that is fed with the gospel of Word and sacrament and that lives in the power of the Spirit will reach what we have come to call apostolic point, when it inevitably "explodes" and begins to evangelize by word and deed the community around it. The institutional church, by the overshadowing of the Holy Spirit, becomes in reality the Body of Christ on earth. It becomes Jesus for the world *now*, doing the things he did, saying the things he said when he first came into Galilee proclaiming the gospel of the kingdom of God and calling people to repent and believe. In our present day, in our community and in our lives, the Church, if you like, is "God with skin on." "What Jesus did in His 'singular' person, He now does through His united 'plural' Body. *Together*, not individually, *we* are the presence of Christ in this world."[1] In place of fragmented individualism, on the one hand, or tyrannical totalitarianism, on the other hand, the Church becomes corporately the Body of Christ (the very opposite of collectively) to form his real and effective presence in the world TODAY.

Such a Church lives in continuous and continual renewal. The renewal movement in the Church in recent decades has brought many congregations alive in the Spirit and to this apostolic point of which we shall speak more at some length.

Individuals on their faith journeys have been brought through many of those "roadblocks" of which I spoke in the previous chapter—roadblocks on that long road from head to heart to will. So much prayer is so often just off the top of our heads. For many who have been "schooled" in this age of rationalism, there have been two equally disastrous situations. There are those who see the head, the mind, and the cerebral processes as determinative of reality: if you cannot prove it rationally, it is not true. Such an idolatry of the cerebral processes is a strange kind of madness. As G.K. Chesterton puts it so strikingly, "The madman is not the man who has lost his reason, but the man who has lost everything except his reason." It's as though everything below the neck could not be taken seriously as giving us evidence of what is really happening. That is certainly a form of madness.

The second and alternative "schizophrenia" is to seek a mindless faith based solely upon intuition, feelings, and hunches and often accompanied by that dangerous ascription, "The Lord told me." Such faith (if that is the right word at all) has no built-in checks and balances from the rational processes. It is totally subjective, out of touch with the mind, and refuses to be open to outside correction from a fuller reading of Scripture, from the traditional teaching and experience of the Church, or even from that wonderful resource of human experience—good, sound, basic, common sense (which may not be such a bad translation after all for that much-used phrase these days—*consensus fidelium*).

One of the good aspects of renewal is the special way in which the Holy Spirit has released rather rigid, uptight Christians, removing those roadblocks of which we have spoken and opening up people's lives to fuller and deeper expressions of their faith through prayer, praise, and passion. "The coming of the rule of God," writes William Abraham, "does indeed mean a profound crisis for the individual. It calls for a death to the old life and a resurrection to a new life in the Spirit; it involves turning from a life of idolatry to one of service to one's neighbor. In such circumstances it is entirely natural to speak of being born again."[2]

Often this experience is very traumatic—certainly at the outset. The foundations of the human personality and, certainly, the foundations of faith are severely shaken. It would seem that whenever we are impacted by that Spirit there is a shaking of the foundations (Isa. 6:4 and Acts 16:26). So *released* are such people in the Spirit that they now can sing (whereas before they persisted in speaking of their tone deafness). Now they can pray and praise—frequently in tongues—whereas before they were rather inhibited and inarticulate, certainly in their prayer language and in many other areas of communication and relationships.

BAPTISM AND CONFIRMATION IN THE SPIRIT

Such experiences are so real and personal to those who receive them that even the word *conversion* seems too bland and flat to describe what has clearly happened. So there has been much talk of baptism in the Spirit. Instead of the old and dangerous shorthand question of revivalist

evangelism ("Have you been converted?"), many insist
these days on putting to other Christians a rather different
question: "Have you been baptized in the Spirit?"

Our Church today needs to meet this situation in a
welcoming way. I want to say, if you like, two cheers for
baptism in the Spirit. You cannot convert and redirect
anything effectively until you first welcome it warmly.
Thank God that people are moving on the road of discipleship to an even more intimate and more committed relationship with the Lord Jesus. For too long we were
notoriously God's frozen people. In the words of the wonderful golden sequence from the medieval mass for Pentecost, we sing the hymn to the Holy Spirit and we pray
that:

> What is frozen warmly tend
> What is rigid gently bend
> Straighten what goes erringly

If the two former petitions, however, are answered, the
chances are that you will have to pray the third petition
more fervently—"straighten what goes erringly." For too
long, God's people did not go erringly, of course, or astray
because they did not go anywhere at all. There is always a
strong possibility that if you do nothing you will never do
any harm. Now God's people are warming up at last.
They are experiencing this release in the Spirit, and all hell
is being let loose. Nevertheless, our first response must
surely be to thank God and to say with eucharist in our
hearts, "It is the Lord's doing and it is marvelous in our
eyes" (Ps. 118:23).

However, to speak rather loosely of baptism in the
Spirit in this context is both dangerous and careless. It
implies two things. In the first place, it implies that you
are not baptized in the Spirit at your first sacramental
baptism. In the second place, it implies that there are two
sorts of Christians—those who are baptized in the Spirit

and those who are not. This second problem is further compounded when we go on to equate baptism in the Spirit with the exclusive gift of speaking in tongues.

In the face of the first error, we need to reaffirm baptism as the once for all, unrepeatable gift from God. In my baptism I was born again as a child of God. My sins were forgiven, and I was reconciled to God through the blood of Jesus and given the gift and sealing of the Holy Spirit. All this is God's initiative, and it is a gift I do not deserve, cannot earn, and certainly cannot begin to understand in purely rational terms.

GOSPEL SACRAMENTS

So baptism is the foundation sacrament. All other sacraments are that double grip of which we spoke in a previous chapter. You cannot repeat baptism any more than the sacrifice of Jesus on Calvary can be repeated. It is once for all and all-sufficient. However, in the course of time I need to be "gripped" by the objective reality of that once-for-all gift, or, as St. Paul would put it, to "take hold of him who first took hold of me" and make this my own increasingly and ever more fully and always only because Christ Jesus has first made me his own (Phil. 3:12ff.).

> Faith is the affirmation and the act
> Which binds eternal truth to present fact.
>
> (Coleridge)

The "eternal truth" is the awesome reality that in my baptism I was made a son of God and an heir of eternal life. God loves me—period. The "present fact," however, that I am experiencing daily is that I am a sinner. That is all too apparent. All sacraments are intended to bind these two apparently opposing realities together. We do not oscillate between being totally holy and utterly sinful. We are at one and the same time both sinners and yet justified. All the sacraments, therefore, are intended to meet us at all sorts of points on our spiritual journey in order to bind these two paradoxical statements together in one whole person and so to release us from the schizophrenic position so many Christians seem to experience: He loves me; he loves me not!

All sacraments are an existential reaffirmation of the once-for-all gift of baptism. Confirmation is intended to meet the renewed Christian in renewal at a point on the long journey of discipleship from being a bad Christian to being that holy person God has always intended me to be. As a sacrament, confirmation equips me with grace, releasing me further in the Spirit, and increasing the life of the Holy Spirit within me. As Terry Fullam so eloquently says, it is not a question of how much of the Holy Spirit you have got but how much the Holy Spirit has got of you. How much of my life is under new management? For if Jesus is not Lord of all, he is not really Lord at all.

So the whole Christian life of discipleship is a journey of confirmation. It is the Christian experience to seek daily confirmation in his salvation. At various turning points along that road of faith, you should reaffirm your baptismal vows. (Notice, you do not *renew* them because, unlike the case of your dog license, they will not run out if you do not renew them). So we should not speak so much of renewing our baptismal vows as reaffirming them. Furthermore, it is not so much a question of you renewing your baptismal vows but rather more a question of your baptismal vows renewing you, whenever you reaffirm them.

Again ideally, the prime minister of renewal (nondivisive renewal) should be the bishop or those delegated by him for this oversight of the good, the bad, and the indifferent. We would do better to speak of these turning points not as baptisms in the Spirit but rather as releases in the Spirit or, better still, confirmations in the Spirit. It would do a great deal to enrich our doctrine and understanding of *the* Sacrament of Confirmation if we would also speak frequently as Christians of the experience of being confirmed in the Spirit. This would root all renewal back to baptism, from which it properly stems, keeping the initiative with Christ's saving work on Calvary and always giving God the glory for the wonderful things he has done and is continuing to do as we "daily increase in his Holy Spirit more and more."

This precious theological insight, incidentally, needs working into a very flexible, pastoral and certainly evangelistic style of confirmation services by our bishops in their dioceses. Such services are right on the frontiers where new Christians are made and where old Christians are being made new. It is the task and responsibility of the bishop to contain and direct renewal in the Episcopal Church today.

Too often in the past we have excommunicated renewal. John Wesley's work was essentially a renewal movement in the Church, and it should never have been allowed to break away. Hopefully, we have learned something from the sad experience of the past that will prevent us from repeating it in the present or in the future.

GIFTS OF THE SPIRIT

The second problem to which we referred previously is even more divisive: namely, "speaking in tongues." There are those in renewal ministry who have set up speaking in tongues as *the* determinative manifestation of what they insist upon calling baptism in the Spirit. They would lead us to suppose that if you do not speak in tongues or have not received your prayer language, you have not yet been fully baptized in the Spirit.

Such a position is neither scriptural, traditional, nor reasonable. Clearly it was a potentially divisive problem in that new little church at Corinth. From Paul's letters, it would appear that people were setting up this one gift as *the* necessary gift. Paul tackles it head on in his First Epistle to the Corinthians. Having spoken first of the unity and diversity of the gifts of the whole Body of Christ within the Church in 1 Corinthians 12, he then seeks to put the particular gift of tongues in its place. To summarize what he says is quite clear and simple: Speaking in tongues is but one of many gifts; all do not possess this particular gift anymore than all possess all the other particular gifts. They do not need to do so since all benefit from one particular gift given to some for the benefit of everybody (1 Cor. 12:26). Hence, there is no need for competition, envy, or rivalry within the Body. In any church, in its fullness there should be manifestations of all the gifts—among which tongues is one that is given to some people. And finally, tongues is not one of the highest gifts to be coveted but one of the rather more lowly gifts, certainly lower than the highest gift of all— namely, love (Cor. 12:31ff.).

We can say this much more positively when we read 1 Cor. 12:27–31 and then run over straight into 1 Corinthians 13, which, in nearly all liturgical readings, has been wrenched out of the context of the whole argument. If you told people at a wedding service that their favorite passage on love was originally intended by the writer to deal with the problem of speaking in tongues in the congregation, they would probably be somewhat surprised.

For in the Greek of this passage, the rhetorical questions at the end of 1 Corinthians 12 are not open-ended as they necessarily appear in the English translation. Greek (like Latin) lets you know (at the front end) whenever you ask a question that it is not a neutral question, and, furthermore, what kind of response the questioner is expecting. Nearly all questions expect the answer yes or no. They imply that response from the outset. From the rhetoric and the argument of this passage in English the questions do clearly imply the answer no, but in the Greek nothing is left to chance. All those questions are prefaced with the little word *me*, which means that the writer is quite clear and that he wishes his readers to be quite clear also. He lets us know that he is not asking an open question but rather a question to which he is expecting, and indeed demanding, the answer no.

So let us read it now in the light both of its rhetorical implications and also of the Greek original. "God has appointed in the church first apostles, second prophets, third teachers, then workers of miracles, then healers, helpers, administrators, speakers in various tongues." Notice that in a church worthy of the name, all these ministries and gifts should be expected and further notice that, in a sentence clearly intended to list priorities, speaking in tongues is the last to be mentioned. The gift of helping and administration is just as important if not more so in Paul's eyes than the gift of tongues.

But then the passage goes on. "Are all apostles?" (No, by implication.) "Are all prophets?" (No.) "Are all teachers?" (No.) "Do all work miracles?" (No.) "Do all persons have the gift of healing?" (No.) "Do all speak in tongues?" (No.) "Do all interpret?" (No.) In order to translate the Greek accurately, we need to write in that little word *no* or find some other way of translating the Greek accurately in order to get the full force of Paul's argument—perhaps along the lines of, "Surely, not all are teachers, are they? Surely, all do not work miracles, do they? Surely, all people do not speak in tongues, do they? Surely, all do not interpret, do they?"

However, we should go on to say that helpers and administrators are certainly high on that list of charismatic gifts along with other gifts that we are so often blinded to or regard as rather inferior gifts, if we regard them as gifts at all. I wonder where we would put the gift of helping and administration on the renewal charts? Yet at the same time, it is important to go on to say that if a congregation

hopes to reach apostolic point it should expect and welcome with praise and gratitude all these gifts, among
which, of course, is the gift of tongues. It is a blessing, this
great gift, to those who receive it and through them for the
whole Church for which God intends the gift to be given.
But, of course, Paul completes and concludes his argument
as he moves into 1 Corinthians 13 with this little phrase:
"But now I will show you a yet better way. Though I speak
with the tongues of men and of angels and have not love
. . . I am nothing."

RELEASED FOR MINISTRY AND MISSION

All the gifts of the Spirit are given for the building up of the
Body to that point I have called apostolic point. It is that
point at which the Church is converted; it turns round from
facing inward to the concerns of ecclesiasticism and begins
to turn outward to the concerns of the kingdom of God and
of the world. The local congregation spills over into
ministry and mission, into passion and compassion. "And
his gifts were . . . to equip the saints for the work and
ministry, for building up the Body of Christ" (Eph. 4:11–12).

All confirmations in the Spirit are intended not to be
hoarded as pious picnics or to provide spiritual massages
for the recipients. We were baptized to be Jesus Christ for
others. This is the great turnaround of history. In
evolution thus far, it has been every man for himself: the
survival of the fittest and the law of the jungle. Look
where it has got us: to the very brink of disaster and self-
destruction. We call it competition. In the revolution of
the kingdom, however, it is every man for others. The
greater love of the kingdom is shown supremely in God's
way of being human (namely, in Jesus) as the cross on
Calvary ("laying down" our lives for our friends) and in
that upper room when he washed the feet of the disciples
("among you as a servant").

Hence, Jesus says (significantly, in the Fourth Gospel and the only Gospel to see the significance of the foot washing, let alone to record it); "Greater love has no man than this, that a man lay down his life for his friends" (John 15:13). The "greater love" is the love and the life for others of which Jesus speaks, and in these last days this greater love has broken in. It has taken over, and it is superceding the old order of every man for himself. From now on, it must increasingly be every man for others.

Hence the word *priesthood* has displaced the old word *manhood* in our vocation to be the priesthood of all believers, which incidentally is not the same thing as the priesthood of every believer. The Church is the priestly community because, as William Temple, the Archbishop of Canterbury during the Second World War, so rightly reminded us, the Church is the only society that exists for the sake of those who are not members of it.

Hence Aaron, from the priestly tribe of Levi in the Old Testament, would go into the sanctuary of God wearing the ephod. Yet we must notice that on that ephod over his heart were the signs and symbols of all the other eleven tribes of Israel. His work (or his liturgy) for the whole state (as in the Greek city-state) was to enter the sanctuary of God on behalf of all the others to make intercession for those who were not members of his own tribe—the tribe of Levi. His worship and his service were for others. So, to belong to the priestly tribe is to live for others and, therefore, to pray for others. All baptized Christians are, therefore, designated rightfully as a "royal priesthood" and a "holy nation" (1 Pet. 2:9).

So intercession is first a way of life before it is a way of prayer. The word *intercession*, etymologically, is derived from the old Roman judiciary courts. To intercede meant to go in before the judge on behalf of others and to plead their cause. For in the kingdom you do not plead your own cause (please notice, members of General Conven-

tion). You leave that to others to do for you. Self-interest
is the way of the world, but it is not the way of the kingdom. Self-interest is manifest in the business news and in
the headlines of our newspapers, and look where it has
got us. No! In the kingdom, you always plead someone
else's cause—life is priestly in that sense.

"All for Jesus" because Jesus lived and died for all and
now "always lives to make intercession for" us (Heb. 7:25).
All those baptized into him are baptized into his own high
priesthood. The ordained priesthood of the ministry of
the Church is there simply to make sure that the Church is
priestly in its outlook. But the Church is priestly in its outlook to make sure that the whole universe eventually
becomes priestly in its outlook and that the kingdom of
this world becomes "the kingdom of our Christ and of his
God" (Rev. 11:15). For the many are saved by the few, as
the few are saved by the one. Apples do not fall out of
thin air, as Austin Farrer would continually remind us.
Rather, they fall from apple trees, and apple trees come
from apple seeds, and apple seeds (which are often discarded and ignored) come from apples. Christ is our great
high priest and it is into his priesthood that priests are ordained and from his priesthood that the ordained priesthood is derived. The ordained priesthood is derived in
order that from it may spring a priestly people.

So we are baptized for others as we live for others,
making intercession for others and even being prepared to
die for others.

It is no accident that the Greek word for witness—
martyreo—is also, of course, translated in English by the
word *martyr*. The Christian witness is the one who lives
for others and whose "greater love" is ready to lay down
his life for his friends. In the Old Testament, Queen Esther
is supremely the priestly, intercessory figure going in
before the king at the risk of her life on behalf of her
people and risking everything to the point of death (since

to go in before the king uninvited was indeed to invite death in the courts of the ancient world). She went in before the king on behalf of others, to plead their cause and to make intercession for her people. She is a truly priestly figure.

To be Christ's witness, then, is no glib evangelization in slick sentences and easy jargon. It is to live for others to the point of death in what we do and in what we say and in what we are. In that sense, all the baptized are baptized for ministry but not for clericalism and not to fill the sanctuaries on Sundays, competing for roles in the eucharist and dressing up accordingly to look as like the clergy as possible! God deliver us from this new form of ecclesiasticism and clericalism that is so rampant in our churches and that parades under the misnomer of the ministry of the laity. The Episcopal Church has far too many ordained priests in its ranks and far too many clericalized laity. (The mission words of Jesus might be parodied: The harvest is pitiful and the laborers are too numerous!) "Are all ordained priests?" to borrow the rhetoric of St. Paul in that Epistle to the Corinthians. The answer might appear to be yes in many churches on Sunday mornings when you take a look at the sanctuary. There simply are not enough jobs to go around in the sanctuary on a Sunday morning in most Episcopal churches!

Rather, we need to ask, "Are all witnesses and therefore martyrs?" Would to God that all God's people were witnessing in the fullest sense of the word. For the witnessing follows the worshiping as inevitably as the service begins when the worship is ended.

THE PASSION OF CHRIST AND THE COMPASSION OF THE PRIESTLY COMMUNITY

There must be no dichotomy between evangelism and mission, between the gospel and the social gospel, once

we have made this gospel connection, since, in the words
of Jesus, "as you did it to the least of one of these my
brethren, you did it to me" (Matt. 25:40). Because of the
first Beatitude, Christ indwells the poor and the poor in
spirit, the prisoners and the captives and those who have
no helper or who most know their need of God. So there
is a real connection between the sanctuary and the slum,
between God and the gutter. It is that gospel connection
of Christ *in* the poor and *in* the sacrament, *in* the slum and
in the sanctuary, *in* the world and *in* the worship. Jesus
calls us to honor, worship, and adore him in *both*, rather
than to ask the banal question, "But, Lord, when did we
see you naked? When did we see you in prison?" Such is
the blindness of most of us, most of the time, in spite of
the mandate of the eucharist, which insists that "heaven
and earth are full of his glory" for "those with eyes to see."
By the Holy Spirit we need to make the connection
between what the world and what religion always try to
keep apart: namely, the secular and the sacred. We must
affirm, in the words of the Manila Manifesto, that "we
must demonstrate God's love by visibly caring for those
who are deprived of justice, dignity, food and shelter."

A Jesuit priest once related to me in the small hours of
the morning how little religious experience he had throughout his Christian life. For him, much of his faith had been
in the mind, that "flame in the mind" of which Justin
Martyr speaks so illuminatingly—much of it, that is, until
the day he went to Calcutta where he had a kind of conversion experience.

He went to visit the community of sisters who work
with Mother Teresa of Calcutta. On the first Sunday
morning, he said the early mass for the community of
nuns. The nuns came forward to receive the Sacrament of
Communion. The Jesuit priest held up the small host for
each nun to receive. "The Body of Christ." Mother Teresa
was at the back of the line. Suddenly she came to stand in

front of the Blessed Sacrament, held out by the Jesuit priest. He told of how a look came over her face of love and adoration and how, in his words, her whole head, now tilted to one side, seemed "displaced" as she adored Christ in the Blessed Sacrament. He would never, he said, forget the look on her face at that moment. But that was not the end of the story.

Later that same day, Mother Teresa volunteered to show the Jesuit priest round the hospice. She saved her own little ward until the last. Her ward was reserved for those patients nearest to death. As she welcomed him into her small room with its small number of patients and was carefully explaining to him about her work, one of the patients cried out suddenly in pain. Mother Teresa went over to the patient and took him in her arms. "At that moment," said the priest, "that same look swept across her face as I had seen in the chapel at mass earlier in the day. Once again her head (as though displaced by love) went onto one side in love and adoration." Yes, of course, it was the same look as she had shown at mass early that day. It was the same look because it was the same Jesus. She was adoring Jesus, worshiping him in the service of the sacrament in the morning, and worshiping him in the sick and the dying, in her care and service to the needy, in the afternoon. Mother Teresa had made the connection and in so doing had witnessed to Jesus and given to that Jesuit a turning point in his own life and ministry.

Mother Teresa has made the connection. Have we?

Would you honour the Body of Christ? Do not despise his nakedness; do not honour him here in the church clothed in silk vestments and then pass him by unclothed and frozen outside. Remember that he who said, "This is my Body," and made good his words, also said, "You saw me hungry and gave me no food," and "Insofar as you did it not to one of these, you did it not to me." In the first sense the Body of Christ does not need clothing, but worship from a pure heart. In the second sense it does need clothing and all the care we can give it. We must learn to be discerning Christians and to honour Christ in the way in which he wants to be honoured. I am not saying you should not give golden altar vessels, but I am insisting that nothing can take the place of almsgiving. What is the use of loading Christ's table with golden cups while he himself is starving? Will you make a cup of gold, and withhold a cup of water? What use is it to adorn the altar with cloth of gold hanging and deny Christ a coat for his back? What would that profit you? Consider that Christ is that tramp who comes in need of a night's lodging. You turn him away and then start laying rugs on the floor, draping the walls, hanging lamps on silver chains from the columns. Adorn the house of God if you will, but do not forget your brother in distress; he is a temple of infinitely greater value.[3]

Bishop Weston of Zanzibar certainly made the connection in an eloquent sermon when he said these words:

Now go out into the highways and hedges, and look for Jesus in the ragged and the naked, in the oppressed and sweated, in those who have lost hope, in those struggling to make good. Look for Jesus in them; and when you find Him, gird yourselves with His towel of fellowship and wash His feet in the person of your brethren.

"Go out"—yes—God's displaced people. "When you were young," says Christ to Peter at his conversion at the end of St. John's Gospel, "you girded yourself and walked where you would; but when you are old, you will stretch out your hands, and another will gird you and carry you where you do not wish to go" (John 21:18). Yes, such would be the death by which Peter would glorify God, but only because he had first learned to live a life that glorified God—the apostolic, priestly life of displacement for others.

So it was that Peter entered into the passion of Christ

and, therefore, into the compassion of God. The baptized, converted Christian cannot be apathetic but must always be sympathetic. Both those words are, of course, at root the Greek version of the Latin word *passio*—giving us our understanding both of passion and compassion, patient and patience. The baptized Christian is baptized into the passion, death, and resurrection of Jesus. The passion of Jesus was Christ's whole way of life, which was so different from apathy, indifference, or hardness of heart. Christ's passion began at his birth. It continued throughout the whole of his earthly ministry, culminating in what we choose to call, in a limited sense, his passion, crucifixion and death.

It was that same passion that led him to be angry with the money changers, yet only after he had first wept over that city. The passion of Christ leads to the passion of the Christ-like and then to the sympathy and compassion of the God-like. "God so loved that he sent" (John 3:16). Of course he did, for love goes out of its way as surely as the Good Samaritan went out of his way and crossed the road to go where the casualty was. Love goes out of its way as surely as Christ crossed that same barrier in his Incarnation—the barrier of sin—to come to be where we are, to bind up our wounds, to pour in oil, to set us up again, and to bring us into one of those resting places (motels, hotels, pubs, or hospices) on the long and hazardous road back to the Father (John 14:2).

WORSHIP AND SERVICE

The challenge is surely this "Go and do likewise" (Luke 10:37). And here again we need to make the connection. Once we have made the connection in that visionlike moment ("when the penny drops") then for us, as for Isaiah in the Old Testament, there is only one prayer: "Lord, here am I. Send me" (Isa. 6:8). Mission comes straight from the heart of God himself, who has been going out of his way (displaced) since the dawn of time, sending his apostolic people on all kinds of crazy journeys to all corners of the earth to minister his love. In these last days, he has *sent* his Son and then his Spirit to represent and to make his Son present, to show the extent of that love and that passion and compassion in the Body of Christ, the Church of God.

So how far will you go with Jesus Christ, who went all the way from heaven to earth, to hell and back again, for love of you and me and all the world? For once you have seen the look of love on his face or heard the words of love from his lips (as Peter did), once you have been to Calvary Hill, there is no going back. Once you have heard him say to *you* that *your* sins (even yours) are forgiven, once you have seen the extent of his great love for you and his tears and his bloody sweat and agony (all very evangelistic language), you are then so grateful (eucharist) that you have to go and try to do for others what he has already done for you—in a word, mission and ministry. Mission and ministry flow from a passionate and thankful, loving heart—and therefore right out of the eucharist. Surely, we are now able to make that other connection summed up in the phrase, "When the worship is ended, the service begins."

Years ago, we used to speak of a passion for souls, but then it suddenly became unpopular and was accused of being paternalistic. It is not paternalistic if we see the source of such a passion. It is nothing less than the love of Jesus—which, according to St. Bernard, "none but his loved ones know."

"We love because he first loved us," says St. John, and he should know. He was at the foot of that cross, and he leant on the breast of Jesus at the moment of his betrayal in the upper room. All preaching, all sacraments are intended to be icons pointing us to the face of Jesus and trying to impress upon us by word, sign, and act the evangelical realities of the gospel—namely, that "Jesus loves me this I know because the Bible tells me so" (Karl Barth). Furthermore, the sacraments show me so, and his love has spoken, showed, and shared it so. Our worship must have about it that "abandonment" of the divine providence (de-Caussade). It must have that passion and that transcendence which alone can release us for God and for others. We need to be intoxicated and inebriated by it—nothing less.

You and I were made for worship, and as the psychologist in Peter Shaffer's play *Equus*, so rightly says it; "If you don't worship, you'll shrink. It's as brutal as that." Love grows cold, however, and hearts get smaller, and a world without saints (like Mother Teresa) "forgets how to praise" (as the hymn says so rightly). It also forgets the overplus of generosity, which always goes that second mile and gives the cloak as well as the coat also. The witness of mission and ministry must never degenerate into those hard-hearted words of mere duty of trying to help the unfortunate. Neither must it degenerate into a political ideology. There is a passion at the heart of real service as there is a passion at the heart of real worship. The two words (*worship* and *service*), of course, in Hebrew and in English happily have a common derivation. But there is only passion in both of these if first there is a passion in our prayer and adoration and only then if by the Holy Spirit we have made the gospel connection. The connection demands that the problems of society are overtaken by the promises of Christ and that the bad news in the newspaper is also connected with the good news of the gospel. In the words of Frederick Buechner, the two so often are to be found in a similar place: you find the good news all among the bad news. However, that is only possible with those who have first been blinded to the light of this world in order to be enlightened by the light of the world to come.

Yet the witness of passion and compassion must issue
in a prophetic as well as a pastoral concern for the needs
of the world, the poor, and the underprivileged. It is not
enough to be compassionate about poverty. We need, at
the same time, to engage in the struggle to remove unjust
poverty. There must be a righteous indignation that we
find in the passionate record of the Old Testament
prophets of the eighth century B.C.: the passion of Amos,
Hosea, and Isaiah. Lay witness will take away from the
altar of worship to the bench and the desk of workaday
life a new determination to make a difference in the world.
We shall not be content simply to dress the wounds but
rather to strive with every muscle to make a world in
which the causes of unjust poverty and undeserved
wounds are removed. So once again the Manila Manifesto
speaks with insight and prophecy when it affirms that
"the proclamation of God's Kingdom of justice and peace
demands the denunciation of all injustice and oppression,
both personal and structural" and that we must not
"shrink from this prophetic witness."

Yet all this flows out of our worship and the words of
our preaching, the sacraments and the Scriptures—for, in
both alike, we need to be "ravished" with the experience
of God's great love for us and for his world. Then,
inevitably, we shall be expelled from the cloisters of the
church for the witness of mission and ministry in the
countries of the world. Every parish church needs to look
again at its preaching, teaching and worship to see if it is
so transcendent that it lifts the church week by week into
the kingdom and so "gospels" the people of God that they
become an apostolic church—a church ready to be sent out
on those impossible errands to wherever and to whomso-
ever the love of God so appoints.

Soul of Christ, sanctify me;
Body of Christ, save me;
Blood of Christ, inebriate me;

Water from the side of Christ, wash me;
Passion of Christ, strengthen me;
O, good Jesu, hear me;
Within thy wounds, hide me;
Suffer me not to be separated from thee;
From the malicious enemy, defend me;
At the hour of my death, call me and bid me come to
  thee;
That with thy saints I may praise thee forever and
  ever.
Amen.

Notes

1. Alison Barfoot, "News," *Celebration*, newsletter of the Fisherfolk (May 1989).
2. Abraham, *Logic of Evangelism*, 34.
3. St. John Chrysostom, *Homily* 50, 3–4.

EIGHT

Parish Missions, Crusades, and the Evangelistic Event

"Mass evangelism has still some value, but it must be mass evangelism of the right kind" (Canon Brian Green).

PLURALISM AND PROSELYTISM

"When people proselytize," writes Martin Marty,

> they represent not just an impulse or an emotion but a world. Through their agency, one world advances and encroaches upon another. An embodiment of one world invites or urges others to become part of it, to see things in a new way, to be uprooted from old communities and contexts and to find new ones.[1]

Little wonder that aggressive evangelism is resented by so many people today, for it IS often seen as serving, to use the words of Gabriel Marcel, a "God of prey whose goal is to annex and enslave," imposing on any converts won by such a method, "a loathsome image of the God whose interpreter I say I am."[2]

In America in the eighties, powerfully aided by the television mass evangelists, we have to admit that evangelism has become a vast industry with big bucks and powerful personalities. Furthermore, in recent years all kinds of scandals have been uncovered in association with this industry. As a result, we should not be surprised that both the word *evangelism* and *evangelist* have become rather soiled words in the vocabulary of a society that would still like to see itself as open-minded, unhypocritical, "as good as those who go to church." The expectant single-mindedness and even the aggressiveness of evangelism do not sit well in an age which cherishes pluralism and the sacredness of every person's conscience. Or put more plainly in the words of Jimmy Durante, "Why doesn't everybody leave everybody else the hell alone?"

Episcopalians in particular, and Anglicans in general, have rather prided themselves on *not* harassing the beliefs and practices of others. As a tradition, Anglicanism has eschewed that very kind of enthusiasm which borders upon fanaticism—the kind of fanaticism that plunged Reformation Europe into so much strife and war and that produced so many martyrs on all sides. The unwritten constitution of Anglicanism places high on its mandate that high-sounding doctrine of reserve—the reserve in the communication of Christian knowledge. The Episcopal Church in the United States, in keeping with the written Constitution of the United States of America, would claim also to prize very highly toleration, while Anglican formulae are derived from a theological process that deliberately permits a wider base of diversity, even eulogizing differing and frequently contradictory theological views.

So much is this so that we might well ask whether the call for a Decade of Evangelism is not a little out of line with the spirit of Anglicanism. Surely evangelism, and certainly evangelistic crusades, are made of sterner stuff than we find in the fabric of Anglicanism. "Pushing the faith" does not sit too well with armchair Anglicans, we might say, who are on the whole happier with the environment of claret in the senior common room rather than the tent crusade mentality or the glittering, slick world of Crystal Cathedral television.

Certainly there is some ground to clear here at the beginning of a chapter that might appear on first sight to buy into the contemporary crusade industry as we begin to look at the place of evangelistic events in a Decade of Evangelism.

In the first place, *mass evangelism* is surely a misleading term, for at its best it does not strictly intend to project an appeal to the masses, since all preaching and proclamation are aimed at individuals. The gospel message makes an essentially personal appeal that is not the same as an individualistic appeal. There is no block voting or surge of the crowd, though in fairness it has to be said that the message to the individual is powerfully aided by the context and peculiar chemistry released in any large crowd. Crowds gather compound interest and people will do and say things in a crowd that they would reject in the cold light of dawn or in their early morning shower. The history of crowd hysteria is not a happy one and presumably would not be the best environment in which to make a serious proposal for marriage, sign a contract, or undertake some other weighty matter of lasting importance.

Nevertheless, Jesus addressed crowds in the name of the gospel. His apostles after Pentecost continued this pattern and undertook similar speaking engagements around Asia Minor and throughout the Roman Empire in the presence of large crowds. For the bald truth is that we do not live in a cold, rational, and open-minded society. The world in which the Word is made flesh is a jungle of well-orchestrated pressure groups and sales techniques, vying for space and time on the media, in the streets, and wherever men and women gather together. Jesus did not spend his life in a quiet place away from the warfare of words. The Word was preached on the same frequencies of the same channels as all the other religious, political, and ideological messages of his day. He and his apostles

were not ashamed to speak in the market place, on the
Acropolis, or, indeed, even at that same corner of the Lake
of Galilee that affords by nature such wonderful acoustical
amplification and where every competing demagogue had
spoken long before A.D. 30 and many times in the years
since. If the crowd is one human way of institutionalizing
communication, then incarnational Christianity will risk
all the possible perversions and distortions afforded by
such an environment in order to get the Word out.

The New Testament understanding of communication
is, in fact, a helpful correction to much of the individualism of the twentieth century and not least that individualism which has tended to take hold of renewal movements
in recent years. "In the New Testament," writes Tom Smail,

> the Spirit typically comes to groups of people together,
> not to individuals alone. Discussions of the so-called
> baptism in the Holy Spirit have often gone awry. They
> have not taken account of that corporate dimension that
> is so evident in the New Testament from Pentecost on;
> they have failed to see that the coming of the Spirit takes
> place when people are together, and that it results in
> new relationships with God and with fellow Christians,
> not as a remote consequence but as the heart and center
> of what the Spirit is doing.[3]

The crowd, the group or the congregation are very much
an integral part of the New Testament understanding of
Christian communication through Word and sacrament.
Indeed, the liturgy itself, which is a vehicle of communication for the gospel, of course always presupposes two or
three gathered together and is not a personal hotline of
spirituality or pietism. The gospel of Easter, it is true, is
directed firmly to individuals in their encounter with the
risen Christ. The gospel of Pentecost, however, speaks
much more directly to the corporate body and, indeed, is
intended to forge and to make the new community. In
both cases it is the same Word that we need to get out, but

the Word is somewhat addressed on a different channel between the Word of the risen Christ and the Word empowered by the Holy Spirit to form the Body of Christ— the Church. In any event, there should be a certain sense of urgency for Christians as there has always been since Pentecost to get the Word out, almost at all costs. For that is the goal. Evangelism is an end in itself and does not become evangelism when the crowd has heard it, received it, or refuted it. Ideally, we are not in the manipulation business. We are, however, most certainly in the communication business, and we must never forget it: anything, so long as we get the Word out, whether they will hear or whether they will forbear.

There is a danger, therefore, in settling on the wrong definition of evangelism. A right definition of evangelism could well rescue us from just the kind of proselytism of which Martin Marty is so critical. Several definitions of evangelism have been promulgated over the years, and they are seriously inadequate and distorted in this way. For example: "Evangelism means the conversion of people from worldliness to Christ-like godliness." Archbishop William Temple spoke of evangelism as "the winning of men to acknowledge Christ as their Savior and King, so that they may give themselves to the service of the fellowship of his church." In 1954, the Evanston Assembly defined evangelism as "the bringing of persons to Christ as Savior and Lord that they may share in his eternal life." The Committee of Enquiry into Evangelistic Work in the church set up by the Archbishops of Canterbury and York defined evangelism as "so to present Christ Jesus in the power of the Holy Spirit that men shall come to put their trust in God through him." If we are caught in this rather loose verbiage from the outset, then we shall certainly be in danger of confusing evangelism with sales techniques, and it will not be long before we are massaging the message and working the crowd. Rather, as John Stott so rightly emphasizes, "Evangelism is neither to convert people nor to win them, nor to bring them to Christ, though this is indeed the first goal of evangelism. Evangelism is to preach the gospel."[4]

When Jesus came into Galilee preaching the gospel, he went where the crowds were to be found. The preacher of the gospel or the evangelist has one overriding concern— to get that Word out, loud and clear. Therefore, he or she is essentially in the business of communication and acoustics. And in communicating, he or she will have an eye and an ear to implement the best means of communication, primarily visual and auditory. He or she will not believe that the end justifies the means and therefore be content to use any means (manipulation or crass emotionalism) in order to win people to Christ. Integrity in his or her calling and vocation as an evangelist will result in something much more subtle than success in numbers and converts. Rather, the evangelist is concerned to preach the gospel of Jesus Christ with integrity, accuracy, and clarity. So St. Paul can say on behalf of all Christian preachers, "Woe to me if I do not preach the gospel!" (1 Cor. 9:16). Notice, that he does not say, "Woe to me if the number of converts this year is not as high as the number of converts last year!"

Yet one further point needs to be made for justification of the evangelistic event and the work of evangelists. There is about Christianity, by its very nature, something necessarily exclusive and apparently arrogant. After all, if Christianity is true, then at least two (unpalatable) truths follow from that statement. First, that all other speculation, reflection, and theological insight from our side of things have been overtaken by a unique initiative and intervention from God's side. However much we may like to probe into the nature of God, Christianity claims that God has stolen our thunder, and therefore the thunder of all serious religions, in the personal revelation of himself in his Son, Jesus Christ. Furthermore—and this is a very difficult matter to come to terms with—when he showed us what he was like, we did not like it! The leading religious men of the day, in fact, got the surprise of their lives. The wise men went to the wrong address (however logical their deductions had been in the first place), and most religious contemporaries of Jesus, far from recognizing him as the Christ, profoundly believed that he was the very opposite—the Antichrist.

So at the dawn of Christianity, the light of day revealed two surprising truths and speculations. Humanmade religion expressing itself through speculation, must give way to a God-given faith expressed through revelation. "The theological faculties" were not well pleased by the intervention of revelation: Such a faith founded on the kind of assurance that only revelation can legitimately foster did not sit well with the doctors of the law. For there is necessarily something of "take it or leave it" about the Christian religion. Put another way, it is not tailored to suit but is rather "straight off the rack" and may not fit very comfortably the vogues and fashions of a particular age. "We affirm," says the Manila Manifesto, "that other religions and ideologies are not alternative paths to God, and that human spirituality, if unredeemed by Christ, leads not to God but to judgement, for Christ is the only Way." Hard words, yet that is what the persecuted Christian martyrs of the first three hundred years profoundly believed, and it was a costly creed for which they paid with nothing less than their lives.

Furthermore, however valid and profound other religions may be, Christianity by its very nature cannot enter the Pantheon arm-in-arm with all the other gods, goddesses, and world religions. The title of Martin Marty's book, *Pushing the Faith: Proselytism and Civility in a Pluralistic World,* already itself begs the question. The implication of that title and subtitle is, I suspect, that civility and a

pluralistic society find something unacceptable about
proselytism, if by that you mean "pushing the faith."

Yet the early apostolic Church lived in precisely such a
pluralistic world—in fact, in a world so similar to our own
that the parallels are at times rather alarming. The Roman
Empire had a very enlightened and open-minded attitude
toward world religions and positively encouraged a
pluralistic, religious worldview. So civilized, indeed was
Rome that it would happily have accepted Christianity in
general and Jesus in particular into the "old boys club" of
the Pantheon. The Roman Empire encouraged this kind of
pluralism in such matters of conscience, so long as no one
religion claimed to be the top dog. It was precisely
because the early Christians insisted (not through their
own prejudices but by the very credentials of their faith)
upon the lordship of Christ and the uniqueness of Christ
in a monotheistic religion that they could not put Jesus up
for election into the Pantheon—that most civilized temple
of the ancient world.

Furthermore, it was not only their exclusive claim that
plunged the early Christians into the troubles of martyrdom. It was their obvious and blatant enthusiasm for what
they had come to know and experience in a white-hot
faith that made their martyrdom inevitable. So for three
hundred years or so, at the cost of millions of lives, Christianity persisted with proselytism, evangelism, witnessing,
and all those other nasty, "narrow-minded" twentieth-
century anathemas. There was and there still is something
about the springtime of Christian faith that demands that
we share it, we talk about it, we sing about it, dragging it
(like a new lover) into our every conversation and coloring
everything that we do with it. Alongside other faiths that
do not need to be quite so single-minded, Christianity
does indeed come across as rather "uncivilized."

I am sure that John Wesley would have been regarded
as somewhat "uncivilized" in the presence of an eigh-

teenth-century latitudinarian, Anglican bishop, crisp and fresh in his lawn sleeves after a very civilized dinner at the House of Lords in Parliament. A latitudinarian bishop had become a bishop first and foremost precisely because he had never been so vulgar as to express any enthusiasm (in either the eighteenth-century meaning of that word or in its contemporary meaning) about his faith in Jesus Christ. Surely, a Christian can be forgiven for enthusiastic rhetoric if he or she believes that the real situation is more akin to a battlefield than a senior common room and then goes on to borrow a little of the princely vocabulary of Henry V exhorting the troops at Agincourt rather than the newly appointed professor of Middle English giving his inaugural lecture. Battles are for winning; lectures are merely presented.

In all this, the reader will realize perhaps by now that the author believes on balance that mass evangelism, evangelistic crusades, and parish missions still have a real and valid place in the overall evangelistic strategy of the Church even today and even in America or in England. I also happen to believe, of course (and, hopefully, it goes without saying), that there are good and bad evangelists and good and bad methods of mass evangelism. Yet I also believe that Paul spoke for our day as well as for his own and for preachers today, as in his own day, when he said those words already quoted: "Woe to me if I do not preach the gospel." Our task is, therefore, not to walk away from bad mass evangelism but rather to seek that which makes for good mass evangelism and how we might the better include it in the overall work of the Church in a Decade of Evangelism. We need to know what good evangelism is, but we also need to know what good evangelism is not.

THE PARISH MISSION

Let it be said from the outset that this book does not purport to be in any way an adequate manual for those who are in the work of the kind of mass evangelism that involves crowds of thousands or that broadcasts to millions. The author has neither the experience nor the backing to undertake that kind of crusade. The Episcopal Church has several notable and fine evangelists who have developed their techniques over the years and who necessarily work through their teams in towns and cities where such evangelistic campaigns are to take place. They provide from their wide experience all the necessary training for such events.

This book is addressed rather to something much more local and much smaller in scale. It is addressed primarily to parishes and congregations in the Decade of Evangelism that wish to mount some evangelistic event in a parish or in a group of parishes as part of the regular round of missions in the life of the congregations in their vicinity. For I am convinced, after several years conducting missions in many parishes throughout the United States and elsewhere, that there is no substitute for the parish mission from time to time, if a parish is to remain healthy and vibrant.

"We are convinced," said the report *Towards the Conversion of England* in 1919,

> that the day of parochial missions is by no means over. The very fact that a parish is prepared to make great efforts to reach the outsider is itself a valuable witness to the conviction that the church has a gospel to proclaim. Even if the outsiders who attend are few in number, the effort to reach them has a most bracing effect upon the congregation. Those who have worked and prayed for the mission will at least have learned to understand their evangelistic responsibilities as members of the Body of Christ.

Canon Brian Green's commentary upon this is helpful. "Mass evangelism, then," he comments, has still some value, but it must be mass evangelism of the right kind. There is no place today for superficial mission work or over-emotional evangelistic campaigns; they can do more harm than good, for people are skeptical enough about the Christian church and its effectiveness. Missions which "flop" or are over-sentimental merely increase cynicism.[5]

In one sense, a parish mission does not say or do any more than is already being done in a living and lively parish week by week. Properly undertaken, the observance of Holy Week, for example, when the preaching is in tandem with the liturgy and when both are showing forth the death and resurrection of Jesus, can be the heart of the church's year and can be a powerful week of mission. Furthermore, because of its climax on Easter Day and with the preceding Easter Vigil, it leads happily and markedly into the making of new Christians at confirmation and baptism on Easter Eve and the reaffirmation of baptismal vows by all of God's people on that same occasion. Such a Holy Week is essentially a week of renewal in the Spirit of Jesus and the resurrection.

Similarly, I believe that the visit of the bishop to a parish—especially for baptism and confirmation—can be a truly evangelistic event. After all, on such occasions there is a large percentage of nonchurchgoers in church— probably more than at almost any other time. The bishop who has an evangelistic fire in his belly has a great opportunity to commend the gospel to the lapsed and to the nonchurchgoer on such occasions.

The bishop can "play the game" of apparently preaching to the confirmation candidates while only inviting the congregation to listen in. Like preaching to children, it can often be the best way of getting something across to the parents. So apparently talking to the new Christians can often be a good way of digging deep into the hearts and lives of lapsed Christians who need to hear the call to

renewal. A confirmation service is a particular opportunity for the bishop to witness and even to relate his own
faith-story or to invite one of the adult confirmation
candidates to tell his or her story and to witness to a new-
found faith in Christ.

Weddings and funerals are a glorious opportunity to
preach the gospel, and again such preaching is often in the
presence of a congregation largely composed of nonchurchgoers.

One of the greatest opportunities for evangelistic
preaching is, of course, an ordination. Here again many of
those present are reluctant hearers who seldom find
themselves in church. The occasion is necessarily charged
with some emotion, and the liturgy is making all the right
noises about commitment, surrender, service, and the
power of the Holy Spirit to take on frail human lives and
enrich and empower them with divine grace. I was once
at a huge ordination at St. Paul's Cathedral, London. Certainly, not less than two thousand people were present. A
bishop, who shall be nameless, mounted the pulpit wearing his mitre. He looked smug and very pleased with
himself indeed. He then proceeded to speak for well over
twenty minutes about "ministerial priesthood" (as he
insisted upon calling it). He spoke endlessly about the
church, the office of the priest, and every other theological
abstraction to the total bewilderment of most of the people
present in the cathedral. Within three minutes he had lost
the congregation! He had thrown away a glorious
opportunity to preach the gospel to the crowds, for he had
substituted a somewhat indifferent talk about the institutional church for a sermon of proclamation about Jesus
and the gospel. He had allowed the institutional church to
displace the challenge of the gospel.

All this serves only to endorse the original point. In
one sense, the parish mission does nothing more than
should already be done week in and week out in all our

parishes and most especially when the apostle and the bishop—the prime minister of baptism—visits the parish or his cathedral.

This still leaves, however, a real place for the outside evangelist and the anointed teacher to come into a parish, a group of parishes, or a diocese to conduct an annual mission. "Mass evangelism," says Canon Brian Green, "must be undertaken at the right time and in the right place when there is the movement of the Holy Spirit. The preaching of the gospel must be clear and thorough, the appeal decisive and the follow-up work after the campaign carefully planned."[6] Where and when all these requirements are in place, the parish mission raises the life of the whole parish by at least one more notch, and the spin-off of that can have ramifications that continue in the life of the parish for many months and even years to come. As on Easter Eve, renewal of the existing Christians and the calling out of new Christians occur together and in the same location. This is not surprising—the vocation and the challenge are the same. New Christians encourage the old Christians in renewal, and renewed Christians generally pick up some new Christians by the process of what we call nowadays osmosis! But it is not a task at any time or in any place to be undertaken "unadvisedly, lightly, or wantonly" or because it is somebody's bright idea.

First, the lay leaders of a parish together with the clergy need to sit down and, with prayer and study, discern the need for such a mission. In the Episcopal Church in America, I only undertake a mission in a parish nowadays where the vestry has voted 100 percent, with no abstentions, in favor of a mission. Some years ago, I found that I was going to parishes where the renewal group (if not the renewal faction) on the vestry had presssed and pressed for a mission. The rector had finally consented in order to keep the renewal group (or the evangelistic committee) happy. In such places and on such occasions, I

used to find that the church wardens, for example, did not
show up during the week of mission until the Sunday
morning when they were "on duty"! Furthermore the
director of music would have deputed his or her assistant
to play each night of the mission and only turn up on the
final Sunday, together with the choir to do their own
thing, while being conspicuous by their absence throughout the whole week.

The Decade for Evangelism will degenerate into somebody's bright idea unless the whole church, beginning
with the bishops, is first won over to be committed to it with
time, money, energy, resources, and, above all, with prayer.

PREPARING FOR MISSION

So the first task in a parish that is looking to evangelism
and for a mission or crusade is to raise the expectation of
every parishioner by prayer and Bible study. One year
ahead of time, a small card (the size of a credit card)
should be produced in the thousands. On one side, the
dates of the mission and the small emblem of the mission
are printed. On the other side is the mission prayer. Here
is an example of the kind of prayer that can be used and
that the Anglican Institute has sent ahead to all parishes
where we are to hold a mission. It is essentially a prayer
of expectation and renewal:

> HEAVENLY FATHER, pour down your Holy Spirit
> upon this Parish (Diocese, Crusade), and grant us a new
> vision of your Glory, a new experience of your power, a
> new faithfulness to your Word, a new consecration to
> your service, so that, through our renewed witness,
> your Holy Name may be glorified and your Kingdom
> advanced; through Jesus Christ our Lord. Amen.

That prayer, which I wrote in 1971 for a mission at All
Saints–Margaret Street, London, is as important for what it
does not say as for what it says.

On a suitable Sunday morning, at a special service, the congregation is asked to commit itself lock, stock, and barrel, corporately to the forthcoming mission and to say the mission prayer for the next year as part of their personal daily prayer. They are given their prayer cards on their way back from receiving communion, and they are invited to put the dates on the family calendar and on their private calendars as soon as they return home.

The Bible study should be a four- or six-week course, either in Lent, Advent, or, better still, on the great fifty days after Eastertide. This Bible study is deliberately aimed at raising the expectations for evangelism throughout the whole congregation.

Financial preparation is also a sacrament of intention and commitment. Some parishes should be encouraged to give out, along with the prayer card, personal collecting tubes or boxes with the phrase "A dime a day!" printed on it. For one whole year leading up to the mission, every member of the parish is asked to put away a dime a day to give God his way! "A dime a day to help us to pray and each day to say THIS PRAYER" is not a bad mandate for mission. For a mission to have no financial problems—and it will not have, if it is undertaken with prayer, fasting, commitment, and giving—means that it can be blessed and anointed in wonderful ways. The whole enterprise needs to be prayed for and paid for before it ever begins if it is to receive the blessing of God. It is not for nothing that, traditionally, the bishop does not consecrate and bless a church building until it is all paid for. We need to have a similar theology for building the Church in the spiritual sense—the Body of Christ.

LOCATION

Where should the mission be held? If the mission is primarily aimed at existing parishioners and their friends, there is a lot to be said for holding it in the parish church. After all, the territory is familiar and everything you need is there on hand. Furthermore, to hold the mission in the parish church can help to put the church building on the map—with banners; possibly with flood-lights outside the church building; with the ringing of the bells—and all this aided by the publicity of the local press or television. Such a mission is often the best kind, especially in the early days of the life of the church or after a new building extension or early on in the pastorate of a new rector. Hopefully, it will gear up everyone, from the ushers to those who do the coffee hour, to a new sense of welcoming hospitality, openness, and expectation of new members and strangers. Furthermore, it will help them to do the job they always do every Sunday but will now do that little bit better and see how their ministry relates to the outreach of the church. Likewise, the follow-up can be focused on the address of the local church more easily, and all this helps the local community to regard their church and its building as the focus of their community life.

However, if more than one parish is involved or if other denominations are really being asked to throw in their weight and commitment and, furthermore, if there is a real expectation that total outsiders will be coming along to the mission; then in all these cases neutral territory is to be preferred above all else. A neutral building reduces the number of denominational signs, symbols, flags, and obstacles, and it is possibly easier for people to come along and remain "anonymous" in such a location, if that should be their wish. It is possibly easier for committed Christians to invite their friends to come with them and to break through the congregational mentality that is so strong in Episcopal churches. Yet there is one further advantage that I believe is important.

Nearly all church buildings have restrictions imposed by the very nature of the floor plan. A good theater, with good seating, professional sound equipment, theatrical lighting and a stage—all these are assets. A larger stage for a larger choir is infinitely preferable to a cramped chancel. Then again it has to be said that the organ is a dubious and hazardous instrument for mass singing—far better a grand piano, timps and trumpets, and, of course, an organ as well, which is always a better instrument for accompanying when it is part of a larger ensemble. The organ is not a percussive instrument in quite the same way that a piano is and, therefore, is not so helpful in leading congregational singing.

However, it is important to check from the outset the acoustics of the theater or a large public building. Too much heavy carpeting or drapery can make a theater or auditorium almost impossible for good congregational singing. The acoustics need to be warm and alive. Sometimes a suitable public building is located with such wonderful centrality to the whole community that an event in it cannot avoid being seen and known by everyone in that community.

That is the aim of the publicity. We should not be content with anything less than maximum saturation, which is that point when it is impossible to live in the locality or in the area and not know that there is going to be an evangelistic crusade or some event of that kind in the church. And by hook or by crook it should be impossible to be a resident in X and not know that there is to be a mission at X's and furthermore that this mission is for *everyone.***

**It is not a bad thing to conduct a survey on the Saturday immediately before the mission in the main shopping area of the town. It will do two things. First, it will tell the planners of the mission whether the publicity has done its job effectively or not. Did everyone who was approached know that a mission was going to take place in their town? Second, it will give ordinary parishioners a last opportunity to hand out further and final notices about the mission and, in so doing, give the opportunity to witness.

The press, banners, a public procession the week before, opinion polls on the streets the Saturday before, or even the local priest standing with the Salvation Army band on a soap box the week before at the shopping mall —everything should be used to publicize the event before it begins.

VISITING BEFOREHAND

A parish mission provides a wonderful opportunity for a full-scale parish visitation. The Billy Graham organization has what it calls the Andrew program. We do well to learn much from their many years of experience. Such a program gives parish visitors from the congregation easy opportunity to go out and talk about the gospel. Episcopalians find themselves talking about Jesus Christ, and that is something worthwhile in itself.

For this exercise, group visitors should be well prepared and well trained. They should go out in pairs and should have the simplest of information sheets about the church, the mission, and the gospel in a few sentences on that handout.

The visitors' task is simply to say that they are from the local Episcopal church, which is to hold a mission. The visitors can then ask the religious affiliation of the household. If the household is a practicing family of another denomination it would still be appropriate for the visitor to give them a prayer card and to ask for their prayers for the mission and for them to consider coming along to one of the evenings and bringing friends. If household members are not churchgoers of any kind, they should be asked whether there and then, or at some other prearranged time, they would like the visitors to come back and tell them about the Christian faith and the part that it could play in their lives. (All this requires careful training and preparation for the parish visitor.)

Recruiting for fringers, lapsed, or nonchurchgoers to go to the mission requires a *two-step decision*. Generally speaking, invitations to attend a parish mission are initially well received. People are polite and well meaning to the parish visitors and probably intend, at the time of the invitation, in all good conscience to attend at least one night of the mission. Sadly, experience proves that almost 90 percent of these well-intentioned people fail to make it at the last minute. They do not show up: the visitors are disappointed, and the numbers attending the mission are sadly below expectations.

It is hard for a regular churchgoer to realize just how alien the territory and the environment of the church are to those who never darken the doors of a church building. Talking about the mission in the warmth of their own homes or over the telephone, they genuinely intend to give it a try and to go to the mission—albeit on one night. Come that night, they shy away, and they do not need many excuses before they are persuaded that it would be better, in fact, not to go along after all.

The truth is that we need to meet such people halfway. The parish can nominate fifty hosts or so each evening. They will give a simple supper party and issue written invitations to that party to half a dozen or so others. Then the whole group will go on together to the mission service. This is, therefore, a two-step decision. The first step is an easy and conventional commitment, leading quite freely into the second commitment, namely, to go to the mission.

Alternatively, the parish itself can host in the parish house each evening a stand-up buffet supper for a hundred or so people. Parishioners can nominate friends, fringers they know, or others they have wanted to invite to the mission to receive invitations to the supper. When the supper is concluded, all will go off to the service next door. It goes without saying that a crèche should be a part of the services offered every evening of the mission, and that one night should be given over to young people exclusively. There will be a special promotion program deliberately designed for that night of the mission to meet them halfway in a similar two-step commitment.

Visitors and welcomers need to go to a special training course, as indeed do the counselors who will match, person-for-person, everyone who comes forward at the end of the mission or each night there is to be an altar call. Sensitivity and awareness are, of course, all necessary. Furthermore, it is important to have one or two obviously weighty men around who could deal kindly yet firmly with any disturbance during the course of the service. We live in an age of great emotional and mental disturbance. We should not be surprised or alarmed, therefore, if—when we are raising the flag of Christ, caring and compassion, and many other highly charged concepts—many disturbed people are attracted and are further disturbed in an environment of this kind. Everyone from the clergy to prayer-partners and ushers needs to be well trained at the outset and to have high expectations that God will be alive and active throughout the mission: things are going to happen; lives will be touched. This preparation is best done by Bible study, prayer, and discussion groups with ample lead time, several weeks before the mission ever begins.

INEVITABLY ECUMENICAL

Evangelism is inevitably ecumenical. For all Christians who recite the creeds, evangelism must be ecumenical. There is no sharp gospel presentation of twenty or thirty minutes that can possibly retreat into denominationalism. Here on the frontiers of faith where the battle is fierce, there is no room for an ecumenism, however, of reductionism; the editing out of any phrase or words that might offend! The evangelist needs to be free to preach Christ out of the crucible of his or her own tradition, knowing that only such a message anointed by the Holy Spirit will have teeth. Neither is there much room in the evangelistic message (nor, indeed, time) to play the Anglican see-saw game: "On the one hand . . . on the other; some people say this, some say that." People want to ask, "But what do *you* think?" So the evangelist who has been brought to his vocation from a particular tradition inevitably speaks from within that tradition. Yet the overriding point is that such a deep-cutting and far reaching message will, in practice, inevitably be ecumenical. What do we mean by this?

In the first place, if the mission is supported by more than one tradition, the counseling and follow-up can insure that newly committed Christians, in the words of Billy Graham, commit themselves to go "to the church of which you tell yourself you are a member!"

Furthermore, the music, the songs, the hymns, and the style of mission service are all in the best sense interdenominational. Roman Catholics, Anglicans, Methodists, and Baptists have an almost-agreed syllabus of renewal music these days. Furthermore, the prayers of the service and the Bible readings can all be done (and, indeed, should all be done) by different colored traditions. All this can help the outsider and inquirer to know that evangelism is not the peculiar property of strange, rather special evangelistic-type Christians. It is especially important that the local bishop should own the campaign and be present on the platform to give the opening prayer or final benediction. Encourage the local Roman Catholic bishop (in full regalia if necessary!) to sit on the platform next to a member of the Salvation Army, who is also in uniform. Each evening have a special guest of honor (lay or ordained) who is obviously a representative of a particular denomination yet who is also present because he or she is truly committed to the Christian faith and to Jesus Christ. A well-known TV personality, newspaper editor, headmaster, mayor, or sheriff who is a committed Christian should always be made welcome and given the opportunity either to read the lessons, lead some prayers, or say a few words of direct witness. Such witness can be most reassuring to timid inquirers. This part of the service, however, should be rather "matter-of-fact," sewn together with traditional prayers, and well-known hymns, all of which are calculated to put the inquirers at their ease. Most of the service should take all those present down the memory lane of traditional, basic, and well-trodden churchgoing. Evangelistic crusades are not the place to be sophisticated, slick, or eccentric. For example, it is not the place to put on a liturgical dance or to have a group that does liturgical miming. The catholic faith in Jesus Christ is for everybody. At its richest (and at its most evangelistically effective), it is inevitably ecumenical without self-consciously setting out to be ecumenical—harmless and nonchallenging, on the one hand, or "with it," sophisticated, and contemporary, on the other.

But all missions and evangelistic events need to be ecumenical in a further sense than this. The practiced evangelist will know how to use a vocabulary that draws on the riches of all the traditions. There is no reason to be afraid to refer to the Mass or the eucharist or to the Blessed Virgin Mary, on the one hand, while being equally happy with the vocabulary of conversion, the love of Jesus, the power of the Holy Spirit, and personal commitment, on the other hand. The gospel that is presented needs to be both broad and deep and needs to draw on all those ingredients in all the traditions we can affirm. After all, no one is interested in what you are against: they want to know what you are for. The way forward, indeed, in ecumenism generally is to be free to say what we can affirm in each other's traditions and to leave unsaid those things to which we are opposed. A colorful, deep, broad, and rich gospel presentation will inevitably therefore be ecumenical.

LET'S GO!

Hymn sheets and the order of events in program form are all available for every person who might conceivably come to the mission. Everything is in place and expectant. Doors are open, and greeters are at the ready no less than forty-five minutes before the service is due to begin.

What is the shape of the service? Episcopalians should be certain from the outset that neither the eucharist nor evening prayer nor evensong form a suitable liturgical context for an evangelistic presentation. All our ecclesiastical "empires" must yield under the one flag—the lordship of Christ—for the sake of these evangelistic events. Musicians, acolytes, and clergy (in England, also bell ringers), to say nothing of those flower arrangers and sacristans, all constitute empires, I fear, in the church! A visit of the local bishop for a large service so often affords a field day for such groups and their leaders. The musicians have to perform some long and indifferently rendered anthem. Flower arrangers somehow have to be busy until the last moment "on stage" agonizing over the flowers and inevitably drawing attention to themselves. All are snatching at self-glorification, so much so that the icon of the gathered Church, far from pointing beyond itself to the glory of God and the lordship of Christ, just gets in the way, blatantly inviting idolatry or irritation. For the truth is that we all need to lay down our arms at the feet of Christ, so that the message of the gospel, anointed by the Holy Spirit, can be given free rein. "Jesus is Lord," the banners should read, and that should set the tone of the evening from first to last.

The organist and the choir should be allowed up front if—and only if—they are willing to throw their weight and their gifts behind the campaign for Christ. If so, then they need to rehearse—organist and choir alike—the hymns and the songs, so that all the musical parts of the service can be done with musical excellence and with sensitivity. Everything from first to last, must be seen as part of the over-arching ministry of making Jesus Christ known *through* the music, *through* the liturgy, *through* the worship, and *through* the Word. In other words, everything and everybody are intended to be icons pointing beyond themselves and never seeking to draw attention to themselves.

For the music is the bicycle of the liturgy and is crucial and essential in evangelistic services.

Before the formal service begins, there should be the warm-up of congregational singing. Not all the hymns should be drawn from what is loosely called renewal music. Start with the familiar, the known, the safe, and the solid. The master of ceremonies or the evangelist himself needs to be out front to teach people the hymns and songs that are, of course, rehearsed while the congregation is still arriving. All this should be done with the congregation seated.

Humor, even a little light-heartedness at this point, helps to reassure the tentative and the apprehensive. If this part of the event is conducted by the evangelist, he can come across as human and as a real person. The decibels rise as the congregation grows in confidence and as they learn first a bit of this hymn and then a bit of that. Then there is the need to risk quiet singing, reflective singing, and to rehearse the congregation in the songs of the heart that will be used at the crucial point in the service.

THE SHAPE OF AN EVANGELISTIC SERVICE

There must be in every evangelistic service a crucial point—a point when the congregation is invited to yield to the promptings of the Holy Spirit and to move into prayer or even to move forward physically, seeking to draw nearer in mind, heart, and will to the Lord, who is present through the faithful preaching of his Word.

So the service is not just a hymn sandwich. It is a liturgy of the Word with its own *epiclesis* and *anaphora* where the Holy Spirit is called down and when Jesus is lifted up and, subsequently, when people are invited to move over into the kingdom of his love and righteousness by coming forward for the altar call.

The following is an order of service the author has used, tried, and tested over many years and over the course of several hundred missions:

Warm up
Silence and waiting
Opening sentence
Congregation stands
Hymn (well-known Episcopal four-square hymn)
Collect for Purity
Kyries or simple meditative round
Collect of the Mission
Congregation sits
Announcements, greetings, reading of telegrams, local
     celebrity
Congregation stands
Hymn (collection either here or later)
Congregation sits
Scripture reading
Congregation stands
Hymn
Congregation sits
Address
Congregation kneels
Prayer, singing of the heart, time of reflection and
     decision
[Altar call]
Congregation stands
Hymn (collection, if not already taken as above)
Blessing

Such an order of service has shape; invites worship, transcendence, and decision; gives ample time for preaching and exposition (under twenty-five minutes—Billy Graham, in fact, preaches only for eighteen minutes); and is all completed well within one hour. An evangelistic service must not last longer than one hour. It requires, of course, particular skill and long experience to achieve the goals of an evangelistic event in such trim timing. Most of us with less experience than Billy Graham probably need nearly twenty-five minutes for the preaching but should be discouraged from going over thirty minutes on any occasion.

The opening sentence can be a phrase from the passage of the Scripture that is to be read and should evoke the same kind of response as the opening introit sentence of the eucharistic liturgy. Said after the silence while people are still sitting, it can be poignant and powerful.

All then stand for the singing of the opening hymn. Please note that neither hymns nor rubrics are announced, as everything is clearly evident on the printed order of service in everybody's hand. Either the preacher or master of ceremonies lifts his or her arms as the organist comes straight in after the opening sentence with the playover of the hymn, and it is very obvious that, as the choir stands punctually on the opening chord given by the organ, everyone else is drawn to their feet. (Announcing hymns and long playovers by organists constitute hiccups and a break in the flow of worship.) After the hymn, while all are standing, the familiar Collect for Purity is said slowly and prayerfully. The Kyries should probably be of the simple folk-song-type setting—possibly unaccompanied—and should be sung very prayerfully, led by the master of ceremonies or evangelist. The point is that such a spiritual song or Kyrie should be an invocation. We are seeking to call down the grace and comfort of the Holy Spirit to anoint this whole gathering. In any event, this song must be sung very simply. If it is rendered by the choir, it needs also to be simply and well done and must flow immediately out of the Collect for Purity. It is not an occasion, however, for Mozart in F or Schubert in G! There are some wonderful and prayerful folk-song hymns that can be learned in all of three or four minutes and that can become the haunting songs and melodies of the mission. The one who teaches the songs in the warm-up should encourage the congregation to expect to find themselves singing these little themes in their cars, at work, or in the bathroom within the next few days of the mission—it really can and really does happen that way.

Still standing, the Collect for the Mission is said, and, subsequently, all sit down.

We've broken in and made a start—we've had the hors d'oeuvre, if you like to mix the metaphor at this point. People should by now be feeling comfortable, relaxed, even pleased to be present and ready and expectant. This is the time for introductions, notices, personalities, etc., and even for a song by a soloist, if such is available. It is also a time, if necessary, for introducing a personality onto the platform for a little personal witness or dialogue with the master of ceremonies or the evangelist. In other words, this first part of the service is largely didactic and informative. Hopefully, it puts everyone present, in the best sense, at their ease. The time has now come to move over into the scripture reading and teaching—the formal liturgy of the Word making its gospel presentation and gospel appeal. In theological terms, this part of the service is the *evangel* or the *kerygma*.

So the service must pick up again. Everyone is brought to their feet for another hymn. After the hymn or a spiritual song all sit for the reading of the passage from the scriptures that will be expounded in the sermon. This must be read *well*. It must be read in such a way that people can hear it and *receive* it. It does not need an introduction or an explanation that will trivialize it. Let the Word of God speak for itself at this point and "stand up" so that the evangelist will easily be able to pick it up later in the service for the theme of his main presentation. A brief sermon hymn follows the reading. This whole first part of the service should not take more than twenty-five minutes at the very most.

The sermon is then given. The sermon should assume zero knowledge of the Scriptures and zero knowledge of the Church, its habits, or its language. Basically, it is a biblical exposition of the Bible passage just read. However, the point of the sermon and the preaching, to use the phrase of Dr. Frank Buchman, is the "personalizing of the audience." Zacchaeus, Bartimaeus, Mary of Magdala, Thomas in the upper room—all become *my* story and what is happening to the biblical characters in the accounts as expounded from Scripture is in a sense being impressed upon me. It relates to and resonates with the story that is in my heart. On most occasions, the passage of Scripture is more powerful in its appeal if it is taken from the Gospels rather than from the Epistles. Such a passage is even better still if it is a narrative portion of Scripture, painting a picture and telling a story. Didactic passages or discourses from the Gospels (and certainly from the Epistles) are generally not so effective. (Of course, this is not an absolute rule, but it is often a helpful suggestion, derived from some years of evangelistic experience.)

As the sermon comes to an end, hopefully it comes to a point. That point is to invite the congregation to kneel or sit in silence and to do their business with God. As Peter invites Jesus into his boat; as Zacchaeus invites Jesus into his home and "receives him joyfully"; as Thomas is invited to reach out and touch the wounds of love and so recommit himself in faith and trust; so NOW we are all invited individually to do just that. So "let us kneel or sit for a time of prayer, reflection, and silence," says the preacher. "This is the time when each one of us has an agenda of the heart with God who is present with us now in the person of Jesus." The preacher can then go on and repeat quietly into the microphone one or two key phrases out of the passage of Scripture from his sermon: "Lord, I believe. Help thou my unbelief." "Lord, that I may receive my sight." "Lord, if thou wilt, thou canst make me clean." "O come to my heart, Lord Jesus, make room in my heart for thee." The whole theme at this point is to invite Jesus into our lives (either for the first time or afresh), to reach out and "take hold of him who first took hold of you."

If there is to be an opportunity for people to come forward to make a commitment to Christ, this is the time to do it. Do not break the action, the silence, or the sense of expectation. As music begins to play quietly, the preacher issues the invitation to come forward and to stand at the altar or at the altar rail. A very simple explanation of why physical movement is necessary is not out of place at this point. "If you felt the Lord touching your life tonight or have felt in any way moved to recommit your life to him as the disciples did in the New Testament, you may like to use this occasion to leave your seat now, as Peter left his nets or Matthew his receipt of custom table, and come forward and stand near the altar of God. You may need sacramentally, that is to say, outward and visibly, to move forward and, as an outward sign of the inward movement of God's spirit in your life, to leave your seat and to come forward to the altar."

As people begin to come forward, counselors should also come forward, matching each and every one who responds to the altar call with a counselor. The counselors should all be sitting together and should be released to go forward so that they, too, end up standing by the altar, near those who have been so moved to respond to the altar call.

Furthermore, as they come forward, the choir can sing

(preferably with everybody still kneeling) with sympathetic organ accompaniment some suitable spiritual hymn or song. "I Want to Walk as a Child of the Light" or "Just as I Am, Without One Plea."

If there is no altar call or invitation to come forward, then it is necessary to mark this moment for those present in some sense and in some sacramental way. Still kneeling, they can sing a hymn such as "I Want to Walk as a Child of the Light," while the preacher can go through the congregation sprinkling everyone with baptismal water. On the last night of a mission, all can be invited at this point to reaffirm their baptismal vows, to be sprinkled with the water of their baptism, and so to make a new start. There and then people who feel so moved can even be encouraged to come forward to be baptized in this water if they have not already been baptized before, providing that they commit themselves to follow up that baptism with a time of study in the faith and with attendance at their local church, intentionally, hopefully to confirmation at the hands of the bishop.

The main thing here is to expect that the preaching has done something: something has happened that cannot be put into words and that, therefore, needs some *sacramental expression*. An evangelistic mission is an event at which things happen. People can be invited to come forward and then to receive the laying-on-of-hands or anointing. In a word, the sermon should reach the same point in the dynamics of the service as is reached in the old Prayer Book at the invitation or altar call at communion. "Draw near with faith." This charge can itself be used slightly adapted so that people make the link between their weekly communion and receiving Jesus joyfully afresh into their lives.

People can be invited to say after the sermon a restyled and shorter version of the Methodist covenant prayer. When this prayer is said in this way—phrase by phrase—

after the preacher, it can be a very powerful statement of recommitment. The introduction in the original prayer is a splendid one: "And now beloved, let us bind ourselves with willing bonds to our covenant God, take the yoke of Christ upon us."

This taking of his yoke upon us means that we are heartily content that he shall appoint us our place and work and that he alone shall be our reward.

Christ has many services to be done. Some are easy, others more difficult. Some bring honor; others bring reproach. Some are suitable to our natural inclinations and temporal interests, others are contrary to both. In some we may please Christ and please ourselves. But there are others in which we cannot please Christ except by denying ourselves. Yet the power to do this is assuredly given us in Christ. We can do all things in him who strengthens us.

Search your hearts, therefore, whether you can now freely make a sincere and unreserved dedication of yourself to God.

Make the covenant of God your own. Engage yourself to him. Resolve to be faithful. Having engaged your heart to the Lord, resolve, not in your own strength nor in the power of your own resolutions but in his might, never to go back.

And here all the people shall join:

I am no longer my own but yours. Put me to what you will, rank me with whom you will. Put me to doing, put me to suffering. Let me be employed for you or laid aside for you; exalted for you or brought low for you. Let me be full; let me be empty. Let me have all things; let me have nothing. I freely and heartily yield all things to your pleasure and disposal.

And now, O glorious and blessed God, Father, Son and Holy Spirit, you are mine and I am yours. So be it. And the covenant that I have made on earth, let it be ratified in heaven.

In any event, there must be a sense in which this whole section of the service must be sealed and completed. It is possible sometimes to use the confirmation prayer from the old Prayer Book in a slightly adapted form:

> Defend, O Lord, these your servants with your heavenly grace and grant that those who this night have been touched afresh with the power of your love may continue yours forever and daily increase in your Holy Spirit more and more until they come to your everlasting kingdom.

In some way or other, the point of evangelistic preaching is to move people one more step along the road of faith. For some, that step may dramatically move them over the ditch between nonchurchgoing and churchgoing; between no faith and a new faith. It may be a step of forgiveness or healing. It may be a step from a time of darkness into a new chapter of light; a time of no prayer into a chapter of new prayer. Hopefully, for all present it will be a time of refreshment and renewal.

If people have come forward or have made an outward declaration of new faith, they need a special word corporately from the preacher. They also need to see a counselor individually for ministry after the service.

By this time, the service may have fragmented a little. It needs to be arrested once more for the corporate conclusion, blessing, and dismissal—all of which will be brief and to the point.

A strong hymn, which brings people to their feet and in its words and marching tune sets people's feet on the road again, is now needed. If need be, the collection could be taken at this point or earlier in the service, as indicated above. Still standing, a powerful and brief blessing and dismissal will mean that people who do not like to be "caught" can easily slip away.

However, if the atmosphere and building can possibly afford an unself-conscious sense of lingering, so much the better. Clergy (in uniform *please*—preferably even a cassock) and counselors will be labeled and should be clearly in evidence. Of course, great care must be taken over each and every individual who comes forward. Therefore, there must be many people lingering behind after the service in the auditorium who look as though they have nothing better to do than simply to wait around. Music in the background, either over the amplifier, from a record player, or live, can all help to keep the atmosphere warm. A few people could unself-consciously go over to light a candle to pray. The side chapel, still lit perhaps (where the Blessed Sacrament is reserved), can also be a place of prayer and ministry.

The prime task of the counselors, of course, is to establish a living link for everyone who has come forward with a living church and, therefore, with a continuing pastoral ministry available. While it may be helpful to pray briefly with each person and also to give them a copy of the Holy Scriptures, it is important to help them to articulate their new-found faith even at this point. Of course, as they are given a copy of the Gospels, the counselor will fill in a card that obtains the necessary basic information to establish a link with another congregation or church. Names, addresses, telephone numbers, and denomination of the church to which they claim allegiance are the barest essentials. After that, all kinds of connections can be made, and the further nurturing in faith that all one-off evangelistic events necessarily presuppose is guaranteed.

It is a small point perhaps but nonetheless an important one: the local bishop must be seen in some way to put his seal on all such evangelistic events. In their turn, these events need to be owned by the church in the person of the bishop and his local representatives—the clergy. On the last night, or preferably, on the following Sunday, it is most helpful if the bishop will consent to attend the church of the mission. When the credit's low, order champagne! Easter Sunday presupposes Low Sunday and missions have to come down to earth in some way or another.

The Sunday after a mission needs to reestablish the place of the local bishop as the local, prime evangelist. If the bishop is willing to preside at the liturgy on that Sunday and visit the parish, it is also helpful for him to be available for a question-and-answer session after the service at which he is the celebrant, of course, and the preacher. So the bishop joins with God's people in thanking God for all the graces of a mission and helps to point everyone—new Christians and those who have been made new—back to the road of discipleship, life in the local community of faith, and continuing commitment to service in the community at large. In other words, business as usual.

Notes

1. Martin E. Marty and Frederick E. Greenspahn, eds., *Pushing the Faith: Proselytism and Civility in a Pluralistic World* (New York: Crossroad, 1988), 155.
2. Gabriel Marcel, *Creative Fidelity*, trans. Robert Rosenthal (new York: Crossroad, 1982), 219.
3. Smail, *Giving Gift*, 20.
4. John R.W. Stott, *Christian Mission in the Modern World: What the Church Should Be Doing Now*, (Downers Grove, IL: Intervarsity Press, 1975), 39.
5. Brian Green, *The Practice of Evangelism* (New York: Charles Scribner's Sons, 1951), 110.
6. Ibid., 110.

NINE

Nurturing God's People in the Gospel: Post Evangelism

"And they devoted themselves to the apostles' teaching and fellowship, to the breaking of bread and the prayers" (Acts 2:42).

POST–PENTECOST

As the days went by after that first day of Pentecost, the newly baptized Christians (all of them formally Jews) developed the life-style of, what we have later come to call, the Church. They were not even known as Christians but simply as "followers of the Way." They stumbled upon the expression of their pentecostal faith in their corporate life, ministry, and mission; only later did they label all of that experience with the one word Church. It did not start, we must notice, the other way around. Ecclesiasticism was not the forerunner of evangelism, but evangelism spawned the life of the Church. It is not so much that the Church, therefore, has a mission. Perhaps it is even more the other way around: the mission has a Church. God's mission (that love which first went out of its way) needs to be embodied, and the catholic Church of Jesus Christ embodies that mission.

Put more theologically and, indeed, even more succinctly: "The mistake of ecclesiasticism through the ages," said Bishop Michael Ramsey,

> has been to believe in the church as a kind of thing-in-itself. The apostles never regarded the church as a thing-in-itself. Their faith was in God, who had raised Jesus from the dead, and they knew the power of His Resurrection to be at work in them and in their fellow believers despite the unworthiness of them all. That is always the nature of true belief in the church. It is a laying hold on the power of the Resurrection.[1]

The power of resurrection-life took hold in the life of that fragile community and forged it into a body—the Church. The Church, furthermore, as it developed was an expression of the gospel in action—the gospel that had touched their own lives and changed their lives—a faith that was now being lived out in all of its implications. Once again, however, we must notice the order: the gospel formed the Church, and that was to be the shape of things to come, as through the ages again and again the gospel has formed and reformed the Church.

So in our own day, evangelism and the power of the gospel will reform all the churches, bringing a new spirit of genuine ecumenism. If the Decade of Evangelism really takes hold, I believe it will be difficult to recognize the continuity between the Church of the twentieth century and the churches of the twenty-first century. They will have been so radically reordered on the front line of evangelism and mission, and in that reordering they will have been drawn closer together than ever before. They will be as different as the pre-Constantine Church was from the church after A.D. 313—this time in reverse. Of course, it is much more difficult to develop in that direction!

So it was that those new Christians in the days and weeks following Pentecost were brought together from the outset as a pretty rough and ready lot! They had been challenged by the preaching of Peter to do something or at least express their readiness to do something. "What shall we do?" they had been asking. "Repent and be baptized," they were bluntly told. So there and then they had undergone the experience of repentance and baptism. It was certainly an experience-orientated and an action-orientated day—that first day of Pentecost. It would have been interesting to have been a fly on the wall and to have listened to what those first Christians said to their families and their friends later on in the evening of that same day. "So what happened?" "What did you do?" "What does it all mean?"

I doubt any of those three thousand newly baptized Christians were able to give very satisfying or satisfactory answers to that barrage of questions.

What is quite certain is that Peter had not preached the whole gospel! It is infuriating to hear the perennial criticism so frequently leveled at the heads of evangelists as they seek to undertake their very special and particular vocation. Of course, he did not preach the whole gospel. "Fancy, he never even mentioned ministry, service in the community, outreach, or the need to care for the poor!" The answer to such critics, of course, is to remind them of how impossible it is to preach the whole gospel in one sermon—a sermon that must not be longer than twenty or twenty-five minutes. I have frequently heard young curates in their first flush of enthusiasm for preaching attempt to preach the whole gospel—and we know the results! As the old lady said to the young curate: "Did you think you had something to say, or did you think you had to say something?" For if you try to say everything you'll end up saying nothing. It is only when you know something you simply are compelled to say that the words of a ramshackle sermon can be taken by the Holy Spirit and become a living Word of God. In one sense, all of us have within us an Epistle to the Romans; that is to say, our personal record of gospel experience, the way in which it has made sense to us and in which it has been effective in recalling us again and again to the full gospel as we have tried to work it throughout the course of our lives. All of our preaching is necessarily fragmentary because all of our "knowledge is partial" (1 Cor. 13:9).

The preacher sharpens up that gospel message that has first spoken to him or to her and then reproduces it with many variations again and again throughout the course of their ministry.

LAY EDUCATION

Yet the people so moved by such preaching have a long way to go in the faith, as indeed does the preacher, before they reach any kind of maturity. The Church is the community of faith in which faith is fostered and in which disciples grow and mature. The converted find that once they have settled down to a life of faith they need to be converted over and over again. The Church is a hospital, a school, and a university all rolled into one. It is the community of wounded surgeons, where everyone is at one and the same time both patient and physician. "He saved others, himself he cannot save," (Luke 23:35). Of course not, precisely because we are saved in saving others. So St. Luke in the events of the day of Pentecost (after the first Christian evangelistic event) tells us the continuing story of how and in what context these new babes in Christ lived, learned, cared, and grew in faith.

In the fellowship of the baptized, the new Christians underwent a continuous course and a refresher course: "They *continued*," we are told, "in the apostles' teaching." The apostles found themselves up to their ears in questions, spending hours each day trying to meet the needs of the newly baptized. They had to rely heavily upon the Holy Spirit. But then, of course, Jesus had told them before his ascension, "I will not leave you comfortless: I will send the Holy Spirit to lead you into all truth: I have many things to tell you but you cannot bear them now" (John 16:12ff.). It is the work of the Holy Spirit, as Jesus foretold, to take the teaching of Jesus and recall it in the memory and in the sub-conscious of the disciples. The Holy Spirit had given them, as it were, almost instant recall—to use the language of the computer. The questions posed by the new Christians pulled out of the apostles their long hours of teaching which they themselves, in turn, had first received from Jesus. Those were precious times when, "in private," Jesus explained everything to them as St. Mark is at such pains to point out (Mark 4:10, 6:32, 9:28, 13:3).

The words of St. Paul expressed their daily experience as apostles: "I hand on to you that which I first received" (1 Cor. 15:3). The Church was the context in which faith was exchanged and in which the gospel was gossiped! "For you I am a bishop," said Augustine, "but among you I am a Christian." The apostles had a particular role to play in all of this process. Yet as Christians themselves they would also need to receive much to strengthen their own faith from the hands of the neophytes. In that sense they were not above the faith but rather lived alongside the faith, giving and receiving—receiving in the giving and vice versa.

> And fear came upon every soul; and many wonders and signs were done through the apostles. And all who believed were together and had all things in common; and they sold their possessions and goods and distributed them to all, as any had need. And day by day, attending the temple together and breaking bread in their homes, they partook of food with glad and generous hearts, praising God and having favor with all the people. And the Lord added to their number day by day those who were being saved (Acts 2:43–47).

EVERYDAY LIFE IN THE COMMUNITY OF FAITH

That is the life-style of the early Church, and clearly it was
a living testimony to the way in which the disciples lived
in fellowship and in the community of the Spirit with
Jesus during his earthly ministry. The Church is the
evidence of the mission—so Jesus turns to inquiring
disciples in St. John's Gospel and invites them to "come
and see" for themselves the evidence. So, we are told,
they go and spend the night. But this process is contagious. The following day, in response to other questions,
they in turn offer the same invitation as vindication of
doctrine: "Come and see," they say to inquirers (John 1:39
and 46). The Church is intended to be the visible evidence
of effective mission as well as the context in which the
integrity of the preached message is vindicated. There
was no credibility gap between the content of the message
and the life-style of the messengers. For Christian
doctrine is not an abstraction written in, or learned from,
books. Rather, it is the experience of the community of
faith, and it is contagious. The apostolic succession looked
at with eyes of reductionism can be a caricature of a game
of tag. Yet, seen properly, it really is the story of who
touched whom. By keeping in touch (literally) with the
faithful, my own faith is sustained and grows. It was as
they came to the Lord and worshiped him, not only in the
sacrament of the "breaking of bread" but also the sacrament of their neighbors and fellow Christians—the sacrament of the Church—that they found their prayers were
answered through the mutual ministry at work in the rank
and file of their membership. Then Jesus was present to
them day by day in a vivid and real way—in his own
Body, the Church, and in the fellowship of the faithful.
The doctrine of the real presence of Jesus was for them a
daily experience: Jesus present in the sacrament; Jesus
present when the Word was studied and preached and

read; Jesus present in the newly baptized in the community of faith and in the poor and the needy and through service in the wider community at large. You could not have an academic discussion about the resurrection when you daily experienced the presence and power of the risen Lord in your midst in the signs and wonders that were so clearly evident! They were literally "witnesses" of the reality that all the things that Jesus had done were still being done (and greater things) just in ways he had promised.

All the things he said were now being said again and again and were being validated in the life of that community. Christianity was not so much words and more words: it was more a new way of life. Little wonder that the apostles were so slow in getting round to writing the gospel narratives: you are not very inclined to write a book while it is all still happening. Biographies are most easily written after the principal subject has died, gone, and been buried. The writing of books about someone is the special role of those who are one step removed from those who are involved in it all. The sign that the writer of Mark's gospel is perhaps only half a step removed from the very events that he is seeking to record is, of course, found in his clumsy, erratic style, continuously punctuated with that little word *immediately*, which occurs no less than thirty-four times in the sixteen chapters of his gospel. Christianity, for that writer, was still primarily an event with a sense of immediacy and urgency. And the finished product of the gospel, in turn, is a rough and ready attempt to put into words an activity that was still in progress: the gospel event was still happening and ringing in his ears as he wrote.

LIFE IN CHRIST

"Fear came on every soul": not fear in the sense of

paralyzing phobia, but rather that sense of awe, that impresses upon everyone concerned the incredible reality of everything that is happening. "It's for real," as we say. Expectations were very high. Yet notice from the outset that the Christian life was a corporate life. In 1 Corinthians 12, we are aware that the writer is not seated at a desk in a study, pursuing the careful and cautious theological dissertation of a scholar or a student. Rather, it is an attempt to put into words the experience of Paul who lived the Christian life in the context of the corporate fellowship of his fellow Christians. In fact, for Paul, you did not live the Christian life: that is far too abstract for him. The Christian life was lived in you. Even that is still too abstract for St. Paul, so he is driven to that strange phrase *in Christ*, which occurs over forty times in his epistles, with the complementarity that Christ, in turn, lived in you. "Christ in you the hope of glory" (Col. 1:27). Paul was overwhelmingly aware that the Christian life was Christ living in him the Christ life—God's way of being human. Furthermore, he realized that his whole life was lived in Christ. Put another way, Paul discovered that he was in his element when he was in the Body of Christ. Donald Coggan, seeking to expound and expand on that strange phrase *in Christ*, gives us a useful analogy.

> We say of a fish that water is its element. In it, it lives, propagates, prospers. Out of it, even for a brief few moments, it dies. We say of a plant that earth is its element. Rooted securely in it, it lives and flourishes. Uprooted, it dies. We might say of the branch of a vine, that the vine is its element. In it, it grows and produces fruit from it. Severed from it, it withers and dies. We say of the members of the animal world, including the members of the human race, that air is their element. It is literally our breath of life. Restrict our access to it, or submerge us in the alien element of water, and we die in a matter of seconds. We say of a man who is supremely

happy in his vocation, fulfilled and absorbed in his
work, reaching the fullness of his potential: "That man
is in his element."

These analogies may help us, even if only partially,
to understand what was in the mind of Paul when he
spoke of a person being "in Christ." When a man is "in
Christ," he is in his element, the element in which
alone he can reach his fulfillment and come to the full
stature of manhood, the destiny which God intended
for him.[2]

To develop that analogy, it is interesting to note that, when
we are born, we move from life in one element in the
womb (water) to life in another element in the world (air).
So when we are born again, our life is now lived in a new
element—in Christ. He is the very air we breathe, and
prayer is the process of inspiration.

So it was that in Christ the new Christians as individuals were forged into a living fellowship in the life of the
Spirit. Our Pentecostal experience binds us together in
Christ, while we receive our resurrection experience on a
more one-to-one-basis. This fellowship of the Spirit in the
common life of the Body of Christ was a revolutionary
reality to the early Church. It is not possible to describe it
by borrowing from secular, ideological philosophies. It
was not communism—it was a little bit like it but something so much greater. It was not hearty fellowship or the
club mentality—though often it can be caricatured in that
way. Even the phrase *esprit de corps*, which is not a bad
paraphrase of the word *koinonia* of the Spirit, does not go
far enough. The analogy of the family will certainly not
do since the family can be a most exclusive and excluding
symbol, as well as being psychologically one of the most
cruel images, responsible perhaps, more than anything
else, for the inhibition of growth rather than for fostering
growth. Significantly, most murders in America are
domestic and still statistically surpass the number of

murders committed on the street. You are probably more in danger of mental cruelty in the family than in the wider community at large.

The only analogy, in fact, that comes anywhere near describing the reality of the experience of this incorporation into Christ is to speak of the cell in relation to the human body. For Christians are not eventually like rivers—subsumed and lost in the sea or the ocean. This is the analogy of incorporation used in all religions *except* Christianity. *Au contraire*, as a Christian, I become more who I am individually the more I engage in the corporate experience of who we all are together. No one part of the Body can pull a fast one over another part of the Body: If one member suffers, all suffer: if one member is honored, all are honored (1 Cor. 12:22ff.).

The story of Ananias and Sapphira, therefore, in chapter 5 of the Book of the Acts of the Apostles, makes all this most explicit. It is a failure in discerning the Body in a similar sense to that of which St. Paul speaks in his teaching about the sacramental Body in his letters to the Corinthian church (1 Cor. 11:27). In cheating the Body, you are cheating yourself. We have in this strange story a case of theological, psychosomatic cancer. Ananias has spoiled his own nose to spite his own face. Such is the fellowship of the Spirit. There is not, and cannot be, anything quite like the Body of Christ on earth. Whether it be totalitarianism or individualism—a plague on both your houses. They both stint growth. Only the Body of Christ, breathing the good air of the Spirit, makes bodily growth possible. So "speaking the truth in love," which Ananias and Sapphira did not do, "we are to grow up in every way to him who is the head, into Christ, from whom the whole body, joined and knit together by every joint by which it is supplied" (the gospel connection at work), "when each part is working properly, makes bodily growth and upbuilds itself in love" (Eph. 4:15ff.).

THE FELLOWSHIP OF THE SPIRIT

Their worship was daily in the Temple where they still enjoyed the worship of the liturgy of the Word with its readings from the Old Testament, the Psalms, and the prayers of God's faithful people. Yet all this for these new followers of the Way was both stimulating and, at the same time, immensely frustrating. Every word in the Old Testament seemed to cry out and to point to the fulfillment of those promises in the person of Christ, already indwelling their hearts, in the breaking of bread, and in the fellowship of their corporate life. How was it, they would continually ask themselves, that their fellow Jews could not see the point of it all?

These new Christians, therefore, spent a great deal of their time together in the fellowship of what they slowly came to call the Church. They did not *go* to church: they *were* the Church. Nurturing new Christians in the faith demands a similar change of life-style. Sunday worship in a renewed parish is so much more than going to Mass. It involves the whole morning. In the course of Sunday morning, the Christians need to experience fellowship, teaching, worship, preaching, and possibly even lunch together—"They partook of food with glad and generous hearts" (Acts 2:46). Full-blooded, catholic Christians have always had a hearty appetite! (Acts 2:46) Furthermore, this pattern of schooling and growth was reproduced under different guises throughout the week in homes and in all the places where the new Christians could come together.***

***The peculiar relationship of the Church to society in places like America, England, and the Western world should probably be pointing us to a new pastoral strategy. Should the committed Christians be meeting at other times in the week for their worship, their teaching, and for life in the Spirit, while Sunday worship should be more predominantly directed toward inquirers and fringe people? If so, do we not want a Liturgy of the Word and a form of worship aimed at

The old model of the parson visiting his parishioners only goes half the way. Much better that the priest in a parish today, between Monday and Saturday, should visit "at all times and in all places" in the parish and constitute Acts 2:42 in small cell groups—groups in which teaching, fellowship, breaking of bread, and prayers are the agenda of the day. We used to say that a visiting parson makes a churchgoing parish. That is a dangerous half-truth and only gets two cheers! "House churches during the week constitute a healthy church on Sunday" would be a better statement of intent. The whole parish is perpetually, if you like, on a confirmation course—at all stages of faith, continually being confirmed in faith by teaching, by prayer, sacrament, ministry, and the fellowship of the Spirit.

Alcoholics Anonymous is a good model for the Church. You are saved only by saving others: you receive only by giving and sharing. And for all of this you need to come together regularly. There is nothing worse than soured sobriety: you end up becoming just a broody old hen. So with the Christian. There is nothing worse than a Christian who is struggling to live the good life and to be kind to his neighbor—but all of this in isolation. He is more concerned with what he is not doing, than with what he is doing: more concerned with what he is avoiding than with what he is undertaking.. You do not necessarily become a Christian by sitting in a pew, week in and week out, anymore than you would become a car by sitting in a garage, week in and week out!

those who have gone to be evangelized with television religion because the mainstream churches insist on providing only the eucharist at all occasions? Have we unchurched whole parts of American society by making the eucharist the exclusive and only fare in our Christian churches? I must ask the readers' forbearance in raising this important question as only a note. It demands much more development and is a question of importance out of all proportion to its place in this book.

VOCATION AND SANCTIFICATION

A kind of joke is at the heart of all Christian vocation. Only in ministering to others, are we ourselves built up. It is as though there is a kind of enlightened selfishness about trying to help others and to serve them. You do not first become a mature Christian and then look around for something to do for others. In ministering to others, you receive, and in helping others to grow, you yourself grow in faith. Furthermore, as we are healed in one area of our life, the Lord then gently focuses the light of his saving love on other scars, and so the pilgrimage goes on. All the gifts of the Spirit are given for the sake of the whole Body and are given like all God's gifts, of course, to be given away. Faith is a process, not an achievement. You undergo the Christian faith; you do not own it, achieve it, or possess it. Discipleship is a lifetime spent carrying your driver's learner permit all the way from baptism to heaven; you must never drive without it.

CHURCH GROWTH

Notice at the end of the second chapter in the Book of the Acts of the Apostles this illuminating sentence: "The Lord added to their number those who were being saved" (Acts 2:47). Put another way, the early Church was the sort of fellowship to which people could be added and feel welcomed, needed, and warmly received. Some groups, cliques, and fellowships are so exclusive that you simply dare not try to add anyone else to them! That early Church was outward looking, open-ended, and therefore truly inclusive.

In a symbolic if not a literal sense, every church building should be like the *Eglise de Reconcilation* of the Taizé community in France. Shortly after they built their community church, they tore out the west wall of that building to put a large, expandable tent on the west end. After all, they realized that they could never be quite sure how many the Lord would be adding to their number next Sunday—let alone the Sunday after that. They needed a building that could adapt to, as well as expect, an increase in numbers. We need to ask ourselves as churches and as congregations again and again, Is our church the sort of church that the Lord could send someone to next Sunday morning and be confident that such a person, or such persons (however many or few), would be *added*, included, and enfolded within the love, fellowship, and hospitality of that church? There may be a sense in which the Lord may not be able to risk church growth with many Episcopal churches as they are now constituted for precisely this reason.

THE LITURGY AND THE CHURCH'S YEAR

Precisely because it is not possible to shoot all the gospel guns at once, the Church evolved what we have come to call the calendar of the Church's year. Everything that is true, of course, about the gospel is true all the time and not just at certain times. But we can only grasp with our finite minds *some* things, *some* times. (Not, of course, that the primary concept of the Christian faith is to be seen as grasping the gospel: you do not need to grasp the gospel, but rather you need to let the gospel grasp you.)

The Church's year not only seeks to present systematically all the themes and aspects of the gospel but also invites us to *celebrate* the gospel in all its richness. Christian truths, as we have seen, are not intended to speak only to the mind but rather to *possess* us in every aspect of our being. They should haunt us and speak to us in our waking moments. So the truths of the gospel trail their coat and are presented in the form of what psychologists refer to as a complex: Experiences, doctrines, and even hymn tunes and scriptural quotations all get stuck together and become related by association. For most teaching is done by association, and, therefore, the Church's teaching should not claim to be an exception. We associate our worship with the seasons of the Church's year, liturgical colors, certain music, certain prayers and scriptural texts. All these become associated and related and woven into a complex pattern that is powerful to convey not only the content of the teaching but also the impressions made by the teaching. This method of learning is quite distinctive and works always by association. All the best advertisements work the same way: they have at least a double meaning and connect (generally rather humorously) with previously unconnected meanings.

That is why the Church deliberately used the seasons of the year and pagan festivals and attached to them the further significance of the Christian season, the Christian celebration, and, therefore, the Christian truth and doctrine. Christmas is a prime example. Coming as it does in the West around the shortest day and the longest night and at the same time as one of the pagan festivals, the birth of Christ marks the end of the darkness and the beginning of the light. Could it be that even birds can appreciate catholic truth, for we are told that they are particularly sensitive to the lengthening and the shortening of the days. So it is that catholic truth makes its appeal by speaking through all of our senses and can be eloquent through the length of days or the hours of sunshine. For certainly Christian truth must be at least as eloquent as the truth of the world around us in order to speak to the world within us. Our gospel message is for the whole universe, which is, according to St. Paul, "groaning and travailing" as it waits and looks to us for our redemption, which in turn will bring about the redemption of the whole created order (Rom. 8).

So with all the Church's year. We learn by association and, therefore, by celebration. Christian doctrine is not orthodox if you cannot sing about it—hence, the glory of Christmas carols.

Each celebration of the Christian year recognizes a year of grace and marks for the Christian pilgrim new insights and new opportunities for growth and maturity. Nurturing in the gospel should be related and attached to our life cycle and should relate to the Church's year. It should afford a glorious opportunity for putting the whole school of Christians into school for Lent, along with those who are preparing for baptism at the Easter vigil. So the new Christians and the renewed Christians get into step from Ash Wednesday onward. Then Holy Week, by Word and sacrament, celebrates the mystery of the passion, death, and resurrection into which the new Christians are baptized and in which the renewed Christians live, move, and have their being. For new and old alike have also been buried with Christ, and their lives are hid with Christ in God.

What an opportunity the season of Eastertide affords, falling as it does in the West at a time of the year when everyone is coming alive again after the long winter and enjoying the first balmy days of early summer. Then follow the great fifty days from Easter to Pentecost to revive us and to lift us up with Ascensiontide in that glorious season, so that we can reflect further upon the Christian life, empowered with the Holy Spirit. Here again is a season for teaching and celebration, for the two should always go hand in hand.

The Christian life and the living out of the gospel demand a rhythm. This is so not only because in some wonderful way Christianity is a dance rather than a dogma but also because rhythm is the pulse of life itself: it is the heartbeat of the universe. *Regula* is not so much a rule as a rhythm, and those who follow Jesus know from experience (sometimes rather bitter experience) that he will lead you in quite a dance—given half the chance!

Hence, the lovely theological lyric of that glorious little hymn of the twentieth century: "The Lord of the Dance." We dance from darkness to light, from a sense of his presence to a sense of his absence, from pain to glory, from silence to words, and from resting to movement and more pilgrimage. "A little while . . . and again a little while . . ." is the pulse and rhythm of growth and maturity (John 16:16ff.).

SPIRITUAL AND GOSPEL FORMATION

You cannot do this all on your own or in isolation. Jesus sent his early missionaries out two by two. Growth is only possible in relationship, hence the emphasis of the Church from early times on the place of what the Celtic Church came to call the soul friend. In Anglican terminology, the phrase *spiritual director* smacks a little too much of the legalistic, streamlined theology of the Roman Catholic Church. Yet at its best, the whole tradition of the duo goes right back to New Testament times. After Paul's dramatic conversion, first Annanias ministers to him as a soul friend, and then Barnabas takes him under his wing. "Brother Saul, the Lord Jesus whom you met on the road sent me to you," says Annanias, "that you may gain your sight and be filled with the Holy Spirit." That is, of course, supremely the text for spiritual direction. The new convert needs to be ministered to before he can then minister (Acts 9:17). We are told Annanias laid hands upon the young Saul. That personal ministry of sharing Jesus is always so important, especially in the early days of new faith. The newly converted Christian may come to church with a lot of baggage: guilt from an abortion many years earlier; an earlier chapter of mucking about with drugs, alcohol, and other religions—or even the demonic. Guilt, anger, sadness may all be part of their previous life. Sacramental confession, anointing, prayer with laying-on-of-hands (sometimes specifically for deliverance from various manias and obsessions and other habits that imprison so many people in the world today). Then the newly converted Christian will need to read the Scriptures. He or she will certainly need some help in this area. At the same time, they will need to learn how to pray —just as Jesus taught his disciples to pray and John the Baptist before him. In a word (to use rather an old, flat phrase from the past), they will need help in developing a *rule of life.*

However, this must not become a yoke or a new law put round the neck of the new Christian. Christ came to deliver us from such bondage—and to save us from the rules of religion. He was eager to tell us that his yoke was easy and his burden was light. A rule of life is not intended to be a heavy burden but rather to be what the spine is to the whole human body: the prime means of movement, spontaneity, and dancing. A rule of life can all too easily become a kiss of death. Yet a baby has to be taught a rhythm to life as it grows up—to be regular—and so does the newborn Christian.

For Anglicans, there is a sevenfold reference that may help us in this important part of growing up in the new life, of the gospel of Jesus Christ. Celebrating the discipline of the new life, we can use the following pegs on which to hang a model for such growth: Scripture, sacraments, Spirit, issuing in study, stewardship, service, and sacrifice.

The full gospel of Jesus Christ is expressed for Anglicans in that threefold cord of life: Scripture, sacraments, and life in the Spirit. Regular Bible reading, the sacramental life of worship, and the prayer life in the Spirit along with the fellowship of the Spirit in the corporate life of Christ's Church—all these constitute the daily bread of sustenance for Christians new and old. But notice that it issues, in a healthy Christian, in a life of study and reflection on the faith; in the stewardship of all our gifts and talents; in service and ministry to others and a sense of sacrifice, perhaps best summed up in the words of Jesus: "For their sakes I sanctify myself"(John 17:19)—in other words, life "laid down" for others.

This way of life evolves best and most unself-consciously in the school of the Church and in the course of the Church's year, together with personal ministry from a soul friend or spiritual director. Spiritual formation is a vital part of the follow-up to all evangelistic events, but it is also a part of the Church's life and ministry at all times and in all places.

For the Christian faith is so very much more than simply a question of believing and swallowing a few improbable doctrines—inserting sacred beliefs into a completely secular outlook. The Christian faith and life constitute a completely new outlook on the whole of life. People who have been brainwashed over many years to see the world in one way (with a secular outlook) do not see it in a totally different way overnight. Conversion at first makes you more aware of blindness than of sight. Like St. Paul, you have to be ministered to in order to begin to see things again with new vision—with eyes of faith. You do not see a different world as you begin to recover your sight. Far from it. But you do begin to see the same old world in a new light and from a new point of view. That is both an instantaneous disclosure and a continuing process: "In thy light may we see light." Or, as the Church has said over the years in its great hymn to the Holy Spirit, "Enable with perpetual light the dullness of our blinded sight."

Parish missions belong together with retreats, conferences, renewal weekends, Cursillo. All have their part to play in the overall evangelistic program of the Church and in this developing ministry of growth and maturity: evangelizing the Church for mission; gospelling the Church so that, in turn, it may minister the gospel to others.

THE PRIESTHOOD OF ALL BELIEVERS

The ministry of healing and the healing of memories also has a particular place, as indeed does counseling—that kind of counseling that expects change and growth and that is not simply the paralysis of analysis.

So we are all caught up in this ongoing process of what we call the ministry of the Church. All are ministers in this, and all need ministering to and always both at the same time. This loving work of the Spirit to make us and to remake us in the life of Christ always takes place between the surgeon's wounded, loving hands. "Teach me as best my soul can bear," says Wesley. I would indeed be blinded and destroyed if I were to see myself as I am—all in a moment. Like all growth, spiritual development is gradual: essentially unself-conscious and not immediately obvious. It is not undertaken with too many mirrors around the place! Yet it is essentially a process of change through reflection, and there are certainly definite turning points and milestones on that long road, that we need to recall and remember "at all times" with thanksgiving. We need tutors in this process, but we need partners as well who will care for us, in prayer for us.

The place of intercession cannot be overestimated. St. Monica, the mother of St. Augustine, having been nine months in travail for the little brat, subsequently spent thirty years in prayer and intercession and continuing travail for him before he was finally born again in A.D. 387. Like Esther in the Old Testament, Monica prayed the prayer of ultimate sacrifice; and, she died almost as soon as Augustine was converted and baptized. For intercession is not so much a form of prayer but more a way of life —life for others. Every parish needs an army of intercessors. Often such people are to be found among the housebound and the elderly, and they form the backbone of any truly evangelistic parish. This is essentially a hidden yet a truly important ministry. The wise pastor of a parish will seek out such people and solicit their ministry for the clergy, for the parish, and for all evangelistic programs in the parish. The intercessor is at the heart of the whole mission and ministry of the Church. Yet it is often most effectively done by those who do not appear to be able to do very much at all: the elderly, the housebound, and the cloistered—and throughout history, predominantly women.

In this context, discernment finds its proper place. As the new Christians are helped to find their true place in the whole orchestra and chorus of the Church and its ministry, a wise and discerning pastor will be listening each day, watching and waiting to help everyone to find his or her proper place and appropriate role in the whole Body of Christ.

So in this way, the Decade of Evangelism is recalling the whole Church to become the sort of Church that Jesus intends his Church to be. The work of the Holy Spirit, informing and reforming the Body, is already manifest for those with eyes to see in the extensive renewal sweeping through all the churches. In all this process of renewal and reformation for evangelism, mission, and ministry, we need the double-edged mandate of the New Testament. On the one hand, we must not "resist the Spirit." Yet, on the other hand, we must "test the spirits." However, most important and all the time and above all, we must *receive* the Spirit if we are to recognize and recall Jesus our risen and ascended Lord, whose presence we recall and represent for the life of the world here and now and in the world to come. That is the true and lasting vocation of the Church of God, and it is inevitably the sort of Church that is also an evangelistic Church—perhaps, almost without knowing it.

Notes

1. Ramsey and Suenens, *Future of the Christian Church*, 38.
2. Donald Coggan, *Paul: Portrait of a Revolutionary* (London: Hodder Christian Paperback, 1986), 76.

BIBLIOGRAPHY

Abraham, William J. *The Logic of Evangelism*. Grand Rapids: Wm. B. Eerdmans, 1989.

Avis, Paul. *Gore: Construction and Conflict*. West Sussex, England: Churchman Publishing, 1988.

Burnett, Bill, ed. *By My Spirit: Renewal in the Worldwide Anglican Church*. London, Hodder & Stoughton, 1988.

Campbell, Alastair V. *Rediscovering Pastoral Care*. London: Darton, Longman & Todd, 1981.

Coburn, John B. *Evangelism: The Task of the Whole Church*. Cincinnati: Forward Movement Publications, 1982.

Coggan, Donald. *Paul: Portrait of a Revolutionary*. London: Hodder Christian Paperback, 1986.

Coleman, Robert E. *The Master Plan of Evangelism*. Old Tappan, NJ: Fleming H. Revell, 1963.

Coleman, Robert E., ed. *Evangelism on the Cutting Edge*. Old Tappan, NJ: Power Books. Fleming H. Revell, 1986.

Colson, Charles W. *Against the Night: Living in the New Dark Age*. Ann Arbor, MI: Servant Publications, 1989.

Dodd, D.H. *The Apostolic Preaching and Its Developments*. New York: Harper & Row, 1936.

Ecclestone, Giles, ed. *The Parish Church? Explorations in the Relationship of the Church and the World*. London and Oxford: Mowbray, 1988.

Gallup, George, Jr., and George O'Connell. *Who Do Americans Say that I Am? What Christians Can Learn from Opinion Polls*. Philadelphia: Westminster Press, 1986.

Gill, Robin. *Beyond Decline: A Challenge to the Churches*. London: SCM Press, 1988.

Gore, Charles. *Jesus of Nazareth*. London: Macmillan, 1927.

Grant, Michael. *Jesus*. New York: Charles Scribner's Sons, 1979.

Green, Bryan. *The Practice of Evangelism*. New York: Charles Scribner's Sons, 1951.

Green, Michael. *Evangelism in the Early Church*. Grand Rapids: Wm. B. Eerdmans, 1970.

———. *I Believe in the Holy Spirit*. Grand Rapids: Wm. B. Eerdmans, 1989.

Henry, Carl F.H. *Twilight of the Great Civilization: The Drift Toward Neo-Paganism*. Westchester, IL: Crossway Books, 1988.

Holmes, Urban T. *Turning to Christ: A Theology of Renewal and Evangelization*. New York: Seabury Press, 1981.

Hooft, Visser't. "Evangelism in the Neo-Pagan Situation." *International Review of Mission* 63 (January 1974).

Howard, Thomas. *Evangelical Is Not Enough: Worship of God in Liturgy and Sacrament*. San Francisco: Ignatius Press, 1984.

Huston, Sterling W. *Crusade Evangelism and the Local Church: An Inside Look at Billy Graham Crusades, Revealing Principles of Evangelism that Can Work for Your Church*. Minneapolis: World Wide, 1984.

Johnson, Ben Campbell. *Rethinking Evangelism: A Theological Approach.* Philadelphia: Westminster Press, 1987.

Kelley, H.N. *No Two Alike: Strength, Diversity and Challenge in Parishes Today.* Wilton, CT: Morehouse Publishing, 1988.

Kelshaw, Terence. *Seed and Harvest: A Newsletter for Friends of Trinity Episcopal School for Ministry,* vol. II, no. 6.

Marty, Martin E., and Frederick E. Greenspahn. *Pushing the Faith: Proselytism and Civility in a Pluralistic World.* New York: Crossroad, 1988.

Newbigin, Lesslie. *The Gospel in a Pluralistic Society.* Grand Rapids: Wm. B. Eerdmans, 1989.

Nichols, Bruce J., ed. *In Word and Deed: Evangelism and Social Responsibility.* Grand Rapids: Wm. B. Eerdmans, 1985.

Oden, Thomas C. "Freedom to Learn." Paper delivered at the International Edinburgh Conference on Pastoral Care and Counseling, 1979.

Poulton, John. *A Today Sort of Evangelism.* London: Lutterworth Press, 1972.

Rainer, Thom. S. *Evangelism in the Twenty-First Century: The Critical Issues.* Wheaton, IL: Shaw, 1988.

Sisson, Dick. *Evangelism Encounter: Bringing the Excitement of Evangelism Back into the Body,* Wheaton, IL: Victor Books, 1988.

Smail, Tom. *The Giving Gift: The Holy Spirit in Person.* London: Hodder & Stoughton, 1988.

Stott, John R.W. *Christian Mission in the Modern World: What the Church Should Be Doing Now.* Downers Grove, IL: Intervarsity Press, 1975.

Taylor, John V. *The Go Between God: The Holy Spirit and the Christian Mission.* London: SCM Press, 1972.

Wagner, C. Peter. *Church Growth and the Whole Gospel: A Biblical Mandate*. San Francisco; Harper & Row, 1981.

_____. *Frontiers in Mission Strategy*. Chicago: Moody, 1971.

Webber, Robert. *Seed and Harvest: A Newsletter for the Friends of Trinity Episcopal School for Ministry*, vol. 11, no. 6.

Wells, David F. *God the Evangelist: How the Holy Spirit Works to Bring Men and Women to Faith*. Grand Rapids: Wm. B. Eerdmans, 1987.

Wimber, John, and Kevin Springer. *Power Evangelism*. San Francisco: Harper & Row, 1986.

Winter, David. *A Battered Bride? The Body of Faith in an Age of Doubt*. Eastbourne: Monarch Publications, 1988.